G. P. Marshall

Social Goals and Economic Perspectives

Penguin Books

Penguin Books Ltd, Harmondsworth,
Middlesex, England
Penguin Books, 625 Madison Avenue,
New York, New York 10022, U.S.A.
Penguin Books Australia Ltd, Ringwood,
Victoria, Australia
Penguin Books Canada Ltd, 2801 John Street,
Markham, Ontario, Canada L3R 1B4
Penguin Books (N.Z.) Ltd, 182–190 Wairau Road,
Auckland 10, New Zealand

First published 1980

Made and printed in Great Britain by
Richard Clay (The Chaucer Press) Ltd
Bungay, Suffolk
Set in Monotype Times Roman

Contents

Preface

This book has been written in the hope that it will make some small contribution to that ever-growing area of study which shelters under the umbrella of 'social economics'. The stimulus to write such a book has derived mainly from trying to convey to final-year undergraduates some of the difficulties, both analytical and empirical, which are encountered when trying to apply the techniques of economic analysis to problems of social welfare. A teacher's efforts to discuss such problems in any sort of detail are usually applied in presenting a course of lectures which ranges over a list of selected topics, and the selection here presented originated in just such a fashion. Thus the topics discussed in this book reflect the author's interests rather than any attempt to compile a comprehensive list of problem areas which contribute essential study for the aspiring social economist. Nevertheless, it is intended that the selection will suggest a 'core' of study and that it will range over some of the major problems facing society in the United Kingdom at the present time.

Despite the origin of intention, however, the analysis presented in the pages which follow is not always given in pedagogical style, for several of the areas covered will not readily lend themselves to that sort of treatment. Rather, the style of the book has been determined by a desire critically to survey and summarize the main contributions to the various areas of study discussed. Within the survey the observer can study certain problems about which there already exists a large body of empirical tests, surveys and results; while in other areas only a theoretical structure (and perhaps a flimsy one) exists as a foundation upon which to offer comment.

The survey is intended for social scientists in general, but it has been written mainly with economists in mind in the belief that most of the problems in a world of scarcity are fundamentally economic in nature. First principles establish that economics is about choice, the rationing device which renders compatible various ends and scarce means. But what sort of choices are available? One of the most notable characteristics of economists' excursions into the analysis of social problems has been the attempt to escape from the strait-jacket imposed by accepting that only problems which readily lend themselves to market evaluation lie within the scope of economic analysis. Thus, during the past two decades, studies by economists have ranged over such diverse areas as 'public' services (housing, health, education and so on), crime, poverty, private charity, marriage and family formation, among various other aspects. Not all of these excursions into the traditional domain of other social sciences have met with unqualified success, and many studies are still in their infancy. However, the present author remains convinced that economic analysis underpins all social science and is the foundation upon which the other disciplines must build. The ensuing survey has been undertaken with a view to justifying this belief.

Given the numerous comments and criticisms offered by both students and colleagues, it is impossible, as always, to detail a list of acknowledgements which does justice to all concerned. Indeed, to be fair one must go back to one's teachers, and in particular to those who fostered early interest in a subject. My overall debt is to the Division of Economic Studies in the University of Sheffield for the enjoyment of several years of working in a friendly yet critical atmosphere. For encouragement to study public finance, I shall be always grateful to Roy Houghton, and for detailed assistance and comment on the current project, I thank Peter Else and Brian McCormick. For continued support and encouragement throughout the preparation of this book, I thank my wife Linda and our children (Andrew, Leigh, Mark and Joseph) to whom I dedicate the remaining pages.

PAUL MARSHALL
December 1978

1. Introduction

As its title suggests, this book aims to discuss social problems from an economic perspective. Economics has made several inroads into the analysis of social aims and policies and has offered at least pointers to the answers to several problems which other disciplines have found difficult to solve on their own. This is not to say that economics stands alone as the one reliable guide to policy-making, for there are many areas where it founders and seeks help from the other social sciences. Indeed, a journey through the problem areas surveyed in this book is a chastening experience for anyone naïve enough to believe that the analytical techniques developed in economics are sufficient for solving the problems of modern industrial society. However, with appropriate caution, it might be claimed that, to solve any of the problems faced by a world of scarcity, economics must provide the analytical bedrock on which to build the structure of policy.

Almost inevitably, a study of social goals becomes a critique of governmental policies, the adjective 'social' usually signifying involvement in some form by the public sector. But this should not mean an automatic presumption that the state's powers must be invoked whenever a problem emerges in the private sector. As a necessary condition for harmonious development and evolution, society has devised a wide array of institutional arrangements to deal with economic problems as they arise. Sometimes these arrangements involve a framework within which individuals can communicate with one another for the purposes of buying and selling – *market arrangements*. Sometimes the exchange process is supplanted by one of *collectivism*, whereby resources are allocated and utilized according to either the dictates of an organizational hierarchy, or the majority wish of a sharing arrangement. Nevertheless, there are several areas of social and economic activity where problem-solving has pointed to the institution of the state as the means of correction (at least in the short term), and the concern of this book is with such areas.

'Social' goals implies that the ensuing analysis will not be concerned with the mechanics of individual or private activities, except to the extent that they result in patterns of resource allocation and income distribution which do not square with society's hierarchy of aims. The reference point is often the individual, or his or her household – the composition of society – but it is the ways in which the individual affects others, the social consequences of his actions or the extent to which the quality of his personal life-style offends socially agreed norms which is of primary interest here. Sometimes the solutions offered, even through the apparatus of a state programme, rely upon individual initiative, while at others a more collective responsibility is adopted. Thus a major aim of this book is to consider a selection of such problem areas and to review the performance of the various programmes offered as solutions. The areas selected for study have been chosen because they represent some of the main areas of social concern in the post-war period, and the search for solutions to the problems discussed has widened considerably the scope of applied economics and has captured the attention of ever-growing numbers of social scientists and of economists in particular.

To attempt any such review, some frame of reference must be established at the outset, and Chapter 2 discusses the issues involved in such a task. At the heart of developments in welfare economics during the post-war period has been a social-welfare function based upon the Paretian ethic with its assumed appeal to the consensus. However, its support of the *status quo* has invited criticism, particularly from those who see income redistribution as an important social goal. Further criticism of the Paretian framework has come from the 'liberal school', who place primary importance upon individual freedom as an end in itself to be traded off against other aims, both private and social. Chapter 2 reviews the liberals' arguments and rejects them as a guide to the formulation of consistent social policies. However, the pragmatism which has appeared in answer to criticisms of the Pareto criterion's lack of relevance to the complex modern society is not without its problems, particularly when 'externalities' are being discussed. Nevertheless, in the absence of feasible alternatives, the Pareto criterion does offer some hope for social remedies.

Perhaps the biggest obstacle to using the Pareto criterion lies in tackling problems of income distribution – if giving to A means taking from B, then a narrow interpretation of the Pareto criterion rules out such a transfer. Chapter 2 discusses application of the criterion when utility functions are interdependent, since both A and B might be better off from the transfer if B derives satisfaction from the improvement in A's welfare. Doubt is cast, however, upon treating income redistribution as another dimension of the externality problem, at least to the extent that such analysis is intended to offer prescriptive guides to policy-making. Chapter 2 suggests that the assumption be accepted that society, for whatever reason, does want to see a more equitable distribution of the rewards of economic activity and offers the reminder that individuals are sometimes motivated by influences beyond the refined mathematical models employed by economists.

As an illustration of the points made in the discussion of the ethical framework, Chapter 3 considers how the microeconomic theory of resource allocation attempts to deal with the problems of pollution and specific underconsumption – health services being the chosen example. The link between these two problem areas, as suggested in Chapter 2, lies in the analysis of external effects. In the case of pollution, it is possible to consider the concept of an 'optimal rate of damage', given the appropriate assumptions, particularly the assumption of zero transactions costs (the small-numbers case), in which case the market-place may solve the problem. However, the assumptions are often difficult to maintain when considering the practicalities of the real world. Analysing 'efficient' allocation of health services in the face of inter-dependence among utility functions – A's consumption of health services has an impact at the margin on B's satisfactions – allows considera-tion of the utility functions of those who finance the organization of a nationalized scheme. Thus, alternatives to cash transfers become a legitimate area of normative study. Furthermore, this might be an area of analysis where the motive force of self-interest is subservient to other determinants of human behaviour and the case for provision through the market mechanism is less than clear. Yet, whenever the market is supplanted by bureaucracy, an efficient system of decision-making can prove elusive when objectives are not clearly specified. Chapter 3 discusses some of the problems arising from trying to specify the aims and costs of allocating resources through an institute such as the UK's National Health Service.

Most of the remainder of the study reviews post-war attempts to reduce the degree of inequality in the UK and to provide a guaranteed standard of living for all. Part of this story relates to issues covered in Chapter 3 in the context of specific underconsumption of health ser-vices and their application to such other areas as education and housing resources. However, most of the ensuing discussion concerns the prob-lems of unequal shares and poverty in a more general sense. Chapter 4 sets the scene for a review of programmes to reduce inequality and underlines both the difficulty of defining 'economic power' and the impossibility of deriving objective measures of equality. In the face of these difficulties, and bearing in mind the abundance of data deficien-cies, Chapter 5 attempts to describe and analyse the changing pattern of income distribution in the UK. Unambiguous conclusions about 'improvements' in income distribution are seen to prove difficult since reductions in shares at the top of the distribution have not been matched by increases at the bottom. In trying to explain the changing pattern of income shares, Chapter 5 considers several social, demographic and economic factors and, in particular, the impact of the income tax system. Again, judgements of improvement prove difficult, since levelling down from the top of the post-tax distribution of incomes must be weighed against little change having occurred in the relative positions of quantile groupings. On the other hand, it would seem to be the case that, when benefits or transfers are also considered, the amount of apparent redistribution is definitely increased.

Inequality of wealth seems even more difficult to assess than that of incomes, given that data sources have depended for the most part upon estate duty returns. Chapter 6 considers the problems arising from this reliance and describes the pattern of concentration which is apparent from recent researches. It would seem that there has been a considerable redistribution of wealth in the UK, particularly since 1960, though again the levelling down at the very top is much greater than for the quantiles immediately below. Part of the reason for this lies in the long-term nature of some of the main determinants of wealth concentration. In the absence of immediate state acquisition of all assets, social, demographic and economic influences on wealth concentration change at a much slower pace than those affecting the pattern of income distribution.

Related to the question of inequality, but a problem calling for different remedies, is that of income maintenance. Society adopts some level of income as a measure of 'minimum standard', that level below which no one is expected to fall. The aim to maintain everyone at or above this standard may or may not derive from a spirit of altruism or sense of social responsibility, but even if it does, this does not preclude steps to ensure that the costs of such a programme should be at a minimum. Thus, for contingencies such as sickness and unemployment, and for certainties such as old age, society may impose upon itself some scheme of compulsory provision whereby individuals are compelled to finance such events by levies upon work incomes. Chapter 7 considers the arguments for compulsory provision of such 'insurance' arrangements through a state-organized scheme, and proceeds to analyse the success of the UK 'pay-as-you-go' programme in the light of its objectives and in relation to its potential effects on the rate of economic activity.

'Insurance' arrangements apart, society's minimum standard may not be reached by some individuals or families, either because they are not eligible for help under such arrangements, or because the help they receive is inadequate and/or their incomes from employment are insufficient. Such problems of poverty require special consideration and separate arrangements for income maintenance. Chapter 8 introduces the discussion with a consideration of the very concept of 'poverty'. Like 'equality', this concept also proves impossible to define in any objective sense, and the level of income designated by the state-offered minimum is taken as the only yardstick by which inter-temporal comparisons can be made. By no means perfect, or even objective, such a yardstick is a second-best alternative. Of course it does not follow that a state programme of income maintenance is the only means by which poverty can be eradicated. Private charities can operate to channel resources to the poor, and state-imposed minimum wages aim to protect incomes from employment. Chapter 9 analyses both these means of protecting the poor, and finds them wanting in both theory and practice – without the check of the market, the charitable firm cannot be relied upon to redistribute incomes in an efficient manner, while minimum wages are likely to lead to either unemployment or higher prices.

Chapters 10 and 11 review the Beveridge programme adopted by the UK as a means of providing a minimum income guarantee to all. Despite the lofty intentions of the original programme, the incidence of poverty has remained stubbornly fixed, with the aged and young children being particularly at risk. Part of the reason lies in demographic changes and part of it in hostile reactions to a system of means-tested benefits. But blame also lies with successive governments which have failed to honour the standards laid down by Beveridge. Chapter 11 takes heed of these causes, and discusses alternative programmes to combat poverty. Considerable attention is paid to the concept of 'negative taxation' as a means of providing a comprehensive scheme of income maintenance in a way which minimizes the social stigma attaching to the means test. Of the schemes considered, the social dividend variant is preferred by the author, though this scheme also highlights the need for society to decide upon the trade-off between the costs of a negative-tax type of plan in terms of the rates of tax needed to finance the transfers against the benefits to be offered. The question of potential disincentives to effort lies at the heart of the discussion.

The discussion of social goals concludes with a lengthy consideration of the role and treatment of women in a mixed economy such as that of the United Kingdom. Many of the issues raised in other chapters relating to inequality are met again in the context of equal pay and opportunities for women in the labour market. Other issues relating to family formation and marital patterns also relate to labour market opportunities as well as to the influence of state tax/transfer programmes. Chapter 12 attempts to survey all of these areas. A model of the household production function is explored and empirical tests of its predictions are summarized and compared. The postwar pattern of female participation in the UK labour market is described, and women's share in market rewards is compared with that of men, the result being a considerable differential. Explaining this differential requires a comparative analysis of models of discrimination. Finally, and returning to some of the issues discussed in earlier chapters, the UK system of income taxation is analysed in relation to its likely impact upon the home/market work choices of women and its relationship with other parts of the state's tax/transfer programme so far as it affects female choice decisions.

2. Normative Ground Rules

The introductory chapter intimated that 'social problems' are, in some sense, those problems which are of such concern to society that they command a dominant place in the social welfare function. This is not to say that the everyday problems of buying and selling are unimportant – on the contrary, they concern the basic requirements of life. However, a well-organized society, whether market-orientated or centrally planned, can usually take it for granted that the essential requirements of life are being satisfied by the system for most of the people most of the time. In one sense, such basic concerns are also social problems in that efficient resource allocation and an acceptable distribution of incomes are usually high in the hierarchy of social requirements. Indeed, when the system fails in these areas, the resultant social and economic upheaval can be catastrophic. For this reason, unemployment, inflation and poor growth performances are considered to be the main enemies of well-ordered society and are usually tackled with all the powers at society's disposal. A survey of the social problems of any society could devote much of its space to considering the causes and cures of such ills. The present aim, on the other hand, is not to embark upon a critique of developments in the field of applied macroeconomics. Rather, it is to consider particular problems of allocation and distribution, which, for some reason or another, are not solved in the day-to-day business of the socio-economic system and require special attention from society's institutions in response to concern which is expressed collectively – that is, through the social welfare function.

The day-to-day problems of individuals are dealt with either through the decision processes within various organizations or 'clubs' (households, firms, etc.), or through the interactions of these institutions in a series of exchange processes or markets. For these processes to operate smoothly, a system of legal rights and redress must first be established – that is, a higher authority is assumed to be a precondition of the well-ordered society. Such authority is referred to under the umbrella of 'the state'. In a system where all economic activity is determined by central dictate the state is supremely powerful as the determinant of resource allocation. However, in a system where exchange processes determine allocation considerable power may be vested in households and firms as the determinants of resource allocation. This power is manifested clearly in the solving of day-to-day problems of 'getting and spending'. But exchange processes may not be able to ensure that all wants are met, and there may exist a need for the higher authority of the state either to be working constantly towards an improvement in the mechanics of exchange or to supplant exchange by dictate where such a need is identified.

If the state is seen as the source of ultimate political power in a society, then it can be designated responsible for social planning and for dealing with those problems which are not solved by processes of private command and exchange. How this job is to be tackled is the root concern of normative social science. In the context of its role as overseer, the state is being represented here as the social consciousness. But if 'the state' is taken to mean no more than a collective representative of society's individuals, and its aims are no more than an embodiment of those wants of individuals that require collective action if they are to be satisfied, why does the real world abound with so many differing examples? History has thrown up several models of the state which have exhibited varying degrees of coercion and repression in pursuing social goals, and the forces of circumstance have not always permitted people to exercise a choice over the model thrust upon them. Even the developed world of the present day, politically mature and economically advanced, offers a varied array of politico-economic systems with differing emphasis being placed upon the market mechanism as a means of exhibiting choices and having them satisfied.

Economics alone cannot answer this question, and the contributions of sociology and political science are of great importance, but it does provide insights into the heart of the problems which cannot be gained through the analytical tools of other disciplines. Hopefully, in the course of this book, such insights will emerge clearly.

The Paretian Framework

The prevailing welfare doctrine of the market-orientated economies has been that the powers of the state do not need to be invoked to increase social welfare unless the market fails in some way to do the job, and there has, consequently, grown up a voluminous literature on the causes and cures of 'market breakdown'. But if we are to judge whether or not the market is coping adequately, some criterion of improvement must be devised, some indication of the social worth of any change in the order of things. Finding such a yardstick against which to measure change is essential to the status of economics as a prescriptive discipline, and most of the developments in the theoretical analysis of 'welfare' have concerned this search. The fundamental problem is that judging the social value of any change is an exercise in ethics, and as such involves the untying of some very complex philosophical knots. The history of the unravelling of some of the main philosophical dilemmas in this area provides fascinating reading, but the present study leapfrogs most of the chronological developments in order to concentrate upon the prevailing doctrine. One important question concerns how some of the social problems of a country such as the United Kingdom can be analysed with the aid of the ethical system adopted by the majority of the current generation of economists – the apparatus of Paretian welfare economics.

In part, the emergence of the Pareto criterion as the means of judging policy changes was the result of a backlash against Pigovian welfare economics and the traces of Utilitarianism which run through Pigou's formulations.[1] Spurred on by Robbins's *Essay*,[2] economists turned to the Paretian framework in an effort to minimize reliance on ethical judgements. The basis of the framework is an assumption that the individual is the best judge of his own welfare – there can be no policy base in someone passing judgement on someone else's metaphysical state – and its prescriptive centre point is the criterion that a change is good, it can be recommended, only if it makes someone (feel) better off and no one worse off. It follows from this judgement that a situation can be described as *optimal* in a Paretian sense if no further Pareto-improvements can be made: in other words, that no change can be made which will benefit at least one person while not making another worse off.

Those who are firm advocates of the Pareto criterion believe that its 'minimal ethical content' renders it acceptable to the consensus within society and thus endows it with prescriptive powers. But the same characteristic ranks as a serious flaw in the criterion so far as its detractors are concerned, for they question how a guideline which sidesteps the issue of interpersonal comparisons can be of use in the real world of policy-making. At the same time, some critics would claim further that the criterion is no more 'scientific' than any other ethical judgement and that to them it might indeed be less acceptable than some other rule, at least in certain circumstances. Sen's example is perhaps the most colourful means of underlying this critique:

If preventing the burning of Rome would have made Emperor Nero worse off, then letting him burn Rome would have been Pareto-optimal. In short, a society can be Pareto-optimal and still be perfectly disgusting.[3]

Before considering further the problems involved in using the Paretian framework as a prescriptive guide, a brief résumé of the prescription seems in order. The essential feature concerns social welfare, which is said to be maximized when the goal of maximum efficiency is attained. This efficiency relates to the allocation of the resources owned by a society, since the Paretian social welfare function defines aggregate welfare in terms of the satisfaction enjoyed by the totality of separate individuals from acts of consumption made possible through a system of transformation of resources into goods. A market system is neither necessary nor sufficient for achieving an optimum so defined, but the model most favoured by Western economists has assumed that the processes of transformation are coordinated through a set of interrelated exchange processes. Optimality is ensured when these processes are perfectly competitive, when the participants within them face smoothly convex utility and production/cost functions, and when there is a complete absence of interdependence among either utility or production functions. Given such a framework, optimality is ensured when certain conditions are satisfied.

The rule that optimality requires all resources to be so allocated that no further reallocation is possible without trading off a welfare gain against a loss results in three main conditions for ensuring that an optimum is reached. These conditions are described in terms of the partial derivatives of the relevant production and utility functions in the following manner:

(i) *efficient consumption:* $\quad \dfrac{\partial U^a}{\partial X^a} \Big/ \dfrac{\partial U^a}{\partial Y^a} = \dfrac{\partial U^b}{\partial X^b} \Big/ \dfrac{\partial U^b}{\partial Y^b}$

(ii) *efficient production:* $\quad \dfrac{\partial X}{\partial L} \Big/ \dfrac{\partial X}{\partial K} = \dfrac{\partial Y}{\partial L} \Big/ \dfrac{\partial Y}{\partial K}$

(iii) *efficient mix:* $\quad \dfrac{\partial U^{a\&b}}{\partial X^{a\&b}} \Big/ \dfrac{\partial U^{a\&b}}{\partial Y^{a\&b}} = \dfrac{\partial Y/\partial K}{\partial X/\partial K}$

Condition (i) defines society's consumption pattern as being efficient when the marginal rates of substitution between any two commodities (X and Y) are the same for any two consumers (a and b) of those commodities. All the possible distributions of a given bundle of goods which satisfy this consumptions (exchange) condition lie on an efficiency frontier termed the 'contract curve'. Condition (ii) requires that the marginal rates of *technical* substitution (ratios of marginal physical products) between any two factors of production (L and K) be equal in all the productive uses (X and Y) of these factors. The efficiency frontier which traces the locus of all such positions is termed the 'transformation curve'. Condition (iii), or 'top-level optimum', brings together (i) and (ii) and requires for an optimal composition of output that the marginal rate of transformation between any two goods (X and Y), given by the slope of the transformation curve, be equal to the common marginal rate of substitution between the same two goods in consumption (given by the slope of a 'community indifference curve').

Market Failure and the Economist as Adviser

Given the assumptions outlined earlier as the framework within which the efficiency conditions might be satisfied, the role of the state is at a minimum – enforcement of the terms of contract and provision and financing of the means of defending lives and property. Thus, within the Paretian structure, activities of government which extend beyond such minimal requirements must be justified on the basis of a model which diverges from the assumed world of neutral economic behaviour and perfect competition. In terms of allocation, such justification usually emerges from a discussion of the problems which result from either monopoly in the market-place or the existence of so-called 'externalities'. It is the latter problem which provides the commonest feature of the topics covered by this book, since externalities pervade the economic processes of the real world and have provided a rationale for a much wider role for governments in the search for solutions to society's economic problems.

However, the presence of externalities does not mean that the Paretian framework must necessarily be abandoned. Indeed, for the past twenty years or so the efforts of welfare economists have been somewhat concentrated on dealing with the theoretical difficulties of analysing problems of allocation within such a framework and in the face of external effects. Perhaps the greatest contribution in this area is the work of Buchanan and Stubblebine, which catalogues externalities in terms of their impact on economic behaviour by using Pareto's condition for valuing change.[4] Within this schema, the presence of some activity by agent B within the utility, production or cost function which influences the actions of individual A denotes the external effect, and where B's activity affects the function at the margin a 'marginal externality' is said to exist. Thus, representing A's utility function by U^a, and activities undertaken by A and B as A^a and A^b respectively, the existence of the external effect is shown in (1) and (2) below, where (1) denotes the presence of an externality and (2) its marginal effect:

$$U^a = f_a(A^a_{1\text{---}n}; A_i^b) \tag{1}$$

$$\frac{\partial U^a}{\partial A_i^b} \gtrless 0 \tag{2}$$

However, the extent to which the presence of such an external effect modifies A's behaviour is not shown in either (1) or (2). For A to want to modify B's behaviour, the marginal externality must persist when A is in equilibrium with respect to all other influences on his activities. When this condition prevails, the externality is described as 'potentially relevant'. Finally, for the marginal externality to be corrected or 'internalized' in a manner compatible with the Pareto criterion, for A to gain without B losing, there must be gains from trade possible when A is in equilibrium. Condition (3) describes such a situation, one said to be showing a 'Pareto-relevant externality':

$$\frac{\partial U^a}{\partial A_i^b} \bigg/ \frac{\partial U^a}{\partial A_i^a} > \frac{\partial U^b}{\partial A_i^b} \bigg/ \frac{\partial U^b}{\partial A_n^b} - \frac{f^b A_i}{f^b A_n} \tag{3}$$

Where $\frac{f^b A_i}{f^b A_n}$ refers to B's marginal cost ratio (A_n is numéraire).

In this way, the analysis of Buchanan and Stubblebine is able to deal with problems which threaten the achievement of the Paretian optimum in a manner which retains the very framework of the Paretian system itself. Yet, in terms of real-world policies, there remains the problem of how to set about correcting for these externalities in situations which might diverge from the idealized framework. Thus, the means of correction can only be chosen by political decision in the absence of any certain method of measuring the relative costs of different programmes of correction. In some circumstances – for example, in the case of public goods – the state may play a dominant role in the provision and/or the financing of the provision of certain commodities. When such cases occur and it proves impossible for the benefits from some commodity to be captured within a single utility function or even a small group of such functions – the commodity is then 'non-rival' in consumption – the Pareto condition for efficiency becomes modified to an equality between the marginal rate of transformation and the *summation* of marginal rates of substitution.[5] Faced with such a situation, the state must seek the answer to the two major questions which form the basis of much of the discussion in the literature of modern public finance:

(a) If consumption is completely non-rival, individual consumers face no incentive to reveal their true preferences, therefore, how is the optimum level of provision to be decided?

(b) Even if (a) can be answered satisfactorily, what is the 'correct' burden of finance to be borne by each consumer?

To tackle these questions in detail is not the present aim, but the issues raised by them recur throughout the discussions in this book. At other times, however, it may be possible to 'internalize' external effects through the processes of market transactions, and the fact that the market is not doing so already may be no more than the reflection of an ill-defined system of property rights which requires only a minimum of state intervention in order to establish a proper framework of such rights. Both channels, state and market, are open to any society, and which one is adopted will reflect relative costs weighed against political as well as economic ends.

A major problem for the economist is that once he is outside the structure of perfect competition he must exercise his skills with extreme caution since any claims to objectivity begin to look flimsy. Theoretical niceties like 'Pareto-relevant externalities' can have only a limited practical relevance unless amenable to measurement. Yet many of the objects of choice do not carry explicit market prices, and values must be assigned to them when aggregating costs and benefits. Very often those who directly experience the costs and benefits are unable themselves to assign the appropriate values, and in such circumstances either the decision-maker or his adviser, the economist, must attempt a valuation. Herein lies the core of the problem, for the assignment of expected values can only be a subjective exercise and as such it threatens the consensus among economists by rendering the measurement exercise value-laden.

The extent to which this stumbling-block is allowed to present an immovable obstacle depends upon the relative importance attached by the economist to efficacy and ethical finesse. In a world of scarce resources, where plans are severely constrained by the limitations of time, pragmatism often prevails. Given this state of affairs, the decision-maker dictates the values and his adviser takes them as given, reducing his own task to that of skilled artisan, collecting relevant information and helping to identify the opportunity costs involved in any proposed reallocation of resources. It is this pragmatic view of things that has fostered the interest of many economists in public sector decision-making, and has led to the development of analytical techniques such as cost-benefit analysis and related frameworks of planning such as planning, programming and budgeting (PPB) systems.[6] The information systems so developed not only guide the decision-maker to arrive at efficient choices, they also enable closer monitoring of the decision-making process and promote public accountability in the political sphere.

A primary aim of the analyst in the above process is to catalogue alternatives so that the most efficient means of achieving any given end might be chosen, though in pursuing this task he faces three major difficulties: (a) the identification and measurement of externalities; (b) identification and measurement of all relevant costs; and (c) the choice of a rate of discount. Since many of the difficulties involved in identifying costs stem from the presence of external effects, the first two parts of the problem are closely related. It is often very difficult to perceive the cut-off point where the total costs (and benefits) of a project can be finally identified, yet too narrow an interpretation may lead to the wrong decision being taken.[7] Indeed, all three problems are interrelated since the rate of discount is itself a measure of opportunity cost in a world of positive time preference. Under perfect competition, one equilibrium rate of interest is established, determined by the dual forces of the marginal social rate of time preference (the rate at which the community is prepared to sacrifice present consumption in return for increased future consumption) and the marginal social opportunity cost of capital (the rate at which current resources actually can be transformed into future consumption possibilities). But in the imperfect capital markets of the real world, the private allocation of resources over time may not coincide with social wants.

A means of lightening the responsibility of the decision-maker is offered by Feldstein, who suggests that, when evaluating capital projects, the social emphasis should be placed on *consumption*, the ultimate rationale for all economic activity.[8] Adopting this approach means that the true costs of any project are the consumption opportunities forgone while the benefits are the consumption opportunities provided. Unfortunately, the theoretical appeal of this approach is not matched by a practical potential. If all the resources used in a given project are released through forgone consumption, and all the benefits are expected to be derived from increases in consumption, then the correct rate of discount to apply is that of the social rate of time preference. But if any of the cost stems from forgone opportunities to invest, and/or expected benefits are in the form of investment increases, then the full benefit/cost calculus must account for a series of investment/consumption chain reactions which render computation impossible. On the other hand, choosing a social discount rate by any other method – for example, using the best available market rate of interest – raises again the spectre of subjectivity.

An Alternative Value System

But pragmatism may not appeal to all, and the inherent values of the policy-making framework are not acceptable to every economist. Indeed, some observers are prepared to substitute their own value judgements for those implied by the Paretian approach, or the quasi-Paretian framework of real-world policy-making.[9] The most vociferous opposers of the established framework are the liberal economists whose voices have been loudly raised in the recently resurrected debate over values in the social welfare function. One important aspect of the liberal viewpoint, the one which has led to much disagreement among students of political economy, concerns a belief in the relative efficiencies of the market-place and the dictates of a central plan. Liberals argue that, since markets allocate resources in response to price signals, there is rarely any occasion when such a mechanism should be replaced by an unwieldy bureaucratic system of resource planning. Left to itself, the market will nearly always satisfy the demands of individual consumers. Such a belief lends support to the view that any programme of income distribution should be as direct as possible, taking the form of, say, cash grants rather than price controls, and that any attempts to encourage consumption of specific commodities like health policies or education services, should not do so through nationalization of resources and allocation at zero user prices. If the problem is an allocative one, the market is likely to be more efficient than any queue system operated within the public sector; if the problem is one of income distribution, potential consumers should receive cash transfers.

Of course, liberals do recognize some types of 'market failure', but either consider such cases to be rare or else believe the methods adopted by the state in correcting the problem to involve unnecessary restrictions on private activities. Thus it has been suggested that policy-makers in the modern industrial economy either overestimate the importance of monopoly in the economy's private sector or, in the case of technical economies of scale, choose public monopoly over the lesser evil of private monopoly. In another area of social problems, pollution could be reduced by a more rational distribution of property rights, while in yet another, the role of private charity could be extended to help in the redistribution of income.[10]

It must be stated here that there is nothing in such views which involves a necessary divide between liberals and followers of Paretian principles. But the point which separates the camps is that such opinion is, when expressed by the liberal, based on a more fundamental belief in the need to preserve individual freedoms, such a need being the overriding consideration within the ethical framework of the social welfare function. In recent years, these values have been writ large as liberals have rallied in support of their principles against an interpretation of their position suggested by Sen in his papers on social choice. Sen's first paper appeared in 1970, and the ensuing debate provoked a further contribution from him in 1976.[11] The main proposition of Sen's work is that it is impossible to satisfy simultaneously both liberal and Paretian values.

Sen defines a set, X, of all possible social states, each being a complete description of society, including every individual's position in it, with each individual, $i(i = 1, \ldots n)$, having a complete preference ordering, R_i, over all possible social states (X). For any set of n individual orderings (one for each individual), there is only one *social* preference relation, R, specified by a 'collective choice rule' which has a range restricted to social preference relations that generate a choice function – a 'social decision function' – in the sense that in every subset of alternatives there must be a 'best' one.[12] Into this framework Sen introduces three conditions: condition U, unrestricted domain – the domain of the collective choice rule includes *all* logically possible sets of individual orderings; condition P, the weak Pareto principal – if every individual prefers alternative x to alternative y (chosen from the range x) then society must prefer x to y; and condition L*, the minimum liberalism condition[13] – there are at least two individuals such that, for each of them, there is at least one pair of alternatives over which the individual is decisive – that is, for the alternative x, y, should i prefer x to y (or y to x), then society should prefer x to y (or y to x).

Now, given the above conditions, Sen demonstrates the impossibility of simultaneously satisfying all of them, in the following way.

Under condition L* there are two individuals, 1 and 2, and two pairs of alternatives (x, y) and (z, w) where x = z. Now assume the following preference orderings:

Individual 1	Individual 2
x, y	z, w
(x = z)	(x = z)
(z =) x > y	w > z(=x)
y > w	y > w
∴ (z=) x > y > w	∴ y > w > z(=x)

Thus, for each individual there is no contradiction. But L* requires for society that $x > y$ and $w > x \ (=z)$; and P requires for society that $y > w$. Here is the dilemma, for $x > w$ for 1, yet for 2 $w > x$, and

$y > x$ for 2, yet for 1 $x > y$. Thus a choice function for this society does not exist.

Now, let x, y, z and w be distinct and assume the following preference orderings:

Individual 1	Individual 2
$x > y$	$z > w$
$w > x$	$w > x$
$y > z$	$y > z$
$w > x > y > z$	$y > z > w > x$

Again, there is no contradiction in the individual orderings. Even so, to satisfy both P and L* proves impossible. L* requires for society that $x > y$ and $z > w$, while P requires that $w > x$ and $y > z$. If the P requirement is applied to each ordering, it means both $w > y$ (for 1) and $y > w$ (for 2). Once more, there is no best alternative and a choice function does not exist.

Sen's theorem has provoked a welter of reactions and comments, some extending his propositions, others challenging them and yet others seeking a compromise between liberalism and the Paretian framework. Most of the criticism has not shifted Sen from his basic position, and he offers an excellent survey of the controversy in his 1976 paper, to which the reader is referred for further detail. But from the point of view of some of the problems dealt with in the public sector, and in view of comments offered by liberals on how the UK authorities should 'solve' social problems, the reactions of British liberals are worth pursuing further at this stage. In the vanguard of the attack from liberals on this side of the Atlantic have been Rowley and Peacock, who have both risen to Sen's arguments with some very positive restatements of the liberal position.[14] Their criticisms of Sen include his failure to recognize the importance of realism in any debate about political economy – since Sen's arguments concern *social* choice, a constitutional issue, the assumption of an unrestricted domain is unjustified; further, in a world where values are being constantly traded off, a social decision rule is unattainable. However, the main contention of Rowley and Peacock is that Sen's condition L* is a gross misrepresentation of liberal philosophy, the true liberal never having regarded his ethical position as being equivalent to Paretian values. They write that the 'essence of liberalism is freedom ... as an ethical value in itself ...',[15] and the value judgement is expressed even more strongly in: 'If certain individuals do not value freedom as highly as liberals would wish, there is no reason why their behaviour should be condoned by the liberal order.'[16] Rowley himself goes further to suggest that the liberal is prepared, within limits, to trade off material welfare as a worthwhile sacrifice for the preservation of freedom.[17] Thus, while Rowley agrees that liberalism and the Paretian ethic share a belief that prescriptive analysis should focus attention on the welfare of individuals, he does not accept the additional Paretian principle which believes the individual to be the best judge of his own welfare, his grounds being that 'there is no guarantee that individuals will necessarily associate their immediate economic requirements with the preservation of freedom in the longer term, even if they should value freedom at all'.[18]

There is no denying the intellectual honesty of statements such as these, but it is difficult to see how they can found a value system which permits any prescriptive analysis of real-world situations. Since the liberal position rests so squarely upon a positive value judgement which does not appeal to the consensus within our society, or even among social scientists, it is unlikely to supplant Paretian principles as a guide to social welfare policies. Part of the problem to be solved by the political system is how to reconcile conflicting values. Some individuals may prefer to have their choices limited, or at least to surrender certain choice decisions to some authority which chooses on their behalf. The reasons for this are varied, and include an inability to make decisions about some of life's less mundane choices, such as in the field of political decisions (foreign affairs, defence expenditure, etc.); political inertia or apathy; and a genuine belief that certain choices regarding society's methods of allocation and distribution cannot be regarded as individual decision problems but must, almost by definition, be treated as social choices, possibly involving a deliberate trade off between freedom and the common good. A completely liberal order would restrict the choices of these individuals who want to surrender decision-making in this way.

As a final note, the prescriptive foundation of the liberal position seems to suffer from a moral inconsistency. That liberals are prepared to proselytize is underlined by Rowley's statement that, in the case of those individuals who do not place the same value on freedom as the liberal, the latter 'will try to persuade them to change their own preference schedules and to introduce freedom into their utility functions'.[19] Yet, in trying so to convert, and bearing in mind his reluctance to accept that the individual is the best judge of his own welfare, Rowley's liberal offers a good example of the *ethical egoist*.[20] The aim of the ethical egoist is to secure for himself the greatest balance of good over bad, and he recognizes the autonomy of others in the normative doctrine that every individual should do what is in his own interest. On the other hand, while he might be able to accept that individuals are behaving reasonably even when their actions conflict with his own interests, the ethical egoist can never use such acceptance as the foundation for prescribing proper behaviour – he is unable to advise any individuals to pursue action x if x conflicts with the ethical egoist's own interest, because to offer advice on this basis offends his moral code. As Glasgow writes:

> Thus for the ethical egoist there is but one autonomous individual (himself) who is also an end in himself. To respect the autonomy of other individuals is to give up this position.[21]

Income Distribution as a Social Goal

By far the greatest deterrent to a wholehearted acceptance of the Paretian framework as a prescriptive guide is the fact that its criterion for judging efficiency cannot be widened into a yardstick of welfare or happiness unless the prevailing distribution of incomes (and wealth) is acceptable to the community. If it is not the case that the income distribution pattern is acceptable, then reallocation will give way to redistribution as an end to be accounted for within the social welfare function. Many of the social problems of the real world have their roots in the prevailing distribution, and this is very true of most of the areas singled out for discussion in this book. Of course, it is impossible to devise an objective means of choosing among distributions. Rather, each society adopts some concept, possibly a hazy one, and devises policies to pursue the chosen objective. Thus the task for the economist in this respect is to advise on the available means of achieving some distributional target and to assess *ex post* the efficiency of distributional programmes. Such programmes will be viewed against other goals, including that of efficient resource allocation.

In recent years a comprehensive attempt has been made to reconcile the Paretian framework with distributional objectives using the analysis of externalities to provide a rationale for programmes of redistribution.[22] Thus, if the income position of any individual or group of individuals enters as an argument into the utility function of some other individual or group, the resulting externality may induce a programme of income redistribution. Of course, the very existence of such an externality does not of itself give rise to any redistribution. In the same way that smoke from a factory chimney induces a change in behaviour, so the position of the poor man invokes a redistribution from the rich man only when the externality is relevant at the margin and when the costs of redistribution are less than the costs of some alternative means of removing the externality. Thus, using two commodities, y and x, and two individuals,

α and β, we can show interdependence by assuming that β's consumption of x appears as an argument in x's utility function:[23]

$$U^\alpha = U^\alpha(x^\alpha, y^\alpha, x^\beta) \tag{1}$$

$$U^\beta = U^\beta (x^\beta, y^\beta) \tag{2}$$

where U represents utility.

For β's consumption to have a potential effect on α's activities, there must be a positive utility gain to α from marginal changes in β's consumption. Such a marginal externality is denoted by:

$$\frac{\partial U^\alpha/\partial x^\beta}{\partial U^\alpha/\partial y^\alpha} > 0 \tag{3}$$

which indicates that a small increase in β's consumption of x yields a small increase in utility to α.

Condition (3) is by no means sufficient to guarantee that α will voluntarily transfer some of his own x to β, for α can enjoy the utility gain no matter how β's consumption is increased. This point is pursued further in a later chapter, but meanwhile it should be clear that the actual means of removing the externality will depend upon the underlying reasons for its existence and the relative costs of alternative programmes of internalizing it. If α enjoys a utility gain from increases of β's consumption of x because, in the absence of the increase, β is unsightly, or a harbinger of infectious disease, or a potential revolutionary threat, the method of internalizing the effect may differ from that chosen when the externality results from α's benevolent nature. History is full of variations on the theme of how the rich have solved the 'problem' of the poor. However, even benevolence does not preclude cost minimization, and the powers of the state may well be invoked to extract transfers from reluctant free-riders or to coerce individuals like β to consume more x (when x represents health or education or similar services).

Thus, later discussion will return to several of these concepts and problems, and much of the framework for discussion will rely upon modifications to the Paretian principles as a means of comparing techniques of income redistribution. But such modifications have not received a totally unqualified acceptance in the literature, and some of the observations of E. J. Mishan are worth underlining in order to maintain a healthy perspective on the powers possessed by the concept of a Pareto-optimal income distribution.[24] The essence of the externality approach is in the sense of a tidying-up operation, to treat all economic problems as allocative so that the same bag of techniques can be used to analyse many varying problems. Mishan challenges this aim if the object of the exercise is ultimately to prescribe redistribution programmes, claiming that 'attempts to derive distributional propositions from efficiency considerations is foredoomed to failure'.[25] Mishan's thesis is that treating the problem as one created by utility interdependence can be no more than of descriptive use. He offers two reasons for his scepticism. First, the approach does not offer anything operational since it requires, in practice, information regarding all the myriad patterns of utility interdependence within any society, anything less than unanimity being rejected as a policy approach. Secondly, the concept itself is invalid since movement towards an optimum is movement from a given position in which there is a prevailing pattern of income distribution. Thus, there are as many Pareto-optimal distributions as there are initial distributions, and the analysis of benevolent interdependence does not provide the means of choosing among optima.

Both of Mishan's arguments support strong reservations about the prescriptive use of utility interdependence as a justification for income transfers. But equally telling is Mishan's warning that, even if it were possible to derive some criterion of efficiency-based distribution which could be made operational, there is no guarantee that negative interdependence – malice, envy and so forth – would not be an equally important policy determinant. If transfers from the rich to the poor lower the utility of the envious or malicious, Pareto-optimal transfers are not possible. Yet to ignore such reactions is to advocate redistribution on some other criterion outside the Paretian framework. Further, even without malice or envy there can be varying degrees of benevolence even within income brackets. Thus, any programme of redistribution would be based on a range of varying contributions from the rich – rich man A might be asked to contribute more than richer man B because the former is more benevolent than the latter – and any redistributive measure (for example, an income tax), based on such principles would be ethically dubious and politically impossible.

Taking the Mishan view, income redistribution must be justified on other grounds. If society wishes it, then it should be done and the major problem is how to do it! To a large extent, much of the later analysis of distribution discussed later in this book adopts this view, assuming that society has a redistributive aim and trying to judge the measures employed in trying to reach this aim. However, interdependence among utility functions is used on several occasions to illustrate arguments for and against state intervention in market affairs, and to illustrate why certain programmes of redistribution take on a particular form. In terms of the overall distribution problem, Mishan's reservations are well justified, and, hopefully, interdependence is used later to describe and illustrate rather than to support any normative suggestions. But in terms of specific commodity interdependence, there does seem to be a case for using interdependence to explain why certain redistributive means have been employed, and the technique is also used to that purpose.

Concluding Remarks

All in all there are several points to bear in mind when describing the type of societal framework assumed to be the model for the UK in later discussions. First, the aim of income redistribution is taken as given, though the desired amount of it is sometimes only vaguely specified. Given the earlier warning that interdependence can be based on several possible causes, it is assumed that the society model to be adopted is humanitarian (the rich do not remove the unsightly poor by hiding them in ghettoes or by some means of destruction) and in some sense egalitarian. The precise aim and character of the social welfare function is never known, though elected governments are assumed to have a set of goals which closely approximate to the wishes of the majority. In pursuing these goals, both equity and efficiency are accompanying objectives, to be assessed by the social scientist as observer. Efficiency requires that the cheapest method of achieving a given aim should be adopted, all other things being equal, and that the method chosen to achieve one aim should not impede the achievement of another. Hence, any interferences with market processes by subsidies or taxes should be neutral in their effects on resource allocation. Equity requires that individuals can only be treated unequally by the state if to do so is furthering a goal of more equality (unequal treatment of unequals); and, as a corollary to this, that individuals of similar incomes and circumstances should be treated equally (equal treatment of equals). This would suggest that any income tax system will be based on ability to pay and that individuals of similar ability will face equal tax demands.

Finally, to pull together one or two threads introduced earlier and to offer a pointer to the analysis of the following chapter, a few further thoughts about 'neutral economic man' are appropriate. Where individuals are motivated by self-interest, and where conditions permit them to pursue their aims unhampered, the Paretian framework may have an appeal. This is the line adopted in certain areas of the ensuing discussions. Where doubt is cast upon this framework, it must be abandoned. This is particularly true whenever distributional considerations are paramount, and it may not be sufficient to assume that problems of distribution can be rendered problems of allocation by treating the former as the results of externalities. It would seem to be the case that individuals are often motivated by 'high ideals', stubbornness, belief in an alternative social structure and so forth. Thus it will not always be possible to discuss behaviour as being the result of an external effect, nor will the liberal order be established if such motivations dominate. A worker may jeopardize his job by striking because he hopes for eventual socialism, an individual may give to charity because 'he was brought up that way', a majority of individuals may prefer to allocate resources to health services through the 'public sector' rather than the market-place, because they believe in a 'social hierarchy of wants', regardless of the relative efficiences of the two sectors.

3. More on Externalities

This chapter immediately picks up the themes pursued in Chapter 2. The subject-matter again is *externalities*, now considered in relation to the consumption of specific commodities. Sometimes individuals consume too much of certain things and sometimes too little, according to the values and objectives of the social welfare function. In other words, consumption or production by one group of individuals affects the utility levels of other individuals who take appropriate steps to alter the prevailing level of economic activity for the sake of conforming to some desired optimum. The analysis underlines some of the doubts expressed in Chapter 2 regarding an unqualified reliance upon the Pareto criterion.

Institutions and Unwanted Spillovers

We begin with the case of undesirable externality – that is, where some activity which raises the utility level of one or more individuals lowers the utility of others. Another way of viewing this case is to consider the activity as creating costs which are additional to those for which the producer is compensated by market proceeds – where, in other words, social costs diverge from private costs. Where such an external effect is relevant in the Pareto sense, institutional arrangements will arise to internalize the externality. The nature of the resultant institutions will depend upon the characteristics of the situation, as we shall see presently.

One obvious institutional arrangement is the state, which can use its powers of taxation to 'correct' unwanted externalities. The most famous theoretical version of this arrangement is that of Pigou's 'corrective tax' whereby an optimum solution (marginal social benefit being equal to marginal social cost) is achieved by the state raising producer costs through imposition of taxes until output is reduced to the optimum level for society.[1] But why invoke the state unless it is absolutely necessary to do so? Is it impossible for the market to solve the problem?

Trading arrangements may permit an optimal solution providing certain conditions are satisfied. First, property rights must be clearly defined and recognized by all economic agents (the 'perfect knowledge' assumption). Secondly, transactions costs must be sufficiently low to permit collective action by those suffering from the externality – and often a simplifying assumption of zero transactions costs is made. Thirdly, no indivisibilities should prevent marginal alterations to output. A fourth condition is that there must be perfect competition in all outputs, *including external effects*. Finally, the distribution of property rights must be acceptable to the social welfare function.

Given that the above conditions can be satisfied, it is possible to demonstrate how the problem is solved within the market sphere. Furthermore, it is possible to show that the optimum level of output is unaffected by who actually pays for the optimum to be attained, whether the sufferer from pollution receives compensation or whether he has to bribe the producer to cut back on his production. This proposition is the essence of the famous 'Coase theorem'[2] and is demonstrated below.

We begin with an example of pollution at a constant rate per unit of output of marketable commodity. This case assumes that marginal social costs outweigh marginal social benefits by some constant amount, t. Thus, t is the *maximum* price per unit of pollution reduction which sufferers are prepared to pay; or, the *minimum* price per unit which sufferers would demand if they were seeking compensation. (It is also the rate of tax which is imposed on producers under Pigou's solution.) To understand fully the mechanics of the problem, it will help to consider a perfectly elastic demand curve for pollution reduction at price t per unit.[3] Consider, first, a case where property rights are owned by the producer – where consumers must bribe producers to cut back the rate of output. Faced with such a bribe, firms will reduce their product output (increase their output of pollution-free environment) by an amount which varies directly with the price per unit of output reduction. Forgone output means forgone profit, therefore the greater the reduction in output from that rate which maximizes profit, the higher must be the unit price for output reduction which will just compensate the firm for reducing its output. Figure 3.1 shows the optimum output of 'cleaner environment' which results from the bribes process. In the figure, D(MV) represents the marginal valuation curve for cleaner environment and S shows the marginal cost, in terms of forgone profit, of providing it. S′ shows the *net* supply curve, forgone profit minus bribe per unit of output. On is the optimum output of cleaner environment (which determines the optimum output of the main product). For outputs below On, the unit bribe is greater than the unit loss of profit, and therefore it pays the producers to carry on reducing output of the main commodity until On is achieved. But increasing cleaner environment, and hence reducing saleable output, beyond On is not worthwhile since the loss of profit per unit is greater than the amount of the bribe.

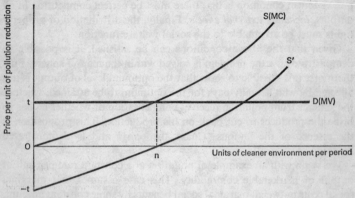

Figure 3.1.

Suppose, now, that environmental property rights are owned by consumers so that producers must compensate consumers for pollution. We find that, as long as the earlier assumptions hold, compensation leads to the same output – that is, resource allocation is unchanged. As output of the main commodity contracts and the amount of cleaner environment expands, so the marginal cost in terms of forgone profit is less than the amount of compensation firms must pay up to On. In other words, the amount producers *save* in compensation not paid is greater than the amount of forgone profit. Beyond On, the loss of profit per unit is greater than the compensation, and so producers are better off producing more of the main commodity (less units of cleaner environment) and paying the compensation – moving back to On.

Changing the example to one where pollution rises at an increasing rate per unit of main output does not alter the Coase proposition, given that the other assumptions continue to hold. If pollution increases as main output increases, this means a downward-sloping demand curve for pollution reduction (units of cleaner environment) since damage per unit decreases the greater is the reduction in output, that is, the more clean environment there is the lower the price that will be offered. As before, there will be some equilibrium price at which demand equals supply for cleaner environment (reduction in main output). Figure 3.2 shows the equilibrium, and S in the figure refers to the supply curve and D(MV) to the marginal valuation curve. The analysis of how equilibrium is established proceeds as in the competitive case – On is the output which satisfies both sides of the market.

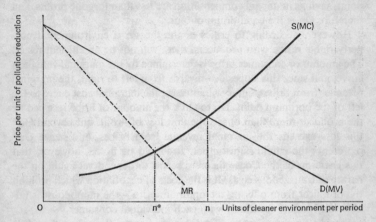

Figure 3.2.

However, the abstractions of the above analysis are unlikely to reflect reality, and this has led some economists to remain suspicious of the Coase theorem. One criticism emphasizes the likelihood of monopoly in the production of pollution.[3] So far the analysis has assumed competition in all markets, including pollution, but is it not likely that a pollution producer will have (at least) local monopoly? Note that the assumption of perfect competition in main product markets is quite compatible with monopoly in the production of secondary, unwanted goods. When monopoly persists, then more pollution (less cleaner environment) can be produced than under perfect competition. This prediction is based on the argument that, since the amount of potential bribe per unit falls as the amount of clean environment expands, so the marginal revenue from bribes will be less than the average revenue. Thus, in Figure 3.2, the equilibrium output of cleaner environment for the monopolist is On*, where the marginal revenue curve (MR) cuts the marginal cost curve S(MC).

Whether more pollution *is* produced under monopoly depends upon who owns the environmental property rights, contrary to the Coase theorem. If consumers own the property rights, then the Coase result still prevails since compensation by producers to consumers will yield an optimal allocation of resources. Since the marginal valuation curve shows the minimum amount consumers will accept in compensation per unit of pollution suffered, output will again settle at On. Prior to this amount, the producer will cut back on those units for which marginal profit (forgone) is less than unit compensation (saved). Beyond this point, savings in unpaid compensation are less than forgone profits, and therefore On is the equilibrium output.

However, according to critics of the theory, if environmental property rights reside with producers, there will not be an efficient result. The amount of consumer bribe is determined by the marginal valuation curve, and since this slopes downwards from left to right, the marginal revenue (from bribes) curve will intersect the marginal cost curve to the left of the optimum point. Up to On*, the amount of bribe received by the producer more than offsets the unit loss of profit, but beyond On* this loss exceeds the marginal revenue from bribes, and hence On* represents the equilibrium output. It should be noted, however, that this criticism of the Coase theorem seems to depend yet again on the nature of transactions costs. It is the costs of negotiation which prohibit the producer from offering the optimum price – the monopolist is unable to negotiate separately with each individual consumer.

Staying on the question of transactions costs, the assumption that they are very low is open to qualification. In the two-person world, such an assumption may be reasonable and the bargaining process may follow a smooth path to agreement. Figure 3.3 shows how bargaining proceeds, the marginal benefits from individual B's activity (producing units of x) being shown by MV^B (B's marginal valuation curve) and

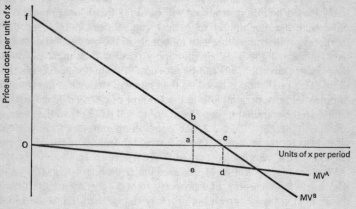

Figure 3.3.

MV^A (individual A's marginal valuation curve). The curves are *net* marginal valuation curves, calculated *after* marginal costs have been accounted for. As the curves show, B enjoys positive benefits at the margin until output Oc is reached; thereafter, marginal benefits are negative. However, A's benefits are negative for all levels of activity. Now, if B, the producer, owns the environmental property rights, he will want to produce Oc and enjoy a total benefit of Ofc. But this output entails Ocd negative benefits for A, who will therefore face an incentive to bribe B in order that production might be cut back. It will pay A to offer bribes to B until the marginal gain from B cutting back equals the amount of bribe A pays at the margin. This results in output Oa, where ae = ab, which is worthwhile for A since his gain of acde exceeds the bribe he has to pay of abc. If, on the other hand, A owns the property right, then he must receive compensation. Without compensation, A would choose zero output, but, responding to B's offers, he will accept output Oa since his loss of Oae is compensated by payments from B. Individual B also finds the arrangement worthwhile because his gain, Ofba, exceeds the compensation which he must forfeit.

But if transactions costs are not zero, then the bargaining process may break down. Transactions costs may be so high for consumers that they outweigh the potential benefits from a reduction in pollution so that it becomes no longer worthwhile for consumers to offer a bribe. High transactions costs result from large numbers on both sides of the market. It may be impossible to isolate individual producers and thereby negotiate with them – for example, how are the individual suppliers of air pollution by motor cars to be isolated? It may be equally difficult for consumers to organize themselves – how does one individual negotiate separately with the thousands of sufferers from air pollution? It seems likely that some form of 'club solution' will emerge whereby a collective negotiating effort becomes possible. However, this does raise the perennial problem of the free-rider, since any reduction in pollution is a collective good, giving benefits to all sufferers, regardless of who actually pays, and true preferences for pollution reduction may not be revealed. Thus the club must be all-embracing and based on well-defined rules of membership – in other words, the state?

A further drawback to the neoclassical position is the existence of production indivisibilities. When infinitely small adjustments to output cannot be made, the optimization rules of marginalism cannot apply. There are, indeed, many products which are likely to create spillovers and which cannot be produced in minute pieces – production is an all-or-nothing decision (witness the concern of the producers of Concorde over the organized protestations of American citizens). When this is the case, neither the bribe nor compensation will prevent the increase in production and more positive action by the state may be required.

Finally, the neoclassical analysis is based upon a given distribution of property rights (income) which is presumed to be acceptable. But what if the distribution of incomes is such that sufferers do not possess the means with which to bribe pollution producers? If property rights reside with producers, then consumers must possess the means of inducing the necessary cut-back in production. Furthermore, the distribution of incomes will determine the relative abilities of the two sides of the market to organize collectively and to undertake effective negotiations.

It should be emphasized that most of the above qualifications do not affect the Pigovian solution, the exception being that of production indivisibilities. However, the conditions which would need to be satisfied so that the precise value of the corrective tax might be decided upon are too complex for this solution to be a real-world possibility. There is, however, a pragmatic way out, suggested by Baumol and Oates,[4] which requires that a set of targets (standards) be set for environmental quality, and that these targets be achieved through a combination of fiscal measures and other 'complementary instruments'. The essence of this proposal is that set standards impose the constraints under which a society operates, and that the society carries a comprehensive portfolio of measures to maintain social and economic goals within these constraints. While taxes may be superior to bargaining, because of, say, transactions costs, direct physical controls on output may sometimes be superior to taxes, because of, say, the complexities of calculating optimal rates of tax, or because the nature of the potential environmental damage from some activity is massive and unpredictable.

Institutions and External Benefits

Externalities also help to create social problems when one group consumes too little of some specific commodity according to the wants of some other group. Prime examples of this situation include the consumption of medical services, education and housing. Most developed nations make some form of public provision for these goods, though the extent of state involvement varies considerably. But even in those countries where the state has a virtual monopoly of provision of these goods, there runs a continuous debate over whether or not the market should be allowed a greater role in the process of allocating resources to the provision of such commodities. In an attempt to survey the main arguments in this area, we concentrate on health care provision.

The model of public provision with which we are concerned is illustrated by the British National Health Service as it has operated since 1946 – medical services offered to everyone free of direct user price and financed and provided through the state, co-existing with a much smaller private sector to which those who possess the means may resort if they choose to by-pass the state monopoly. Two major criticisms have been aimed at this system, both arguments being constantly used against any state monopoly which offers services at zero user price: (a) provision at zero user price inflates demand beyond the level of supply during any time period with a consequent reduction in both the quantity and quality of services offered; (b) monopoly provision restricts consumer choice, and, therefore consumers are prevented from learning by experience. Resources are thus allocated according to producer sovereignty and not consumer sovereignty.

Both arguments raise the problems discussed in Chapter 2. The first criticism has been expressed most forcefully by Buchanan,[5] who argues that excess demand is inevitable since there are forces at work in the system to both expand demand and restrict supply at zero price. So long as price elasticity of demand is positive, rational consumers will continue consuming until the marginal utility from medical services is zero. But consumers as voter/taxpayers, balancing benefits against costs, will vote to supply an amount of services that falls below satiation level – and excess demand must result. Given this problem and the other arguments referred to, a neoclassical answer is that, if the primary aim is to redistribute income, then cash transfers from high-income groups to low-income groups would permit the price mechanism to operate and resources could be allocated according to consumer sovereignty without violating Paretian principles. Let us now qualify these arguments, and in doing so take a closer look at the model provided by the National Health Service.

As a positive proposition, consumer sovereignty suggests that all economic activity is directed towards satisfying the wants of consumers. As a normative proposition, consumer sovereignty asserts that the efficiency of an economy should be judged in terms of how well it satisfies the wants of consumers. Qualifications of the positive proposition relate to the presence of rigidities and imperfections in the economic system and are not discussed in any detail in the present context. We shall, however, give an airing to the normative arguments.

The normative proposition seems based on two major assumptions, each of which has relevance to the area of health care. First, there is the assumption that wants are known and that the objects of choice satisfy those wants. Generally, this assumption may be unrealistic, since some commodities may fail to satisfy wants because of consumer ignorance and the high costs of acquiring information. Furthermore, individuals may not possess definite wants above a certain level of satisfactions, and 'shopping around' may refer as much to acquiring wants as it does to satisfying them – at least, this might be true of the rich consumer, the wants of the poor being more circumscribed. Medical services would seem a prime example of the information problem. The chain of knowledge by which an actual want becomes defined is not the simple one-to-one relationship by which, say, hunger or thirst is satisfied. An individual consumer must know that he is ill (not always easy); know what is the real nature of the illness; know what the best treatment is and how to get it. This represents a complicated shopping-list, particularly since the last two items may involve considering several alternatives.

As it has been pointed out elsewhere,[6] the health services are not unique with respect to the problem of information, and many commodities are consumed under varying degrees of ignorance and uncertainty. However, it might be argued that good health is the primary want of most individuals, and to that extent a ready way is sought to reduce the uncertainty surrounding health service requirements. Whether this mechanism relies upon, or completely supplants, the market will depend on factors not yet considered. For the moment it should be noted that an *a priori* case cannot be made in favour of either the state or the market on the basis of information problems.

A second observation on the neoclassical assumptions is that the doctrine of consumer sovereignty says nothing about how consumer preferences are to be aggregated whereas Pareto–optimality does. As we have observed before, the new welfare economics was couched in terms of independent utility functions – *neutral* economic behaviour – which lent support to the neoclassical split between allocation and distribution. This belief in neutrality meant that economics was hamstrung as a policy-making science, since no income redistribution could be permitted, in the belief that inter-personal comparisons of utility could not be made.

Reaction to the denial of inter-personal comparisons began in the 1950s, much of the impetus being provided by Little,[7] who contended that individuals *do* make such comparisons, that they are a fact and hence that their assumption does not entail a value judgement. But real progress on this front had to wait until the attack on the notion that utility is homogeneous and a substitution of the view that different wants give rise to different kinds of utilities. A major contributor to developments along these lines is Georgescu-Roegen, who underlines two important points. First, he stresses the existence of the hierarchy of wants which makes possible objective measures of need and allows for the well-being of others to be a direct objective of economic activity. These results emerge from the observation that the hierarchy of wants seems to be identical for all men up to a certain level of income. Above this level, wants may become intensely individualistic and therefore non-comparable, but this does not deny the common objectivity of the basic wants – food, shelter, *good health* and so on.

Any observer understands why there is welfare sense (not necessarily imply-ing obligatory policies) in taxing people who spend their summers on the Riviera, in order to help undernourished people; but most observers will question that there is sense in taxing the same people to help others to go each Sunday to a football game.[8]

Secondly, self-interest and neutral economic behaviour are not neces-sarily facts of life or even of human nature, such motivations being largely determined by the nature of society itself.[9] We are reminded that societies have differed in their emphasis upon the need for the individual to recognize the greater welfare of the community. Furthermore, a society could not last long under any 'prolonged eclipse of the social variable' – the criterion by which any individual regards the welfare of his community. This fact is attested to by the gradual emergence of the 'cartel of the welfare state'.[10]

We may add to the view of economic man as a neutral agent a third qualification which seems to be suggested by the two points already made – that people derive utility from the mode of acquisition of goods as well as the actual act of consumption. This allows for different insti-tutional frameworks to yield different utilities. Hence, a society may *prefer* to allocate resources for health care (housing, or education) in a non-marketing mode.

Now, if these three observations are relevant, voluntary income redis-tribution becomes feasible, and points along a Pareto-efficient trading contract curve may now be compared on the basis of the degree of in-equality in income distribution given by each point. Such a comparison, as referred to in Chapter 2, blurs the distinction between allocation and distribution, and policies to achieve improvements in one may require changes in the other. Given these requirements, lump-sum transfers, price subsidies and even coercion may be compared as means of raising the consumption level of specific goods for a particular section of the community.

An important argument developed by Pauly is that utility interdependence weakens the case for transfers in cash, as opposed to other means of redistribution, because it rests upon the maximization of the recipient's welfare unconstrained by the utility function of the giver.[11] A lump-sum transfer creates only an income effect, whereas, say, an equal-amount price subsidy creates both an income effect and a substitution effect. The combined forces of the price subsidy will create a greater increase in consumption than the income effect of the cash transfer, and this will be the case even with the Giffen good, since the (posi-

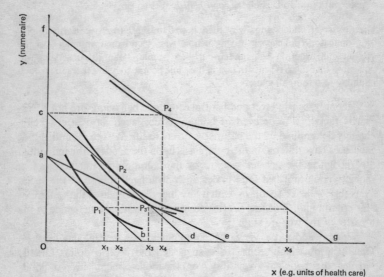

Figure 3.4.

tive) substitution effect will pull in the direction of increased consumption. Yet even the price subsidy may fail to induce the recipient to raise his level of consumption to that demanded by the giver, and some form of 'all-or-nothing' scheme may be called for whereby the potential recipient is offered the choice of either a subsidy, which enables him to achieve approximately the same level of utility as he would gain in the absence of any redistributive measures, or nothing at all. This method assures the largest possible increase in the recipient's consumption for a given amount of subsidy. Figure 3.4 illustrates the various transfer possibilities. The figure shows part of the preference map of individual B, representative of some group of individuals, who, in the view of another group in society, represented by individual A, consumes too little of commodity x (say, health care). Faced with his preference map and his own income constraint, ab, individual B consumes at point P_1. A lump-sum transfer of income from A takes him to P_2 (budget line cd), while an equal-sum price subsidy takes him to P_3 (budget line ae) – the combined income and substitution effects induce him to consume more x with the price subsidy than with the lump-sum income transfer ($x_2 - x_3$ more).

However, as Pauly points out, a lump-sum transfer in kind *can* promote the desired increase in consumption if resale of the transferred commodity is prohibited *and* the amount transferred is large relative to the amount purchased in the absence of any transfer arrangements. Figure 3.4 shows such a transfer, $x_1 - x_5$. By reducing his own purchases of x, individual B is able to move leftwards along fg, but is prevented from reaching a tangency point to the left of P_4 since he cannot reduce his own expenditure on x below zero.[12]

The best point that B can reach under the above arrangements is P_4, where he consumes a quantity of x which is greater than could be achieved through price subsidies. Yet an all-or-nothing scheme takes B to P_4 with a smaller transfer than x_1 to x_5. Faced with a no-subsidy alternative, B would accept a transfer of $x_1 - x_4$, which takes him to P_4 at a saving of $x_4 - x_5$ for A.

Another way to view the various transfer arrangements is in terms of relative costs for A — a given increase in consumption of x by B is achieved most cheaply for A by the all-or-nothing method. Looking at the problem from this angle serves to underline a basic dilemma facing the policy-maker: B's preference is for the lump-sum transfer, but this proves to be the most wasteful from A's standpoint. Considered in terms of costs, Pauly's analysis looks similar to that of Lindsay, who goes so far as suggesting that his model may offer a rationale for arranging medical care along the lines of the National Health Service.[13]

Lindsay's model specifies some degree of equality in consumption of some commodity as part of A's objective function, whereas Pauly's analysis assumes that an unspecified increase in consumption by B is one of the arguments. The analysis of relative costs in each case would, however, be the same. Lindsay identifies four methods by which A (the rich man) can increase the degree of equality in the consumption of some specific commodity x: (a) at the going price A buys x according to his marginal valuation of x and then destroys some of his acquisition – the 'burnt offering' method; (b) A buys x and gives some to B – the gift method; (c) A abstains from buying that amount of x which equates price and marginal valuation; (d) A subsidizes an increase in B's consumption of x.

Of the four possibilities, method (a) is most expensive for A since he loses the full value of the units sacrificed. Method (b) is half as cheap as (a) since it produces twice as much equality. Method (c) produces the same degree of equality as method (a), but this third method costs no more than the consumer surplus sacrificed since units of x are not purchased as with method (a). Finally, method (d) is the cost of inducing B to buy more x, a cost which cannot be greater than the price of x, but which may be as low as the difference between this price and B's own marginal valuation of x – in fact, A pays the difference. Now, since the

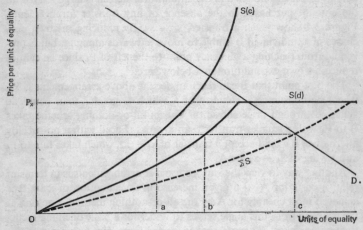

Figure 3.5.

first three methods, all of which reduce the rich man's holdings of x, are mutually exclusive, his least-cost method involves a combination of method (d) and the cheapest of the first three methods, which, up to the ceiling imposed by the price of x, must be method (c). In other words, the cheapest strategy for A combines subsidy with rationing (abstention). Figure 3.5 summarizes how the costs of increasing equality are allocated between the two methods, A's demand curve for equality in consumption of x being shown by D. The supply (marginal cost) of equality by abstention is shown by S(c), and for the subsidy method S(d) is the relevant supply curve. ΣS represents the horizontal sum of S(c) and S(d). Oc is the amount of equality which equates A's marginal evaluation of equality with his marginal cost of providing it, and A achieves this amount by providing Oa units of equality by the abstention method and Ob units by the subsidy.

In rather similar fashion, Pauly's least-cost method involves an all-or-nothing subsidy, though his final scheme of things does not include abstention since he is more interested in the increase in B's consumption *per se* rather than in the resulting degree of equality. Pauly's example is a scheme which extracts B's consumer surplus – that is, a scheme by which the marginal cost to A equals the difference between the maximum price B is prepared to pay for an additional unit and the marginal cost of producing that unit (the price of the unit). Given that B's demand curve is 'normal', A's marginal cost curve will slope upwards from left to right and intersect the curve which represents A's demands for increases in the private consumption of the commodity by B.

Thus both models offer serious qualifications to the arguments of the New Welfare Economics. According to Lindsay, his model offers a rationale for the National Health Service, resolving inequalities in consumption of health care through the collective provision of subsidized services, financed through progressive taxation (which also removes the free-rider problem), with access to such services being offered to *all*, regardless of means. This free access means that the rich are prevented from acquiring the 'lion's share' of scarce medical resources, and so, to gain an increase over their National Health Service 'ration', they must gain access to the private medical sector by paying the relatively higher prices which private services can command.

However, Lindsay's analysis ignores the more detailed nature of the rationing mechanism.[14] It has been suggested that the rationing system for publicly provided services may be less efficient than the system used by the market-place. Culyer has pursued this point, comparing the market system of rationing by price with that of the National Health Service, which rations by the queue, time prices, in other words, being substituted for money prices.[15]

Culyer argues that while queueing reduces effective demand for medical resources, it is a less efficient rationing method than user prices since waiting costs are dead-weight welfare losses, the costs incurred not inducing an increased supply of resources. It might be argued that, since a wait of a given length is relatively more costly for those with higher earnings, queueing works to redistribute income. But this argument ignores three important points. First, institutional arrangements in the labour market separate wage-earners from salaried employees and the former are more likly to be employed at hourly rates of pay. Thus queueing discriminates against the wage-earner and in favour of the salaried employee. Indeed, the latter may face no opportunity cost as measured by forgone earnings if allowed time off without penalty for sickness during any salary month. Secondly, separating high earners from low earners is not necessarily a separation of rich from poor since the former may receive large incomes from wealth holdings. Queueing discriminates in favour of individuals with large wealth holdings but low earnings. Thirdly, whether the rich suffer more than the poor from this system of allocation ultimately depends upon relative income utilities at the margin. Only if the marginal utility of income to the rich is greater than the marginal utility of income to the poor can it be said that real marginal time costs will be relatively higher for the rich. But to make such a judgement is to introduce interpersonal utility comparisons.

As a final qualification to Lindsay's arguments, more in support of Lindsay than Culyer, we note the latter's argument that the rich cannot avoid their time costs by buying private medicine (assuming they pay an amount equal to their time costs) since they still have to pay National Health Service taxes – they cannot contract out. Thus whether the rich *would* transfer to the private sector depends on whether the resulting net gain in consumer surplus would outweigh the fiscal cost of National Health Service provision. There is no *a priori* way of knowing the likelihood of this net gain being sufficient, though there may be a strong suspicion that price-discriminating monopolist suppliers of health care would tap a large portion of the potential consumer surplus. The argument should also be tempered by the fact that it ignores interdependence. The rich may accept the tax price to redistribute towards the poor, but then use the private system to reduce their own time costs. In other words, the rich accept coercive transfers as a means of trapping the free-riders, but prefer the price mechanism to allocate resources among themselves. To some extent, this would seem to lend support to Lindsay's thesis.

The conclusion must be that we cannot make *a priori* judgements until we know more of the nature of the various utility and production functions which go towards determining the allocation of health resources. Need for such information has spawned a huge output of research material over the past decade or so. These researches have ranged over the full spectrum of problems in both the demand for and supply of medical services, and have covered both abstract difficulties such as the elusive definition of 'good health' and concrete technical problems such as the logistics of ambulance services in the case of hospital out-patients.[16] However, while answers have been provided to certain problems of technical detail, the wider issues covered in this chapter remain unresolved.

Allocating Resources without Markets

Before leaving this area of applied economics, we must briefly consider another problem: one which arises from the nature of publicly provided services. If, as in the United Kingdom, the state assumes the role of the market as the means of resource allocation, *how* are these resources then allocated? How do the authorities plan for the future consumption of health services?

The techniques which have evolved as aids to evaluation and planning in public expenditure are usually lumped under the heading of 'cost-benefit analysis', a technique which attempts to identify relevant gains and losses from a given project and to measure the project's ratio of benefits to costs. On the assumption that an acceptable system of compensation operates to placate the losers in the implementation of any plan, community welfare is assumed to increase if a project's benefit-cost ratio is greater than one. But this is not the end of the planning problem. Usually there are several routes by which a particular allocation problem can be solved, involving projects of differing size (outlay) and differing benefit-cost ratios, yet only one can be used. Thus a choice must be made. In principle, marginalist analysis provides a guideline: by equating costs with benefits *at the margin*, the authorities can undertake projects of efficient size; and where projects are of a given size (outlay), the project which yields the greatest benefit from the given outlay would be chosen. However, pursuing such a rule is, in practice, rarely so easy, given the nature of the information problem.

An obvious problem in the identifying and measuring of costs is the one which lies at the heart of our present discussion: externalities. The presence of external effects often makes it extremely difficult to trace the 'cut-off' point where the *total* costs and benefits of a given project can be identified, and decisions based only on those costs and benefits which are easily traced may be incorrect because they have ducked a serious problem. Related to this difficulty is the fact that, since the real costs to be measured are opportunity costs, a means must be found whereby alternatives can be ranked. Since they are rejected satisfactions, costs are subjective, and the ranking of alternatives can therefore only be done with reference to the wants of the individuals affected by a project. When externalities prevail and/or costs and benefits are intangible, evaluation must still be undertaken; and without a clear knowledge of consumer wants, there is a danger that resources will be allocated according to the aims of producers. As we have seen, this argument has been used to criticize the National Health Service.

Another difficulty facing health-care planners is the fact that the returns on an immediate resource outlay will flow over time. Thus, what rate of discount should be chosen? Under conditions of perfect competition, one equilibrium rate of interest emerges which has a two-fold determinant: (a) the marginal social rate of time preference; and (b) the marginal social opportunity cost of capital. However, real-world capital markets are not perfect, and the distribution of incomes among income classes *and* over time may not coincide with the social welfare function. So how is the social rate of discount to be decided? Economists are as yet unable to agree on a common basis for comparing different kinds of projects, though Feldstein's approach[17] has found much support. According to Feldstein, since the ultimate aim of all economic activity is *consumption*, then this is what the valuation of capital projects should emphasize. This means that the real costs of any project are the sacrificed consumption possibilities, while the real benefits are consumption opportunities offered by the project. Now, whenever some proportion of the resource outlay on a project is financed by sacrificed investment opportunities, then the real total benefits must include all the expected increases in consumption created by the increased investment.

Like many theoretical niceties, Feldstein's approach has only a limited practical application because of the difficulties involved in calculating the costs and benefits of successive changes in investment and their ultimate effects on consumption. Government decision-makers usually adopt a pragmatic approach to such problems, and in the case of the United Kingdom this has meant the adoption of a rate of return on capital projects which is at least equal to the minimum rate expected on a marginal low-risk project in the private sector,[18] in recognition of the potential trade-off between public and private projects. To account for a politically determined total volume of investment, the U K authorities adjust the minimum rate to produce a 'test rate of discount' which is then applied to all public sector projects, amid much resultant debate. One obvious reservation is that there is no guarantee that the test rate is superior to any other of the market rates as a true measure of social time preference. It is also the case that such a system assumes a definite trade-off between public and private projects, while quite often there may be a considerable degree of complementarity between them. Furthermore, a test rate of discount for the public sector may be determined by private schemes which themselves are likely to reflect government influence in the private sector as a result of government stabilization policies. Finally, the test-rate approach may ignore the fact that public sector projects may well pursue some redistribution of incomes as part of their objective.

Since the beginning of the 1960s, numerous project evaluations have been undertaken involving the skills of researchers in both the private and public sectors. These studies have ranged over a wide area in which purely 'commercial' criteria are felt to be misleading and where there is a lack, or absence, of signals from the price mechanism. Thus, not only have there been studies of health and educational services, but also of road and rail traffic systems, urban renewal programmes and of alternatives for the siting of a third London airport. Indeed, many of the areas studied provide useful illustrations of problems encountered in the earlier section on pollution.[19] What the various studies emphasize is that the greatest problems do surround the evaluation of externalities and intangible costs and benefits. Indeed, such difficulties have often resulted in evaluations taking the form of 'cost-effective' studies where the aim of the chosen project is clearly defined and the scheme which can match this aim by the least use of resources is chosen. This is not to deny, however, that there have been several success stories in the history of the development of cost-benefit techniques, particularly in the area of transport studies where similar evaluations have emerged from different researchers trying to assess time savings and reductions in accident rates.

Yet, by itself, even an accurate and comprehensive cost-benefit programme can be no more than a guide to the formulation of a plan – it cannot constitute a plan in itself. Nowhere is this more true than in the case of health services. For plans to be devised and assessed, it is essential that final outputs be defined. But, as shown by several cost-benefit studies of government projects, this is where the planning exercise becomes extremely difficult. This difficulty stems partly from the prevalence of externalities, but is mainly due to the fact that the output from government spending is not supplied through a market process and does not carry a market valuation as in the case of private goods. Because of this factor, the annual accounts of public sector income and expenditure try to measure the relative importance of the government sector by measuring the value of the inputs into that sector during the relevant period. But this method is a poor substitute for a system of accounting which links input expenditure to clearly defined objectives ('functional' accounting) and in response the system known as 'planning, programming, budgeting' (PPB), or 'output budgeting', has been developing.[20] As a method of presenting information which links resources to 'needs' (however defined), PPB not only guides the decision-makers, it also permits more efficient checks to be made by the voters upon the decisions of their representatives in government.

The system has four basic aims:

(a) To identify the *objectives* of government activities.
(b) To identify and analyse the *outputs* of government programmes in relation to objectives.
(c) To measure the full *social costs* of government programmes, a task which meets the problems encountered by cost-benefit analysis.
(d) To identify and analyse all the *alternative means* by which any given programme objective can be achieved. This aim is to isolate the least-cost method of gaining an objective.

Clearly such a system can provide a sound planning framework so long as these aims can be satisfied, though, as is so often the case, real-world efforts have so far produced imperfect results. The UK authorities have been flirting with PPB for some fifteen years or so, but despite concrete developments in the field of defence, where PPB was introduced in 1964, following the apparent success of experiments with its use in the Department of Defense in the United States, progress has been rather sporadic. Furthermore, where serious attempts have been made to implement a PPB system, the results have not always been encouraging. For example, in 1968 the Home Office instigated feasibility studies of several police forces with a view to allocating expenditures to clearly defined activities such as traffic control; crime investigation and control; ground cover; and so forth. But instead of the anticipated benefits, the results tended to reaffirm the difficulties involved in trying to measure intangible outputs, a clear example being the impossibility of establishing how much of traffic control costs are devoted to accident prevention as opposed to traffic offences.[21]

Similar disappointments had to be faced elsewhere in the public sector, the experiment conducted by the Department of Education and Science being a major example.[22] But a firm belief in the potential of PPB systems has been adhered to by the Expenditure Committee in strong pleas for a more rational approach to the planning of public expenditures;[23] and in 1974 some sort of answer was provided by the Department of Health and Social Security (DHSS) with the introduction of a planning system for health and personal social services in an attempt to relate priorities to resources through a programme budget. In 1976, the system was extended to the National Health Service. So far the experiment must be judged on the basis of two publications: a Consultative Document in 1976 and a follow-up document in 1977.[24]

The spirit of the DHSS planning exercise reflects a significant movement away from conventional methods of accounting with its emphasis upon input expenditures. The essence of the expenditure projections is to underline priorities in the light of expectations of resource allocation determined by the social and economic plans of central government while also taking account of population trends as estimated by the Office of Population Censuses and Surveys. By using this 'non-financial' data, a more comprehensive guide to resource needs can be arrived at, and when such needs are further based on comparisons between past and present expenditures, the projections should be more reliable than conventional forecasts. This type of budgeting has enabled the Department of Health and Social Security to be more cognizant of the complimentarity which can exist among medical user services and has permitted 'client groupings' to which it is possible to allocate expenditures in some detail.

However, identifying client service areas is not quite the same thing as defining outputs. The real-world system is still somewhat removed from the theoretical ideal. Table 3.1 presents a comparison between the DHSS categories and a hypothetical programme suggested by Else.[25]

Table 3.1.[a]

Hypothetical output programmes[b]	DHSS service programmes[c]
1. Treatment of illness and injury	1. Primary care services
2. Prevention and control of diseases	2. General and acute hospital and maternity services
3. Prevention of accidents	3. Services mainly for the elderly and physically handicapped
4. Long-term care	4. Services for the mentally handicapped
5. Training of medical staff, etc.	5. Services for the mentally ill
6. Research	6. Services mainly for children
7. Expansion and improvement of facilities	7. Other services
8. Unspecified administrative and other expenditure	

NOTES: [a] This comparison is also presented in P. K. Else and G. P. Marshall, *The Management of Public Expenditure*, Policy Studies Institute, London, 1979, Chapter 7.
[b] ibid., Table XII, p. 65.
[c] DHSS, *Priorities for Health and Personal Social Services in England,* Annexe 2, Table 1, p. 82.

Comparing the DHSS breakdown with that of the hypothetical example, it can be seen that the former does not indicate why expenditure is being allocated in a given manner; rather, it merely indicates *where* public outlays are being spent. In this respect, then, the system does not permit a degree of accountability which is likely to conform to consumer preferences. It is true that when such service allocations are compared along a time-stream it is possible to observe trends. For example, it would be possible to discover whether expenditure on, say, day centres for the mentally handicapped is rising or falling, and to project, given expected population trends, whether such outlays are likely to increase during some specified future time period. But such data do not permit discussion of whether or not this particular allocation *should* change because there is no indication of objectives. We need to know what life-style has been chosen for the mentally handicapped so that we can judge the extent to which government spending on services for this section of the population fits the chosen model. It is only by moving more towards the definitions offered by the hypothetical example that judgements about efficiency in public spending can be made.

Conclusions

This chapter has probably raised more questions than answers. However, two clear points emerge. First, whether the problem is one of undesirable externalities or whether it involves external benefits, there is no room for dogma in the search for solutions. Neither the market nor the state is sole keeper of the key which unlocks the door to efficiency in the allocation of resources when externalities are present. Different institutional arrangements offer differing kinds of help, and society's aim must be to choose the best mix. Secondly, replacing the market by the state may solve one set of problems but it raises another in relation to the search for information. If resources are to be allocated without reference to a price mechanism, then information on costs and benefits must be extracted by other means. Accounting conventions which dodge the main issue and offer measurements in terms of inputs are not the stuff by which good planning emerges. It is essential that the search for output measures should not lose momentum.

4. Inequality (1):
Some Conceptual Difficulties

A major area of research for social scientists is that of income distribution. We have already outlined a case for such concern, and we now consider some of the difficulties surrounding the measurement of distribution before actually looking at the distribution reflected in the official statistics of the United Kingdom.

Concern about a community's income distribution is usually a concern about inequality in the shares of economic power enjoyed by the various members of that community. This is not to say that income inequality is more important than some other form of inequality – discriminatory barriers may prevent a rich black immigrant from enjoying the social opportunities readily available to a poor white native; and the wife of a millionaire may not face the same range of labour-market opportunities as a male graduate whose parents are dependent upon social security.[1] However, when other variables are assumed away (for example, we can assume a racially homogeneous population with equal opportunities for the sexes), there remains concern that a society can exhibit severe discrepancies in the degree of economic power enjoyed by the various members of that society.

Defining 'Economic Power'

By a person's 'economic power' we refer to his command over scarce resources. Such power may stem from political strength,[2] from the fruits of the services of factors of production sold in the market place (wages, rents and profits) or from inherited wealth. Thus, command over resources may lie in the dictatorial powers of a ruling despot who has no need to own the medium of exchange so long as his wants can be satisfied by domestic production. In the more democratic framework of conventional assumption, on the other hand, command over resources is usually determined by access to goods markets financed either from the sales of productive services or by the proceeds from inherited wealth.

Measuring Economic Power

It is not clear so far how we are to measure economic power. Yet some measure must be decided upon if we are to make relative comparisons among individuals and among income classes. One measure which finds favour with some observers is that of *expenditure*, on the grounds that any individual's command over economic resources can only be properly gauged when he uses up community goods and services for his own consumption purposes. However, *income* has normally been adopted as the measure of real economic power because it is income which determines *opportunities* to exercise command over economic sources. What any one individual chooses to do with such opportunities is irrelevant to the definition of inequality, since those who are 'more unequal than others' necessarily face a reduced array of alternatives compared with the opportunities available to the 'others'. Indeed, this argument is often further extended to cover not just the *flow* of economic power to any individual unit, but also the total *stock* of potential command over resources possessed by that unit – that is, holdings of wealth. As long as we are emphasizing *opportunities* as the determinant of in-equality, this seems a logical extension. Yet even in a world where wealth is equally distributed there could be inequality in the distribution of incomes, and it seems sensible to consider the latter problem before looking at the former.

The concept of income itself poses further problems. How are we to define the base from which economic power derives, whether the object be one of calculating the distribution of economic power or that of demarcating a source of government revenue (a tax base)? Again, if it is *potential* economic power with which we are primarily concerned, then we might agree with Henry Simons that the calculation of an income base implies:

... estimate (a) of the amount by which the value of a person's store of property rights would have increased as between the beginning and end of the period, if he had consumed (destroyed) nothing, or (b) the nature of rights which he might have exercised in consumption without altering the value of his store of rights.

And:

Personal income may be defined as the algebraic sum of (a) the market value of rights exercised in consumption and (b) the change in the value of the store of property rights between the beginning and the end of the period in question.[3]

What the above statements underline, certainly for purposes of the income tax, but also for the aim of measuring income as a guide to real economic power, is that the definition of income should be comprehensive and it should relate to a clearly defined time period. We might add that there is also the implication of a clearly defined income unit. Obviously, the less comprehensive the income definition, the less reliance we can place on the measure of distribution (or on the success of an income tax in penalizing real ability to pay). But how comprehensive should be the definition? In principle, the measure should be all-embracing. For example, in computing a base for income taxation an ideal principle to follow might be:

... a taxpayer's income in any one year is the value of what he could have consumed during the year without living on and so diminishing his capital wealth in the process.[4]

Such a definition would be equally suited to the measurement of inequality, and the similarity with Simons's definition is clear. The definition would embrace: capital gains (and losses); fringe benefits from employment; the imputed rent from physical capital owned and used by the chosen income unit (a substantial supplement to the income of house owner-occupiers); imputed income from domestically produced goods and services; and social insurance benefits. Furthermore, income so described is defined in real terms, particularly important when comparing the relative positions of classes within a given distribution of incomes since changes in relative prices may have different effects upon the consumption patterns reflected by these different classes. Very often these relative effects are geographical. For example, there is a considerable disparity in property values throughout the United Kingdom, the costs of living in London are much higher than those in the provinces, and so forth.

Clearly, the above principles represent an ideal, and attempts to calculate the distribution of incomes in any real-world situation are bound to be dogged by measurement problems. This is certainly true for the United Kingdom, and, as we shall see later, since the calculations for the United Kingdom are based on data collected for income tax purposes, they reflect the definition of income sanctioned by the Inland Revenue rather than the idealized picture presented above. In the following chapter we shall take up this issue and give closer consideration to the deficiencies of the definition of income adopted by the authorities.

At this point we should also note two further problems which must be resolved when income distributions are being calculated. First, there is the problem of choosing the time period to which the data is to refer.

This choice is made for us when we use real-world data collected by the Inland Revenue – income tax returns are made annually. It has been clearly underlined elsewhere[5] that the choice of time period can be a crucial determinant of the degree of income dispersion. For example, weekly income is likely to be more dispersed than monthly or annual income. The influences of shift working, overtime, sickness, the vagaries of the weather, and so on, are felt much more strongly on weekly distribution than on, say, the annual pattern. Moreover, a *lifetime* measure may give a truer picture of income distribution and may be nearer to the real source of society's concern about inequality – a poor pensioner may be suffering the consequences of a myopic, profligate youth; a university student, currently in dire poverty, may be expecting very high financial rewards from his graduate career.

Thus, whatever time period is adopted, it is likely to have different consequences for the various income classes. While a lifetime picture may yield more accurate long-term comparisons, the weekly view may be more relevant in depicting the plight of the very poor. The rich are able to tide themselves over a lean patch either by borrowing or by the sale of assets, but the poor may have no resources to fall back upon during bad times and the imperfections of the capital market may ensure that the rates of interest offered to the poor are a sufficient deterrent to borrowing. Therefore we seem to return to the basic question of whether or not it is *wealth* (the availability of assets) which is the primary determinant of economic power. We must realize that several distribution measures are necessary in order to arrive at the true relative picture, and also that calculations of both income and wealth distributions are essential to a true understanding of the degree of inequality within any particular society.

Finally, there is the choice of the income unit. Should we choose the *individual*, the *family* or the *household*? For the time being, we note merely that we cannot be dogmatic on this issue since the definition may not be able simultaneously to differentiate between income units in which the majority of members are dependants and those in which there are, say, several earners and incomes are shared among all members of the unit, whether earning or not. It may be the case that differing definitions are best suited for differing tasks. We shall return to further detail on this question when we consider the real-world picture for the United Kingdom.

Interpreting Real-World Data: UK Example

Statisticians and social commentators are continually wrestling with the problems outlined above, and any example of calculating real-world income distribution is bound to illustrate our earlier comments. In the United Kingdom, knowledge of the state of income distribution derives from various sources, the most relied upon being that of the annual survey of personal incomes undertaken by the Inland Revenue. Information from this source is supplemented by the Family Expenditure Survey, and further supplementation, with specific regard to the influences of the labour market, is provided by the New Earnings Survey.

'Official' (i.e. originating from government departments) estimates of income distribution in the United Kingdom are published annually in the *Blue Book* (*National Income and Expenditure*). The post-war distribution of personal incomes in the United Kingdom was tracked by the *Blue Book* until 1967, when the series was ended because of estimating difficulties. However, continued pressure from social observers, in addition to the impetus to interest in this area which was provided by the Royal Commission on the Distribution of Income and Wealth, helped towards a reintroduction of the series in 1976, the first of the new calculations pertaining to the tax year 1972/3. Broadly speaking, the current methods of estimating the distribution are similar to those used in the pre-1967 series, though the use of an income tax year rather than a calendar year as the period of reference is felt to remove one source of estimating problems.[6]

As a guide to the true distribution picture, these official estimates are far from perfect and have been the object of some heavy criticisms.[7] Such criticisms stem mainly from the fact that Inland Revenue data comprise information from personal income tax returns and there is no guarantee that the information collected for one purpose is suitable for another. The most obvious example in this respect is that of the definition of income. We have argued for a comprehensive definition of income so as to gauge the degree of inequality, and later we shall argue for this in relation to defining the tax base. But, in reality, income is defined more narrowly for income tax purposes. Of the many sources of income omitted from the definition determined by the income tax statutes, those most often quoted are: capital gains; imputed net rent from home ownership; imputed income from home production; certain fringe benefits and certain government transfers. Clearly, any definition of income which does not include these items must produce a distorted picture of the distribution of incomes unless it can be guaranteed that these additional income sources are equally distributed throughout the population.

Furthermore, data collected by the Inland Revenue do not take into account the other effects which influence the real nature of income distribution, namely, the importance of needs in relation to income and the differential impact of price inflation. While the income tax system does help to adjust the post-tax distribution of incomes by exemptions and allowances which do relate to needs (number of dependants, and so on), the income figures do not reflect any such allowances. Thus, if low-income families tend to have more children than high-income families, then the degree of income dispersion may be worse than that which is reflected by calculations referring to income tax units. Similarly, if the rate of price inflation on, say, food is higher than that on, say, consumer durables, then any measure of changes in income distribution over time which relies on calculations of *money* incomes will underestimate the dispersion of real economic power. As we shall see, it is not always possible to combat these drawbacks, but at least the observer can maintain a healthy suspicion about the true nature of things when studying official estimates.

The Measure of Inequality

The problems of measuring inequality do not end with the difficulties of calculating an income distribution. Even if we choose the best definition of income unit and the most comprehensive definition of income and even if a system of data collection exists which is also comprehensive and perfectly accurate, there remains the problem of actually measuring the degree of inequality. On the face of it, this appears to be a straightforward statistical and therefore objective exercise. But, in reality, the task is surrounded by the pitfalls of subjectivity, that recurrent bane of the social commentator who wishes to be 'scientific' in his judgements.

In a world in which there is no more than a blurred distinction between factors of production, analysing the distribution of incomes among capitalists, labourers and rentiers may still have uses, but is probably less instructive of the degree of inequality than some measure of the size distribution of incomes. Such a measure has then to be analysed by an index of inequality, a summary indicator of the extent to which income is distributed in unequal amounts among income recipients. Unfortunately, there is no single index of inequality which is free from criticism. Broadly, we can distinguish between indices which compare extremes – for example, the share of the top 10 per cent of income earners as a ratio of the share enjoyed by the bottom 10 per cent – and those which survey the whole distribution. The former type of measure might provide a reasonable guide to how much relative poverty persists, and to this extent it can be a useful indicator of social progress. However, to record a comprehensive picture of the shares enjoyed by all income levels, we need a much broader summary measure of the whole income distribution.

Unfortunately, the summary indices which analyse the whole distribution are sensitive (to different degrees) to changes in particular parts of any given distribution, and income distributions may consequently be ranked according to the degree of inequality embodied within them in a different order, depending on which index of inequality is used. We shall not consider a detailed comparison of the summary measures,[8] but we shall take a close look at the Gini coefficient as the index which finds most favour among statisticians, and the one which is used extensively in official reports. In order to do so, we first consider a popular method of representing distributions – the Lorenz curve, which permits in graphical form a comparative analysis of the distributions, for example, between countries at some point in time or between two different points in time in a given country.

The basic information provided by the Lorenz curve (when applied to incomes) is that of cumulative (percentage) income shares: the bottom (top) 10 per cent of the population (income units) receive x per cent of total income; the bottom 20 per cent receive y per cent (y > x), and so on. When this curve is then compared with the *line of income equality*, the degree of inequality can readily be seen. This measuring rod is the curve which would result if all incomes were equal – every x per cent of the population receives x per cent of total income. Thus, if the bottom x per cent of the population receives less than x per cent of total income (and 1 — x per cent receive more than 1 — x per cent of income), the Lorenz curve lies below the diagonal, how far below being determined by the degree of inequality. In the extreme case of one individual receiving all the income, the curve follows the horizontal until the last person is reached, whence it approximates to the vertical. Hence we can arrive at a comparative measure – given two Lorenz curves to compare, that which is nearer to the diagonal shows a more equal distribution of incomes.

Figure 4.1 provides an example of the Lorenz curve. The unbroken curve shows the cumulative income shares in the United Kingdom in 1971/2 as calculated for the Royal Commission on the Distribution of Income and Wealth, while the broken line is a hypothetical curve for comparative purposes.

To show how comparisons can be made, consider points A, B and C. Point A shows that, if there were complete equality, then half the population would receive half the total income. Point B shows that, in year 1971/2, the bottom half of the population received only just over 25 per cent of total income. Point C shows that in year 1971/2, the bottom half of the population received considerably less than they would have done in the absence of inequality, but at the same time received a

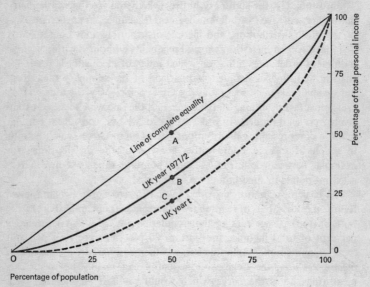

Figure 4.1. Lorenz curve (personal income before tax)
for the United Kingdom, 1971/2, and hypothetical curve for year t.

bigger share than in year t. As we can see, the curve for year t lies further from the diagonal than the 1971/2 curve, not just at point C but at all points. In other words, the degree of inequality was greater in year t than in 1971/2.

However, while the Lorenz curve offers a ready visual guide, the dual requirements of analytical precision and speed demand a numerative summary measure of inequality. This is provided by the Gini coefficient, which measures the ratio of the area between the Lorenz curve and the diagonal to the total area beneath the diagonal. Obviously, when the Lorenz curve follows the diagonal (incomes completely equal), this coefficient has a value of 0, while the other extreme (all income held by one individual) produces a value of 1. Thus, for purposes of comparison, a distribution of incomes which has a Gini coefficient of 0·45 is more equal than one which has a coefficient of 0·75.

Unfortunately, the analyst's task is more difficult than the above type of comparison suggests. Indeed, the comparison turns out to be a naïve one since it assumes a particular sort of relationship between the two Lorenz curves, namely, that one lies above the other for the full range of population precentiles. Unless this assumption is satisfied, an ambiguity persists. For example, suppose that we compare the distribution

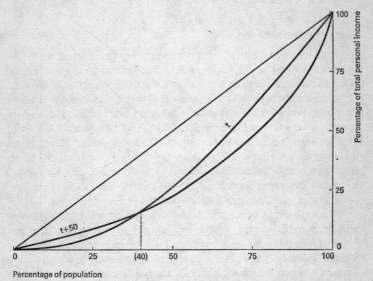

Percentage of population

Figure 4.2. Hypothetical Lorenz curves for years t and t + 50.

profiles of a particular country at two points in time, t and t + 50, and we plot two Lorenz curves as in Figure 4.2.

These two Lorenz curves show that, for all percentile groups up to the bottom 40 per cent, the share of total income was higher in t + 50 than in t, but that above this point shares were higher in t than in t + 50. At the same time, the Gini coefficient for t + 50 is higher than the coefficient for t. Thus, according to the Gini coefficient, incomes were less equal in t + 50 than they were in t. Yet, some other measure of inequality which affords more weight to improvements in the share of total income enjoyed by the lower income groups would register t + 50 as the year of greater equality. The conclusion must be that, in measuring the degree of inequality, we cannot avoid introducing value judgements about the 'desired' state of distribution. Any two social observers with differing views on the weight which should be given by the social welfare function to improving the economic position of the lower income groups would place two different interpretations on any decrease in the Gini coefficient between two points in time. Thus it seems that, although the Gini coefficient provides a neat and numerical index, it does so at the cost of providing inadequate information. Only if the coefficient is used in conjunction with the original data on percentile shares is an adequate comparative picture likely to emerge.

Improving the Index

It should be noted, however, that criticism has not gone unaccompanied by efforts to find an alternative index. The deficiency in the Gini coefficient has attracted the attention of several researchers in the field of income distribution. One contribution which has created a lot of interest is that of A. B. Atkinson, who offers a pragmatic index of inequality in the form of an insertion into the social welfare function of explicit weights attached to varying states of inequality.[9] He proposes a parameter ε which represents such a weighting and takes on values from zero (society is indifferent about the state of income distribution) to infinity (society is concerned only with the position of the lowest income group – a 'Rawlsian position').[10]

Atkinson's explicit recognition of social welfare weighting derives in part from an earlier contribution by Dalton,[11] who postulated that any index of inequality can only be relevant if it is concerned with economic welfare. In support of this view, he suggested a measure based on a comparison between the actual level of social welfare and that level which could be achieved if income were equally distributed; Dalton's 'welfare' was measured in terms of utility functions (strictly concave), and his index was defined as:

$$D_{(\varepsilon)} = \frac{\sum_{i=1}^{n} U(y_i)}{nU(\mu)}$$

where U represents the utility function; y_i is the income of the ith individual; and μ is the mean of the distribution of incomes.

However, Atkinson is unhappy about the detail of the above index, since it is sensitive to the level from which social utility is measured. For example, if a positive constant is added to all the U functions, then the index changes.[12] Thus, he rectifies the measure so that it becomes

invariant with respect to linear transformations. His alternative definition adopts the concept of the 'equally distributed equivalent income'
of any given distribution of total income – that is, that level of income
per head which, if distributed equally throughout the population, would
yield the same level of social welfare as that given by the prevailing distribution. The new index becomes:

$$A_{(\varepsilon)} = \frac{1 - Y_e}{\mu}$$

where Y_e represents the equally distributed equivalent income.

This new index conveniently lies between zero and unity. When income is equally distributed, $Ye = \mu$ and the index will have a value of
zero. If the distribution is completely unequal (one man receives all
income), then the index has a value of unity. Thus, if the index falls,
then distribution has become more equal – to achieve the same level of
social welfare as that generated by the existing distribution, the level
of equally distributed income must be higher relative to the mean.

Atkinson's claims for the use of the index rest not only on its rigour
but also on its intuitive appeal. For example, if $A(\varepsilon)$ has a value of
0·25, this indicates that an equal distribution of community income
would require only 75 per cent of the prevailing total income to maintain the same level of social welfare. We can further show this intuitive
appeal by illustrating the link between the index and the parameter ε
in relation to our earlier example of distributions at two points in time,
t and $t + 50$. What the index tells us about the relative inequality of
these two distributions depends upon the value attaching to ε.

Table 4.1.   Possible indices of inequality at different points in time.[13]

ε value	$A_{(\varepsilon)}$ at $t + 50$	$A_{(\varepsilon)}$ at t
0·5	0·10	0·15
1·0	0·20	0·25
1·5	0·30	0·32
2·0	0·40	0·38

What Table 4.1 demonstrates is that the index can only become relatively higher for the year in which the share of total income enjoyed by
the lower income groups (the bottom deciles) is highest when society's
preference weighting for the position of the lowest income groups has
risen sufficiently high. In Table 4.1, this point appears to be reached
when $\varepsilon = 2\cdot0$; prior to this, the inequality index is lower in $t + 50$, but

for ε values of 2·0 and above, the index has a lower value in year t. This underlines Atkinson's introductory point – whether or not we describe distribution at time t + 50 as being more equal than distribution at time t depends upon the value attached to ε, society's weighting of the position of the lower declines of the income distribution.

Concluding Remarks

The search for a totally acceptable index of inequality is far from over. We have concentrated upon Atkinson's measure because it highlights a defect in the Gini coefficient as an unambiguous index, and it is this coefficient which is most popular among statisticians of income distribution. To formulate a practical version of Atkinson's index, however, depends upon a knowledge of real-world social welfare functions and, in particular, the preferences regarding redistribution towards the lower income groups.[14] As yet, such detail has not been attempted. Indeed, it would be a major political step to attempt it.

Thus, the following chapter attempts to summarize a real-world distribution picture (that of the United Kingdom) with an index which is known to be defective and with the help of data which is far from comprehensive and occasionally dubious in its accuracy. At some stage we are bound to face the question of whether inadequate measurement is better than no measurement at all. A tentative answer here and now suggests that qualified reasoning, cognizant of data deficiencies, will usually be more likely to approximate to the truth than uninformed opinion, guesswork, or dogmatic value judgements.

5. Inequality (2):
The Post-war Distribution of Incomes in the United Kingdom

Inevitably, any attempt to chart a pattern of real-world income distribution must be confounded to some extent by the difficulties encountered in the previous chapter and by others not envisaged there. Nevertheless, research has not been deterred by such problems, though its progress may have been retarded from time to time. The post-war years are studied because this has been the time when statistics have been gathered of a nature permitting reasonable estimates of distribution patterns to be made. It has also been the period of the Welfare State, and therefore an era in which the distribution of incomes (and wealth) is expected to have become more equal.[1]

The increasing interest in the problems of income distribution led, in 1974, to the appointment of a Royal Commission on the subject, and the material published by this commission has presented us with the most comprehensive picture ever provided of the prevailing distribution pattern.[2] This chapter and the following are attempts to summarize and comment upon the main findings of this commission. Under the chairmanship of Lord Diamond, the aim of the commission has been to

... undertake for the United Kingdom an analysis of the current distribution of personal income and wealth, and of available information on past trends in that distribution which would cover personal incomes at all levels, earned income of all kinds (including fringe and non-monetary benefits), unearned income of all kinds, capital gains, and all forms of personal wealth.[3]

Tracking the post-war situation in the way suggested by the above warrant is made difficult by the nature of official data. Comparisons over time can only be made properly if there is a continuation of measurement techniques. But it is inevitable that, as changes are made in the compilation of real-world data, intertemporal comparisons become less clear cut. As mentioned in the previous chapter, the official *Blue Book* estimates of distribution were halted after 1967 because of the increasing difficulties of estimation. However, the pressing concern of researchers in this field plus the impetus provided by the Diamond Commission resulted in a decision to resurrect the series in a modified and improved form, beginning with 1972/3,[4] the gap between 1968 and

1972/3 being eventually filled in by the Fifth Report from the Diamond Commission. The new series is felt to be improved because it makes more use of the various alternative sources of data available to government statisticians; and since it adopts the tax year rather than the calendar year, it avoids the problems of converting data on incomes which relate to the former into a form which approximates the income of the latter.

The *Blue Book* data, presented by the Central Statistical Office (CSO), are the best available official estimates since they are the only ones compiled solely for the purpose of depicting personal income distribution. It is possible to derive estimates from other sources, the main ones being the Inland Revenue's Survey of Personal Incomes (SPI) and the annual Family Expenditure Survey (FES).[5] Both these sources, however, have deficiencies owing to the fact that they are undertaken for purposes other than estimating income distribution.[6] The SPI is a product of data collected for purposes of taxing personal incomes, while the primary aim of the FES is to compile patterns of expenditure for the construction of the Retail Prices Index. Estimates provided in the *Blue Book* do rely extensively on the SPI, but with supplementation from other sources which are likely to be helpful in achieving a true picture of the distribution of incomes. The new series (post-1967), for example, makes considerable use of data collected for the FES.[7]

While accepting that the *Blue Book* estimates are the most reliable of all the official series, it should be remembered that they rely heavily on data collected for purposes of income tax assessment and, hence, that deficiences remain from the point of view of estimating the distribution of incomes. The definition of income for income tax purposes omits a number of categories of income, for example: social insurance benefits such as unemployment and sickness benefits; educational grants; certain employee fringe benefits; income excluded under allowable deduction for tax purposes, such as mortgage interest and superannuation contributions; the imputed rental value of owner-occupied housing (excluded since 1963).[8] This list is by no means complete, but it contains the major omissions and combines with other factors such as tax evasion and under-recording of part-time earnings of a spouse to render suspect any distribution of incomes calculated on the basis of such data. Perhaps most glaring of all is the omission of incomes which are below the effective tax exemption limit (outside the 'tax net'). These drawbacks must be borne in mind when we discuss the distribution pattern which apparently emerges from post-war data.

Distribution of Incomes before Income Tax

While the Diamond Commission has surveyed all of the post-war period, it is not the sole guide to the picture, and there have been several other attempts, notably by Paish,[9] Lydall,[10] Nicholson[11] and Walsh,[12] to use the CSO estimates as a means of depicting the post-war distribution pattern and commenting upon the factors influencing this pattern. From various sources comes the summary of the pre-tax situation presented in Table 5.1.

Table 5.1. Cumulative distribution of personal income (*Blue Book*) 1949 to 1974–5: before tax

Quartile group of income recipients	Share of total personal income in year							
	1949[a]	1957[b]	1959[b]	1963[b]	1967[a]	1972–73[a]	1973–74[c]	1974–75[d]
	%	%	%	%	%	%	%	%
Top 1%	11·2	8·2	8·4	7·9	7·4	6·4	6·5	6·2
5%	23·8	19·1	19·9	19·1	18·4	17·2	17·1	16·8
10%	33·2	28·1	29·4	28·7	28·0	26·9	26·8	26·6
40%	68·1	65·7	67·8	67·7	66·9	66·8	66·5	66·5
70%	87·3	88·8	90·3	90·3	89·7	89·4	89·1	89·2
Bottom 30%	12·7	11·3	9·7	9·7	10·3	10·6	10·9	10·8

SOURCES: [a] Diamond Commission, Report No. 1.
[b] R. J. Nicholson, 'Tax Allowances and Fiscal Policy', *Lloyds Bank Review*, January 1967.
[c] Diamond Commission, Report No. 4.
[d] CSO, *Social Trends*, 1977.

Taking the figures in Table 5.1 at face value, what sort of pre-tax distribution emerges for the post-war years? Up to 1957, there appears to have been some movement towards less inequality in the distribution of incomes. Between 1949 and 1957, the share of the top 10 per cent of income recipients fell by more than a seventh, while the share of the top 1 per cent fell by over a quarter (nearly 27 per cent). The position of the bottom 30 per cent, on the other hand, worsened during the same period, from a share of 12·7 per cent in 1949 to 11·3 per cent in 1957. Taking a broader income range, Table 5.1 shows that the relative position of the top 40 per cent of income recipients worsened slightly while that of the top 70 per cent improved. In other words, what redistribution there was tended to shuffle incomes from the top of the range towards the middle, with the middle also making gains upon the bottom quantiles.[13]

Over the next decade, 1957–67, the apparent trend towards equality slowed down, and even the positions of the top percentile groupings changed little. The share of the top 1 per cent fell from 8·2 per cent to 7·4 per cent, and the share of the top 5 per cent fell from 19·1 per cent to 18·4 per cent, but the share of the top 10 per cent fell by only one tenth of a percentage point. If we extend the quantile grouping to consider the top 40 per cent, we see from the table that this group's share actually increased over the decade – from 65·7 per cent to 66·9 per cent. Finally, the position of the bottom 30 per cent worsened still further, in a fall from 11·3 per cent to 10·3 per cent.

The distribution pattern after 1967 exhibited changes which appear as small as those of the preceding decade, though the overall reduction in inequality seems less ambiguous. Each of the chosen percentile groupings up to 40 per cent shows a reduced share with the size of the reduction diminishing as the percentile grouping increases from 1 to 70, while the share of the bottom 30 per cent of income recipients increased from 10·3 per cent to 10·8 per cent, thanks to a sharp rise in 1972–3 following a fall over the period 1967 to 1971–2.

What, then, emerges as the *general* impression regarding the postwar pattern of income distribution? It would seem that there has undeniably been a re-distribution of income away from the top quantile groupings, but the result is not an unambiguous reduction in inequality since the bottom grouping of 30 per cent had a lower share in 1974–5 than in 1949. Indeed, a substantial fall in the share of the bottom 30 per cent of income recipients between the years 1949 and 1959 has still to be rectified – a reasonably sized increase in share for the bottom 30 per cent between 1963 and 1967 has been followed by only a very small increase since that time. In other words, we meet head-on the problem outlined in the previous chapter – our judgement of the degree of inequality prevailing over the period depends upon how much weight we attach to the relative position of the lower income groups.

To further illustrate the difficulty of interpreting distribution patterns, Table 5.2 presents measures of both the size and direction of change in the percentile shares. The changes in size are proportional – that is, the change in the size of a share over a period is expressed as a percentage of the share at the beginning of the period and the changes are rounded off to the nearest whole number.

Table 5.2 underlines the fact that there has been a marked movement towards equality during the period in question in that the shares of the top percentile have been considerably reduced. The rate of reduction has not been constant, and in fact there was a distinct slowing down in the period from the late 1950s and through most of the 1960s. Nevertheless, taking the period from 1949 as a whole, the top 1 per cent saw its share almost halved while the share of the top 10 per cent fell by a fifth. At the same time, the fall in share experienced by the bottom 40 per cent was minimal while the share of the top 70 per cent actually rose slightly. It would seem that the income reshuffle has been of most benefit to the middle income groupings (40–70 per cent). The changing fortunes of the bottom 30 per cent bear out this finding and provide

Table 5.2. **Proportional changes in income shares 1949 to 1974–5: before tax**

Quantile grouping	1949–57 %	1957–67 %	1967–74/5 %	1949–74/5 %
Top 1%	−27	−10	−16	−45
5%	−20	−4	−9	−29
10%	−12	0	−5	−20
40%	−4	+2	−1	−2
70%	+2	+1	−1	+2
Bottom 30%	−11	−9	+5	−15

SOURCES: Derived from the sources used for Table 5.1.

illustration of the difficulty in interpreting measures of inequality. During the whole of the period since 1949, the Gini coefficient value has fallen steadily (from 41·1 per cent in 1949 to 33·1 per cent in 1972/3)[14] yet the share of the bottom 30 per cent of income recipients has fallen by 15 per cent. Indeed, the share of this bottom grouping increases in only one of the three periods separated out by Table 5.2, the period being that since 1967.

It would seem that, up to 1963, the (pre-tax) Lorenz curve is creeping towards the diagonal, but continues to cross the 1949 curve in the region of the lower income groupings. After this time, the Gini coefficient changes may represent unambiguous reductions in inequality – such a reduction for the same period could also be confirmed by an Atkinson index as long as ε is greater than zero. But, taking the whole of the period since 1949, the reduction in the Gini coefficient must be reconciled with a fall in the share of the bottom 30 per cent.

Social and Demographic Explanations

The causes of the shape of the post-war distribution of pre-tax incomes are several and often difficult to separate. A summary view would suggest that there is no single all-important determinant but many different ones, and that it is the sum total of the small effects of these various determinants which has created the changes in inequality. These various factors may be summarized under the groupings of *social and demographic* and *changes in factor shares*.

A detailed and comprehensive analysis of social and demographic factors has been undertaken for the Diamond Commission by Dinwiddy and Reed.[15] In this study, the authors compare the actual distribution at the end of their period of study, 1951–71, with the distribution which would have prevailed at the end of the period had the demographic and social patterns in force at the beginning of the period remained unchanged. In this way, the effects of the various demographic and social changes upon the distribution of incomes can be identified. The findings tend to bear out the observation made above that there is no startling change which can be contributed to any single factor.

The main forces identified by Dinwiddy and Reed are: (a) changes in the age structure of the population; (b) changes in the activity rates of various sections of the population (identified by sex and age); (c) changes in marital patterns; and (d) changes in education patterns. Not surprisingly, the study found that changes in the pattern of income distribution were often attributable to some combination of these separately identified factors, but it did prove possible to differentiate those changes which had a multiple cause from those which were induced by only one cause.

Over the course of the study period, the age structure of the population underwent significant changes at its extremes – there was an increase in the proportions of the population aged 55 and over and 25 and under, while the population aged 25–54 declined. The effect of the increase in the elderly population bears out intuitive expectations, tending to increase the extent of inequality, though the increase is only small. However, an interesting feature of this change is that the extent of inequality accounted for by the age factor was found by Dinwiddy and Reed to be greater in the distribution of incomes among tax units than the distribution among individuals. The reason for this underlines the interplay among the various determinants, because it relates to another paradoxical finding from the study: the age factor causes an increase in the share of the bottom of the income distribution among individuals. This paradox is resolved by the fact that the bottom two deciles of the distribution based on individuals are 'dominated by non-pensioner married women', and therefore the increased proportion of the elderly tends not directly to affect the bottom two deciles but to *lower the average of the top eight deciles*, hence increasing the share of the bottom 20 per cent.

The increase in the proportion at the other extreme of the age structure, 25 and under, combined with another change, in numbers in full-time education, to influence the state of income distribution. Dinwiddy and Reed attempt to assess the effect of changes in the proportion of the population in full-time education over the two decades as they were reflected through changes in the average activity rate of the whole population. The effect of a rise in the 'student' age group (15–24) of 1·7 million as a consequence of demographic change, plus an increase of four million in the numbers undertaking full-time education, was concentrated at the bottom of the distribution – the bottom 20 per cent experienced a fall of 14 per cent due to this factor.[16]

Marital patterns are also analysed in the study, but again the magnitude of the changes wrought by this factor is not great, with increases in the Gini coefficient of 1 to 1·5 per cent, depending on the data base adopted.[17] This small overall increase in inequality reflects an increase in the share of the top 1 per cent (when the joint impact of marriage rates and demographic changes is allowed for this share increases by some 2½ per cent), and also a change at the bottom of the distribution where the share of the bottom quantile fell over the period (despite a slight increase in the share of the bottom decile).

Finally, perhaps the most significant socio-economic change over the period was a change in the pattern of economic activity resulting from the increasing proportion of women, particularly married women, who went out to work. The impact of this on the distribution of individual incomes is calculated by Dinwiddy and Reed to be 'dramatically concentrated in the 8th decile group', which suggests that 'it is above all in that group that the additional economically active women, associated with rising labour force participation between 1951 and 1971, appear'.[18] The overall effect is to increase the shares of the bottom 50 per cent, but the effect weakens as we move from the eighth up to the fifth decile. Necessarily, therefore, the female activity effect reduces the income shares of the higher quantile groupings, the biggest share reduction being that of the top 1 per cent. However, if the distribution is further modified to allow for the increased part-time participation of women, the income share of the bottom 20 per cent increases mainly at the expense of the eighth decile and the overall effect is to moderate the distributional effects of the increased economic activity among females. To round off, we can refer to the general conclusion that, in terms of the individual distribution of incomes, '. . . the rise in female activity rates had a positive influence on the income share of groups below the median, but little influence on the income share of the bottom decile'.[19]

In the case of the distribution of income among tax units, there is no dramatic impact on any single quantile grouping. Instead, there is an increase in the shares of the middle and upper ranges (second to seventh deciles) and a reduction in the shares of the very top and bottom. The general conclusion regarding tax units reflects the fact that the bulk of the increase in female activity during the period came from married women. As a result the increased income shares are enjoyed by higher groupings than in the individual distribution and the reduced shares at the very bottom are more pronounced. Hence, the reduction in the Gini coefficient is greater in the case of the individual distribution.

Factor Market Patterns

The analysis has concentrated upon the size distribution of incomes, but a full account of this pattern also requires some reference to factor shares. When discussing the distribution of pre-tax incomes in an economy such as that of the United Kingdom, the analysis is necessarily concerned with the shape of things determined largely by market processes. Whatever the nature of social and demographic changes, the rewards ultimately enjoyed by individuals in a market-orientated economy must reflect the nature of markets. Thus, there seem to be at least two important questions to discuss: (a) how are the total rewards from economic processes shared out among the various factors of production; and (b) if one type of reward dominates, what forces help to determine *its* distribution? The answer to the first part guides towards the answer to the second. To understand the forces which determine the distribution of incomes, we need to know the dominant source of income. An increase in the share of income going to rentiers is likely to have an impact on overall size distribution different from an increase in the share enjoyed by salaried employees. Furthermore, if salaries account for, say, more than half the rewards in an economy, then any change in the dispersion of salaries might well determine a change in the overall dispersion of incomes.

Bearing the above points in mind, what of the post-war pattern in Britain? According to Lydall,[20] the trend towards equality in the distribution of incomes, which was apparent during the immediate post-war years and which continued until the second half of the 1950s, owed much to the postwar economic expansion and the consequently improved fortunes of labour. During this period, the sustained high level of employment meant that earned income rose faster than any other form of personal income, and Lydall saw such a pattern, if it were to continue, as being the prime mover behind a continuing tendency towards equality. However, for the period 1957–63 this pattern changed, with the rate of growth of employment income slowing down relative to that of self-employment, and within the former the rate of growth of wages slowed down relatively to that of salaries; and, most strikingly, with rent, dividends and interest becoming the most rapidly growing sector of personal income.[21] This period, as we have seen, was one in which the trend towards equality apparently slowed down.

Table 5.3. **Percentage shares of main components in total personal income, 1963–76**

	1963 %	1965 %	1967 %	1968 %	1969 %	1970 %	1971 %	1972 %	1973 %	1974 %	1975 %	1976 %
Labour (market) income												
(a) Income from employment	71·2	70·8	70·1	69·6	69·5	70·2	70·2	69·4	69·1	69·4	70·8	70·0
(b) Income from self-employment	8·6	8·3	8·4	8·5	8·6	8·7	9·1	9·9	10·6	10·1	9·2	9·1
(c) Total employment Income	79·8	79·1	78·5	78·1	78·1	78·9	79·3	79·3	79·7	79·5	80·0	79·1
Non-labour (market) income												
Rent, dividends and net interest	11·1	11·8	11·3	11·2	11·2	10·3	9·8	9·1	10·2	10·4	9·1	9·0
Transfer income												
National insurance and other cash benefits from public authorities	8·3	8·6	9·4	10·1	10·1	10·0	10·0	10·7	10·2	10·4	10·5	11·4

SOURCES: Diamond Commission, Report No. 4, Table 3, p. 9; and Report No. 5, Table 2, p. 17.

After 1963, according to the *Blue Book* estimates, the pattern of factor shares emerges as shown in Table 5.3. This table shows that, for the period after 1963, we can again observe a correspondence between changes in the size distribution and changes in the component shares. Over the whole of the period since 1963, there has been little change in the share of total income going to employment income, though an interesting pattern does emerge within this component category. From 1963 to 1967, the share of self-employment income remained fairly static, but from that point up to 1973, it steadily increased until it reached a peak of 10·6 per cent. After 1973, the component share fell but remained in 1976 above the level of 1963. The 'investment' (rent dividends and net interest) component of income rose between 1963 and 1967, but thereafter it fell from 11·3 per cent to its lowest level for the period, 9·0 per cent in 1976. However, of the four income categories shown in Table 5.3, the component showing the most marked change is that of transfer incomes, this share increasing over the period by over 30 per cent.

Figure 5.1 gives a clear indication of the relative rates of change of each component during the first half of the 1970s. Based on estimates presented by the Diamond Commission, the graphs plot the various components of personal income expressed as an index, with 1971 = 100.

The patterns in the figure clearly show the faster rate of growth of income from self-employment relative to employment income until 1975, and the relatively sluggish increase in 'investment' income; but perhaps most clearly outlined is the rapid rise in transfer income. The figure also underlines the trend in the index of property income – imputed rent of owner-occupiers. This item appears in the Family Expenditure Survey, where it is added to the income and expenditure of each household in owner-occupied accommodation to place such households on a comparable basis with those paying rents. It is interesting to note that this component of income has been growing faster than 'investment' income for the period shown; indeed, its index value lies above that of each component of employment income after 1973, and above that of employee income for the whole of the period. This reflects, in part, the great increase in owner-occupation during the 1970s, but note that in the view of the Diamond Commission the inclusion of imputed rent makes little difference to the observed inequality in the distribution of incomes.[22]

Finally, on the question of the relative growth rates of various income components, the trends apparent since 1963 continue the longer-term pattern of a rise in the share enjoyed by labour relative to that of capital – from 1:1 at the beginning of the century to just over 3:1. This trend reflects the relative growth of salaries since the First World War, and works against the long-term constancy of relative factor shares believed in by certain economists. Reviewing the evidence on the trends in factor shares observed in the United Kingdom and other countries, Atkinson has concluded '. . . the evidence suggests that in most advanced countries labour received between $\frac{2}{3}$ and $\frac{3}{4}$ of national income and that its share has shown a long-run tendency to rise over time.'[23]

We now consider the second question raised at the beginning of the discussion of factor shares: the distribution of the largest component of total income. It would seem that a proper understanding of the state of income distribution requires an account of the distribution of the returns to market labour, that is *earnings*. Earnings data can tell us much about income dispersion at both a point in time and over some time scale.

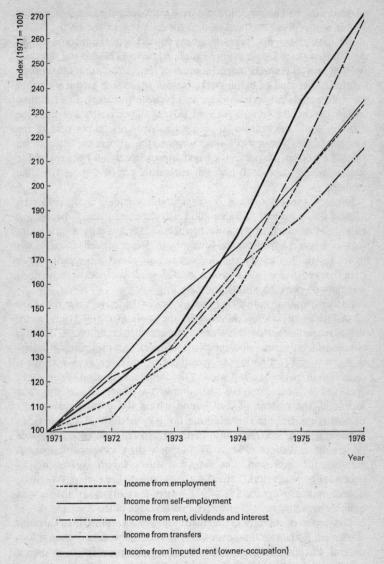

Figure 5.1. Rates of growth of income components, 1971–6.

According to Table 5.3, income from employment has approximated 70 per cent of total personal income for each year of the 1970s. Thus a closer look at any one year should say much about the income dispersion in that year. Latest available data relate to 1977 and suggest that, for that year, there were several sources of inequality within the market-determined spread of earnings. Two main sources of inequality lay in the differentials between workers and between the sexes. For full-time male workers, the top 10 per cent earned 58 per cent more than the median, while the bottom 10 per cent earned only 68 per cent of the median figure. Among full-time women, the dispersion was similar since the bottom 10 per cent earned approximately 69 per cent of the median while the top 10 per cent earned 62 per cent more than the median.

Between the sexes there is considerable inequality. In 1977, the highest decile among full-time adult women earned nearly two and a half times as much as the lowest female decile, but only a little more than one and a half times the lowest male decile. Indeed, the earnings figure for the highest female decile was only about 5 per cent higher than the median for full-time men in 1977, while the median for women was only 65 per cent of that for men.

Earlier it was suggested that, broadly, over the longer term the share of profits and rents has fallen while the share of earnings has risen. While recognizing that there exists a somewhat complex relationship between factor shares and the distribution of incomes among individuals, it might still be argued that these trends must work towards a reduction in inequality. But what of the actual distribution of earnings? Available evidence suggests that, while the share of earnings has increased, the pattern of distribution within this earnings share has been altering. But the alteration has not been uniform and some types of earning have changed little in their dispersion while others have undergone a distinct change. Within one large component, manual earnings, the dispersion of earnings has shown a remarkable stability over a long time period. Table 5.4 shows data on the earnings distribution of manual workers, 1886–1977, where the earnings of the various quantile groupings are expressed as percentages of the median.

The degree of stability in the distribution pattern of manual earnings is reflected in the fact that, over the long period, this distribution is lognormal. Earnings in general, however, do not approximate to such a regular pattern, though Lydall, mainly on the basis of his studies of France, Hungary and the United States, has suggested that the standard distribution of earnings is close to lognormal in the central part of the distribution – 'from perhaps the tenth to the eightieth percentile from the top',[24] while the upper tail of the distribution 'often approximately follows the Pareto law, for at least the top 20 per cent of the aggregate frequency'.[25]

Table 5.4. Manual earnings distribution, 1886–1977

Year	Lowest decile (% of median)	Lower quartile (% of median)	Upper quartile (% of median)	Highest decile (% of median)
1886	69	83	122	143
1906	67	80	127	157
1938	68	82	119	140
1960	71	83	122	145
1970	67	81	122	147
1977	68	82	121	146

sources: Diamond Commission, Report No. 1, Table 22; and *New Earnings Survey*, 1977.

Over the course of this century, there seems to have been a definite worsening of the relative position of the earnings groups at the top of the distribution.[26] Yet this apparent reduction in inequality has not been uniform. Drawing conclusions from his own work, and from the studies by Routh, Lydall concludes: (a) over the period 1910–60 there was some decline in earnings dispersion among males (but in an irregular fashion) and an *increase* in dispersion for females; and (b) there was some decline in over-all dispersion in the United Kingdom during this period, but not a dramatic one.[27] The lack of uniformity within earnings shares can be emphasized by reference to the fact that there is even a considerable dispersion of earnings within defined occupational groupings. Atkinson captures the essence of the problem when he remarks that there is such a variation in earnings within occupations that 'knowing what a man's job is tells us relatively little about his likely earnings, which may be rather surprising, since we are accustomed to thinking that it does'.[28]

Distribution of Incomes after Income Tax

If social and demographic factors combined with the influences of the market-place have not removed inequality, might we expect the income tax system to do the job? Given the progressive rates structure of the UK income tax, one would perhaps expect that the post-tax distribution of incomes would be less unequal than the distribution of incomes before the effects of income tax. Yet reality has not borne out this expectation. Indeed, the changes in the postwar pattern of income dispersion after taxes on personal income have been accounted for are very similar to those observed in the pattern of pre-tax incomes. Adopting the same time scale as previously, Table 5.5 summarizes the post-war shares in after-tax incomes for various percentile groupings.

Table 5.5. Cumulative distribution of personal income (*Blue Book*), 1949 to 1974–75: after tax

Quantile group of income recipients	1949 %	1957 %	1959 %	1963 %	1967 %	1972–3 %	1973–4 %	1974–5 %
Top 10%	6·4	5·0	5·3	5·2	4·9	4·4	4·5	4·0
5%	17·7	14·9	15·8	15·7	14·8	14·2	14·3	13·7
10%	27·1	24·0	25·2	25·2	24·3	23·6	23·6	23·2
40%	64·1	62·5	65·0	64·7	63·5	63·8	63·5	63·6
70%	85·4	86·5	88·7	88·2	88·0	87·8	87·2	87·2
Bottom 30%	14·6	13·5	11·2	11·8	12·0	12·3	12·8	12·8

SOURCES: As for Table 5.1.

Table 5.5 exhibits a levelling down of incomes as a result of the income tax, but it also shows that the relative share sizes of the quantile groupings remained virtually unchanged over the period. If we compare the proportionate changes in the size of shares and the direction of change in shares for the three 'decades' covered in the time stream, the point should be even clearer. Table 5.6 presents such a comparison and underlines the close similarity in the pre- and post-tax changes. It would seem that the pattern of shares over time has not been significantly altered by the operation of the personal income tax.

The apparent similarity between the two distributions does not mean that the income tax does not reduce inequality – Table 5.6 shows that it does. But it does raise the question of how far inequality *can be* reduced by the income tax. In principle, the UK system does aim to level out income shares, and the Diamond Commission single out three main direct effects of the income tax on the distribution of incomes.[29] First, the system causes a 're-ranking' of tax units through the variations in the amounts of tax paid at the same level of income. Secondly, excepting those at the bottom of the distribution (who pay no income tax), all income groups face a reduction in their income. Thirdly, the progressive nature of the income tax reduces inequality.

Not all of these features are immediately apparent from the distribution figures already presented. For example, there might be a considerable re-ranking of individual tax units as a result of income taxation, but this need not affect the size distribution of incomes if it merely re-

Table 5.6. **Proportional changes in income shares, 1949 to 1974–5: before and after tax**

Quantile grouping		1949–57 %	1957–67 %	1967–74/5 %	1949–74/5 %
Top 1%	(a)	−27	−10	−16	−45
	(b)	−22	−2	−18	−38
10%	(a)	−12	0	−5	−20
	(b)	−11	+1	−5	−14
40%	(a)	−4	+2	−1	−2
	(b)	−2	+2	0	−1
70%	(a)	+2	+1	−1	+2
	(b)	+1	+2	−1	+2
Bottom 30%	(a)	−11	−9	+5	−15
	(b)	−8	−11	+7	−7

(a) = before tax.
(b) = after tax.

SOURCES: Derived from the sources used for Table 5.1.

shuffles the rankings *within* the percentile groupings. Another qualification is that the income tax does not exhibit a uniform progression in fact, though it does in principle. The UK system certainly exhibits the characteristics of progression since the marginal rate of tax is greater than the average rate, and the average rate increases as income rises. But, over time, the increases in the actual average rates imposed upon different income groups have not been uniform. Table 5.7 shows the changes in average tax rates for various quantile groups over the period since 1959.

Table 5.7 shows that, over the course of the period, all income groups experienced an increased tax burden as reflected in the higher average rates of tax imposed upon each group. The increases have provided an impetus to the movement towards less inequality by favouring the bottom 20 per cent, relatively to the higher groups. The increase in average rates, however, has featured more in groups below the top 10 per cent. The average tax rate of the top 10 per cent increased from 23·5 per cent in 1959 to 29·1 per cent in 1974–5, while the average rate for the next decile in 1974–5 was two and a half times that for the same group in 1959. Even greater was the increase for the next two quintiles: the average tax rate increased by three times for the 21–40 per cent income group, while that for the middle quintile (41–60 per cent) underwent a more than three-fold increase. Thus it would seem that the brunt of the burden in increased average rates of tax was not borne by the very top of the distribution but by the 11–80 per cent group.

The burden of actual tax paid also shifted ground relatively over the period. This was partly due to reduced income shares at the top of the distribution, but it also reflected the differential increases in average tax rates. In 1959, the top 1 per cent of tax units paid 34·5 per cent of all income tax but only 15·8 per cent in 1974–5, while the top 10 per cent's burden fell from 64·9 per cent to 42·2 per cent over the same period.

Table 5.7. Average tax rates for various percentile income groups, 1959 to 1974/5

Quantile group of income before tax	Average tax paid as percentage of income before tax				
	1959 %	1967 %	1972–73 %	1973–4 %	1974–5 %
Top 1%	43·2	43·3	41·6	42·0	47·1
10%	23·5	24·5	25·1	25·6	29·1
11–20%	7·8	13·3	15·1	15·8	19·3
21–40%	5·7	11·1	12·9	14·5	17·2
41–60%	4·9	9·1	10·4	12·1	15·2
61–80%	2·6	4·7	3·8	5·3	7·2
81–100%	0·1	0·8	—	0·4	1·0

SOURCE: Diamond Commission, Report No. 5, Table 7, p. 26.

Consequently, the share of total income tax paid by the remaining 90 per cent of tax units increased during the period from 35·1 per cent to 57·8 per cent.[30] It would appear that the income tax system has been 'softer' on the extremes of the distribution than on the top to middle ground.

Despite the slight reductions in inequality shown by the figures on tax burdens, the earlier comparison of distributions suggests that the degree of progression in the UK income tax is limited. But what more can be done to reduce inequality through direct taxation of incomes? The emphasis on equality tends to obscure the objective of efficiency, and it may not be possible to further reduce inequality by increasing the *rates* of income tax without creating adverse effects on economic activity. Reduced net rewards for effort may result in less effort. This problem of disincentives has fuelled an ongoing debate in the field of applied economics, where resolving the issue has proved difficult in the face of ambiguous conclusions from both theoretical predictions and empirical investigations.

An income tax reduces the total cost of a given amount of leisure, and a progressive (or proportional) rates structure also reduces leisure costs at the margin. How a potential supplier of effort (measured in man-hours) reacts to the consequent change in the relative prices of effort and leisure depends upon the relative strengths of the resultant income and substitution effects. While the substitution effect induces increased consumption of leisure, following the reduction in its price, the income effect may induce either an increase or a decrease in leisure consumption, depending on its sign, while its strength relative to that of the substitution effect determines the final consumption outcome.

Empirical findings lend support to these either/or possibilities rather than isolating a definite influence. With the possible exceptions of a finding that there is a definite disincentive effect for those individuals who are subject to the top marginal rates of income tax,[31] empirical findings suggest that tax considerations are not usually a major determinant of effort and that where tax does have an effect, it encourages effort among some taxpayers and discourages it among others.[32]

Nevertheless, the *potential* disincentive to effort, coupled with a possible discouragement to savings and also the possible inflationary effects of tax-induced higher wages bargaining, render further increases in marginal tax rates on the middle to top income groups impractical (apart from the political limitations of such a policy). There is a trade-off between efficiency and equity, and whether or not it is accepted that the terms of trade have already swung against further increases in tax rates, most would accept that a limit exists.

The other avenue through which a reduction of inequality might be pursued is to maintain (or even reduce) existing tax rates and widen the tax base. The real base upon which the UK income tax rates is applied is a far cry from a comprehensive definition of income. A real danger which results from a narrow definition of income is that taxable capacity comes to be defined according to a legal definition of income established through case law. Hence there results a steady erosion of the tax base as concessions to one group of income recipients are matched by concessions to another in an attempt to maintain post-tax parity. Over time, the diminishing tax base forces governments to raise tax rates to high levels for the sake of maintaining revenue yields. Higher tax rates lead to further enactments of tax privileges and may have adverses effects on economic incentives.

There is such a wide range of deductions and allowances and sources of income exempt from penalty under the UK income tax system that present purposes do not permit a detailed discussion. From time to time in later analysis some of them are underlined. Meanwhile three points might be stressed. First, accounting for special needs through tax allowances is less efficient than direct income transfers since allowances only benefit taxpayers. Furthermore, under a progressive rates structure, inequality increases since the higher the marginal rate of income tax the higher the net value of the allowance to the tax-payer. Recognition of these drawbacks has led in Britain to the eventual phasing out of child tax allowances in favour of direct 'child benefits'. Secondly, in following the road towards the 'property-owning democracy', society becomes divided into those who own property and those who live in rented accommodation. Under the UK income tax, owner-occupiers enjoy a double 'subsidy' – tax-free imputed income (rent which they would otherwise have to pay) and a tax allowance on the interest paid on mortgages. In 1972–3, mortgage payments accounted for about 75 per cent of all tax deductions, and over the period from 1950 to 1974, mortgage interest payments grew faster than incomes[33] – the unequal treatment of income units who do not own their own home seems to have intensified over the post-war period. Finally, the truly comprehensive tax base 'attacks' wealth as well as income. We shall pursue this point further in the following chapter.

Distribution after Taxes and Benefits

If income tax were the only means by which inequalities are removed from the income distribution, then it might be concluded that Britain's postwar record in this respect is one of failure. However, the 'Welfare State' also entails a programme of benefits, and a full assessment of redistributive measures must account for these. The official estimates of the incidence of taxes and benefits, published annually in *Economic Trends*, are prepared by the CSO from data collected by the Family Expenditure Survey. Three definitions of income stages are used in these estimates: *original income*, *net income* and *final income*, and their components are as follows:

$A = $ *original income* $= $ 'market income' (income from employment, self (employment and investments) + imputed rent from owner-occupied (or rent-free) housing.

$B = $ *net income* $= A + $ direct cash benefits − direct taxes.

$C = $ *final income* $= B + $ direct and indirect benefits in kind − indirect taxes.

Direct cash benefits are defined to include all the major social security benefits in cash (family allowances, unemployment benefit, supplementary benefit and old-age and retirement pensions are all covered by the definition). *Direct taxes* are defined to cover income tax, employee national insurance contributions and national insurance contributions of the self-employed, but taxes on capital or on undistributed company profits are excluded. *Direct benefits in kind* include benefits from the National Health Service, School Health Service, scholarships, school meals, milk and other welfare foods and state education. *Indirect benefits in kind* covers food subsidies and housing subsidies (those received by local authority tenants and including rent rebates). Finally, *indirect taxes* include both taxes paid by households at the time of purchasing and taxes passed on by producers of goods and services – VAT, import duties, domestic rates, motor-vehicle licences, business rates and employer's national insurance contributions.

The pattern of benefits and taxes, expressed as a proportion of both GDP at factor cost and public expenditure and revenue over the years 1961–75, is shown in Figure 5.2. Since benefits are introduced as a new consideration in this section, the figure shows the trends in both types of benefit, cash and kind, as well as the total benefits allocated in the estimating process.

Figure 5.2 shows that the steadiest upward trend for the period covered is that of benefits. As a proportion of GDP allocated benefits rose every year, with the exception of 1963–4, the total rise being from 14·1 per cent in 1961 to 23·3 per cent in 1975. The trend in benefits expressed as a proportion of public expenditure was also steadily upwards, moving from 33·2 per cent in 1961 to 39·8 per cent in 1975. The trends in taxation, however, did not show the same consistency, nor was the magnitude of change so great. Erratic changes in the proportionate size of both direct and indirect taxes resulted in a similarly erratic pattern for the proportion of all allocated taxes and a final proportionate size which was only 4·2 percentage points higher than the 1961 position (31·3 as opposed to 27·1). As a percentage of public revenue, all allocated taxes again followed an erratic path, with the general trend being downwards from 63·6 per cent in 1961 to 53·5 per cent in 1975. Figure 5.2 clearly shows this downward path. Equally clear from Figure 5.2 is the resultant upward spiral in the ratio of benefits to taxes over the period: from 52·2 per cent in 1961 to 74·4 per cent in 1975. It would seem that benefits have become an increasingly important sector of public spending during the past fifteen to twenty years, and with this fact as a backcloth, it is interesting to check whether or not this increased importance has had any major impact on the pattern of income distribution.

However, before considering the redistributive impact of benefits it is

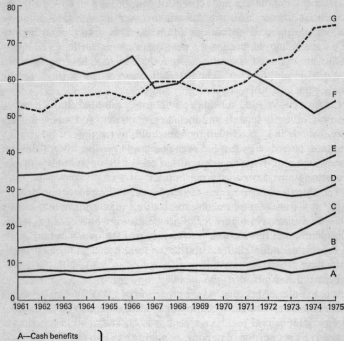

A—Cash benefits
B—Benefits in kind $\Big\}$ as percentage of GDP at factor cost
C—All benefits
D—All taxes as percentage of GDP at factor cost
E—All benefits as percentage of public expenditure
F—All taxes as percentage of public revenue
G—Ratio of benefits to taxes

*Figure 5.2. Trends in benefits and taxes allocated to households
in CSO studies of incidence, 1961–75.*

important to allow for qualifications arising out of the assumptions[34]
on which various taxes and benefits are allocated to the definitions
adopted by the CSO. In relation to taxes, the CSO studies assume that
the burden of any tax is equivalent to the amount paid by the household
and that indirect taxes paid by intermediate producers are passed on to
final consumers. Thus an omission which is immediately apparent concerns the fact that taxes (and subsidies) affect the amount of goods purchased by households, and this in turn will affect the incomes of suppliers, which may cause further changes in output and incomes. The
chain of subsidiary effects from a tax may be very lengthy and com-

plicated, but no allowance for this is made in the official estimates. The assumption that the burden of taxes falls squarely on consumers is also suspect, and this is recognized – the Diamond Commission points out, such an assumption might be a reasonable one to make when estimating the incidence of *marginal* changes in taxation, but it is highly unrealistic for the task of calculating the total effect of direct and indirect taxation.

On the other side of the calculation, benefits (in kind) to individuals are assumed equal to the average cost of provision and are allocated to households on the basis of assumed needs. For example, highest benefits from the National Health Service are assumed to be enjoyed by the very young and the very old, and the costs of the various sectors of education are allocated to those households with children within the relevant age categories. Such assumptions, while reasonable in principle, may grossly misstate the real state of affairs prevailing in any given time period since the allocations are made regardless of the actual consumption patterns of the households covered by the survey. Furthermore, individual subjective valuations of benefits in kind may well differ from the average cost of provision: the means of obtaining such information are not as yet available.

It might also be argued that the range of benefits allocated to households is too narrow, given the wide and varied range of total benefits provided through the public sector – roads, transport subsidies, defence, police and fire services, museums, libraries and so forth. The practical difficulties of allocating to households the benefits from such provisions are immense. Moreover, there is no guarantee that the resultant distribution pattern would differ greatly. Whereas J. L. Nicholson found that, by assuming that such benefits are accruing equally to all (itself a dubious approach), the weighted average Gini coefficient for six main types of family can be reduced by 5·0 percentage points,[35] the Diamond Commission remain uncertain that the results would be much changed.[36]

However one views the approach of the CSO, the actual distribution trends which result from the surveys must be treated with caution, as in the case of the other distributions discussed so far. With this proviso, the pattern of income shares presented in Table 5.8 may be discussed.

In contrast to the patterns shown in Table 5.1, the situation facing the bottom 30 per cent group in Table 5.8 is one of a marked decline in share of original income over the period 1961–75. Given the nature of original income, this is to some extent expected – 'original income', unlike 'income before tax' in the *Blue Book* distribution, excludes all state transfer payments and therefore shows a smaller share of total income going to the lowest income groups. Nevertheless, the decline in share of total original income received by the bottom 30 per cent was of the order of 39 per cent over the course of the period 1961–75, which might be explained by the increase in the number of pensioner households during the period, combined with rising unemployment, particularly in the second half. It might be added that a reduction in share of original income over the period was also experienced by the decile immediately above the bottom 30 per cent. For all decile groups above the bottom 40 per cent, however, the share in original income rose over the period and the Gini coefficient value increased by 2·3 percentage points.

Table 5.8. Effect of taxes and benefits on the distribution of household income; average of 1961–3, 1971–3 and 1975. Percentage shares of original, net and final income by decile groups

	Original income			Net income			Final income		
	1961–3	1971–3	1975	1961–3	1971–3	1975	1961–3	1971–3	1975
	%	%	%	%	%	%	%	%	%
Top 10 %	27·4	26·9	26·6	23·6	23·5	22·7	23·5	23·4	22·4
11–20 %	15·7	16·8	17·1	15·1	15·5	15·5	15·2	15·5	15·4
21–30 %	13·0	13·9	14·1	13·0	12·9	13·0	12·8	12·9	13·0
31–40 %	11·5	11·8	12·0	11·1	11·0	11·3	11·1	11·1	11·2
41–50 %	9·3	10·0	10·1	9·1	9·7	9·7	9·8	9·6	9·7
51–60 %	8·0	8·4	8·5	8·2	8·4	8·5	8·5	8·3	8·4
61–70 %	7·0	6·6	6·5	7·3	7·0	7·1	7·2	6·9	7·0
71–80 %	5·4	4·2	3·6	6·0	5·6	5·6	5·9	5·5	5·7
81–90 %	2·4	1·3	1·0	4·2	4·0	4·0	4·2	4·2	4·3
91–100 %	0·2	0·1	0·3	2·4	2·6	2·6	1·8	2·6	2·9
Gini coefficient	40·3	42·3	42·6	32·6	32·6	31·9	32·8	32·4	31·1

SOURCES: Diamond Commission, Report No. 1, Table 24, p. 62; and Report No. 5, Table 22, p. 51.

The apparent redistribution towards the top half of the distribution of original income since 1961 reflects, to some extent, the definition of original income. It is after taxes and benefits have been accounted for that a reversal of this pattern of redistribution might be expected. Indeed, it does appear that taxes and benefits have been responsible for such a redistribution over the period, for although the Gini coefficients relating to each point in the time period are similar within each income category, the difference between the values of the coefficients for original income and final income in 1961–3 (7·5 percentage points) is much less than the difference in 1975 (11·5 percentage points). We can also appreciate the influence of taxes and benefits by calculating proportionate changes in shares caused by these factors and by comparing these changes for the three time points chosen in Table 5.8. By calculating the differences between net and original income and final and original income, expressing the differences as a percentage of original income in each case, we are able to compare the size of the changes wrought by taxes and benefits in various years. Table 5.9 presents the results.

Table 5.9. **Proportional changes in income shares caused by taxes and benefits, 1961–3, 1971–3 and 1975**

| | Proportional changes | | | | | |
| | Original/net | | | Original/final | | |
Quantile grouping	1961–3 %	1971–3 %	1975 %	1961–3 %	1971–3 %	1975 %
Top 10 %	−14	−13	−15	−14	−13	−16
11–20 %	−4	−8	−9	−3	−8	−10
21–30 %	0	−7	−6	−2	−7	−8
31–40 %	−3	−7	−6	−3	−6	−7
41–50 %	−2	−3	−4	+5	−4	−4
51–60 %	+2	0	0	+6	−1	−1
61–70 %	+4	+6	+9	+3	+5	+8
Bottom 30 %	+57	+118	+149	+49	+120	+163

SOURCES: As for Table 5.8 (figures rounded off to the nearest whole number).

This table has two important features. First, there is a marked similarity in the magnitude of the proportionate changes between original and net income and between original and final income. This feature is a further reflection of the similarity between the distributions of net and final incomes which can be observed in Table 5.8. (Presently, we shall give further consideration to this feature.) Secondly, there is a very large increase in the magnitude of the proportionate changes in income share of the bottom 30 per cent group over the course of the time period. In 1961–3, the share of this group in net income was more than half as much again the share in original income, but by 1971–3 the net income share was more than twice the share in original income, and by 1975 it was approaching three times. Changes in the relative size of the share in final income for this group were again of a very similar magnitude to those of net income.

In addition to the second observation made above, it can be seen from Table 5.9 that the direction of change in the shares of the top four deciles is downwards, though much reduced in magnitude when in comparison with the gains of the bottom 30 per cent; while gains are made in the two deciles above the bottom 30 per cent, again small in relation to those of the bottom three deciles taken together. The suggestion would seem to be that taxes and benefits have induced a considerable redistribution of incomes, through original to final, over the course of the period considered.[37]

It should be noted, however, that the redistributive forces at work within the definitions of 'net' and 'final' incomes can be pulling in different directions. A calculation prepared for Report No. 1 from the Diamond Commission[38] shows that, for 1972, changes in the Gini coefficient wrought by various taxes and benefits were as follows: direct benefits in cash, −5·53; direct benefits in kind, −2·18; indirect benefits (housing subsidies), −0·38; direct taxes, −2·23; indirect taxes on final goods and services, +1·43; and indirect taxes on intermediate goods and services, +0·34. As can be seen from these estimates, the effect of all taxes on the distribution is small with the progressive effects of direct taxes being largely offset by the regressive effects of indirect taxes. Thus the real impetus towards reducing inequality comes from the benefits side of the picture, where there are substantial reductions in the Gini coefficient values. The opposing forces created by direct benefits and taxes and indirect taxes help to explain the earlier observation from Tables 5.8 and 5.9, that moving from net to final income makes little impact on the distribution between households at different levels of income, and the shapes of these two distributions are very similar.

Concluding Remarks

The survey undertaken in this chapter has been made difficult by the problems of measuring distributions and defining income units and income determinants. Consequently, all conclusions are to some degree tentative. However, given that observers retain this cautionary note, it might be decided that, so far as income redistribution is concerned, the benefits side of the Welfare State has met with some success. Market forces, combined with social and demographic influences, have reduced incomes at the very top of the distribution during the post-war period, though the bottom third of the distribution has also had its share reduced. Thus the reduction in the Gini coefficient may give a misleading picture of the trend towards greater equality.

Income tax has further reduced shares at the top, but it has failed to improve the relative position of the bottom group. Indeed, the post-tax distribution of incomes bears a striking resemblance in shape to the distribution of incomes before deductions of income tax. The combined effect of tax and benefits, however, does seem unambiguously progressive and a powerful force in working towards less inequality. Bearing in mind the deficiencies, data on postwar trends in the incidence of direct and indirect taxes and benefits suggest a large reduction in the Gini coefficient without the ambiguity of being coupled with a worsening of the relative position of the lower income groups.

6. Inequality (3): The Concentration of Wealth in the United Kingdom

In the view of many observers, inequality in wealth shares within a society gives a more accurate picture of the nature of inequality because the full extent of any individual's economic (and political) power is determined ultimately by his potential command over available resources, which must reflect his ownership of assets as well as his current income. Thus, it is held that any society concerned with social justice will be concerned about both wealth and income shares, and this chapter attempts to survey the situation in the United Kingdom on the assumption that such concern characterizes a policy aim. In terms of measurement, the difficulties encountered in estimating wealth concentration are even bigger obstacles than those met when trying to calculate patterns of income distribution.

The Definition of Wealth

The problems raised by the task of defining wealth are similar to those met when trying to define income, and as a result there is an inevitable divergence between measurements in principle and estimates in practice. Thus researchers usually offer more than one estimate of distribution to account for differing inclusions in the definition of wealth adopted for purposes of calculating wealth concentrations from data collected in the real world. Wealth and incomes are, of course, the different dimensions of one set of means by which individuals (or institutions) satisfy their wants. *Wealth* refers to the stock of means available, while *income* refers to the flow of means which stem from the given stock. Another term for wealth is 'net worth', which perhaps better emphasizes the point that wealth relates to a *net* stock, the difference between a set of assets and a set of liabilities.

Given that any stock of means of command over resources is measured by the total (capitalized) value of the various items within the stock, the essential preliminary step in empirical work is to determine which assets are to be included in the definition of the wealth stock. The Diamond Commission sees the crux of the problem in the relationship between 'value' and 'ownership', the key concept being that of 'marketability'. An individual may own the right to income flow from a given asset yet he may not be able to realize the market value of that asset because it is non-transferable. A prime example of this is the state pension – the asset has a value to its owner because it bestows him with income, but he cannot trade his pension right in the market-place. Should such rights be included in the calculation of a comprehensive wealth stock? Less difficult to handle in empirical work are those assets which confer income benefits upon their owner and are disposable at an exchange price – cash, bank deposits, company shares, government bonds, dwellings and so forth. Clearly, such assets must be included in any definition of personal wealth.

Since definitions of wealth differ according to which assets are included in the wealth base, they may present differing pictures of wealth concentration. However, this does not, in the opinion of the Diamond Commission, mean that different definitions of personal wealth are necessarily conflicting or mutually exclusive. Indeed, definitions are likely to differ according to their purpose. Hence, where the prime concern is the distribution of immediate command over resources, the definitions of personal wealth may best be defined in terms only of ownership of assets which are easily traded; but where the definition has a wider purpose – say, measuring the distribution of 'welfare' – it may well embrace non-marketable assets.[1]

Aware of the problems posed by variations in asset values according to their marketability, Atkinson and Harrison pay more detailed attention to defining the basis for valuation, which is a problem closely related to that of defining wealth. Two bases are chosen: a 'realization' basis – an asset is valued by the amount it would fetch on the open market, at the date in question; and a 'going concern' basis – an asset's value to its owner if it is retained. These two valuations are bound to differ. Even in a perfect-market framework some assets will yield benefits to their (intra-marginal) owners in excess of their market price, while the real-world of market imperfections produces a set of asset prices which can greatly differ from the owners' valuations; moreover, some assets (certain pension rights) cannot be traded and have a realization value of zero. Clearly, there is a relationship between the concepts adopted by Atkinson and Harrison and those used by the Diamond Commission. Yet while the Diamond Commission opt for estimates of marketable assets only, Atkinson and Harrison consider both realization and 'going concern' values because they 'can see little case for attaching special significance to zero realization value, preferring to treat marketability as varying continually and the feeling that our realization value corresponds more closely to "everyday usage" ...

than the Commission's own procedure'.[2] The significance of such differences will emerge later, but the important thing to note at this stage is that definitions which are suitable for empirical analysis are likely to be narrower than the comprehensive definitions of theoretical analysis. This restriction should be borne in mind when weighing the implications of empirical findings.

As in the case of income measurement, it is important to establish a clearly defined ownership *unit* and to choose a time period during which economic power is assumed to accrue. On the question of the appropriate unit – individual, household or family – there is little to add to the earlier comments about measuring income, and the reader should note again that different tasks may require different definitions. Since a good deal of wealth is in joint ownership, any estimates of individual wealth holdings require appropriate adjustments to be made – a point returned to later. On the question of time-scale, the importance of life-cycle effects may be even greater in the case of wealth than in the case of income. Whether such effects do significantly alter the distribution pattern calculated at a point in time is debatable, but the *potential* impact of their life-cycle effects is clear: individuals accumulate wealth during their lifetime as a result of savings accumulated to finance the years of retirement. Hence even holding everything else equal (life expectancy, tastes, earnings and so on) the distribution of wealth would exhibit inequalities because of age differentials in the population.

The UK Data Sources

The data available from official sources offer even less detail about the distribution of wealth than they do about the distribution of income. A major reason for this is that the United Kingdom has never had a properly defined wealth tax, and hence there does not exist a bank of comprehensive information on the nation's wealth holdings. The main data source is statistics compiled by the Inland Revenue from estate duty returns, since the full extent of any individual's net worth is only declared to the revenue authorities when he dies. Introduced in 1894, estate duty has remained the only tax on individual wealth holdings in the United Kingdom. In spite of many specific alterations to its base, there was no real structural change until 1974, when the estate duty was replaced by capital transfer tax. Thus, for all but the very recent past, estate duty has been the main provider of data concerning wealth holdings, and it is the nature of this data which suggests caution when using estate returns as the base for deriving wealth distributions. As with income, data collected for one purpose does not always lend itself readily to other aims, and researchers have found it necessary to make several 'adjustments' when trying to measure patterns of wealth concentration.

Some of the problems arising from the use of estate duty returns result from a reliance on a sample of the total population which is based on the numbers dying in any one year, while others are caused by the nature of the tax on estates. Sampling error makes any interpretation of sample surveys difficult, but in the case of estate duty, this problem can be severe, given the very small samples which may emerge for particular ranges of wealth.[3] Further, there is no guarantee that the sample from any particular age or sex grouping is a true representation of the living population of that particular grouping. Other difficulties arise from some of the technicalities of estate duty. One obvious problem concerns the fact that certain estates may be relatively substantial, yet go unrecorded because they fall below the exemption limit for estate duty and are not thoroughly checked by the authorities. Less obvious is the fact that many estates are not covered by revenue statistics because no grant of probate is obtained. Altogether, over half the estates in any one year (the bulk belonging to the lower range of wealth) are 'missing'.[4]

Gaps in the official data are not limited to omitted estates, however, since revenue returns do not record all sources of wealth, estate-duty being somewhat removed from a comprehensive tax on wealth. The list of exemptions is lengthy, but three items are usually singled out as likely to have a substantial effect on wealth distribution if included in the estimates: property held under discretionary trusts (prior to the Finance Act of 1969); property settled on a surviving spouse; and both occupational and state pension rights. The latter omission is the result of the Inland Revenue's exclusion of non-marketable (non-transferable) assets – under a 'going concern' approach to valuation such assets may be an important component in the structure of wealth holdings. Finally, to re-emphasize an earlier point, many physical assets – such as consumer durables and dwellings – are assessed at market prices, yet imperfections in the markets for certain commodities, particularly for secondhand goods, may suggest valuations far below those based on 'going concern'.

Trends in Wealth Distribution

When trying to estimate trends in the distribution of wealth over time, the problems already outlined again present obstacles, but there are some further difficulties. For example, comparisons over time require a consistent series of calculations, yet official estimates were not available before 1960, and the efforts of private researchers prior to this date, though generally based on the estate multiplier method, differed in several respects (geographical coverage, choice of mortality multipliers and treatment of small estates and 'missing wealth') from the estimates eventually offered by the Inland Revenue. For this reason, the Diamond Commission found it useful to separate their time series into two distinct periods with 1960 as the watershed. Of course, as was seen in the case of the data on incomes, an official series does not guarantee consistency when there are changes to the tax base and/or to the methods of collecting taxes, and there have been several changes in estate duty legislation over the years.

The two main sources on wealth distribution are again the works of the Diamond Commission and of Atkinson and Harrison, though both do make extensive use of the findings of other researchers. The definition of wealth adopted by the Diamond Commission is narrow,[5] but in the case of omitted items which are believed to be very important, estimates are attempted which include these items so that comparisons can be made with results based on the narrower definition. Pension rights, both state and occupational, are the two major items to receive such treatment. Despite the accompanying problems, estimates based on estate duty returns and published by the Inland Revenue form the basis for the Diamond Commission's survey of wealth distribution. Such estimates are based on the estate multiplier method, whereby the estates of persons who die during a given year are used as the sample base for estimating the wealth of the living at that particular point in time. Since the age at death of someone leaving an estate is known, and it is possible to assess the probability of dying at that age, total personal wealth and its distribution can be calculated by multiplying the value of estates in each sex and age group by the reciprocal of the relevant mortality rate.[6] By using this method, the data employed by the Diamond Commission is based on wealth valuation in terms of marketable assets only.

The estimates made by Atkinson and Harrison exclude pension rights and rights to communal property (schools, hospitals and so on) because of the conceptual difficulties involved. While eschewing a naïve reliance upon the official estate multipliers, these authors recognize that such a technique is a useful statistical tool and are concerned more with trying to quantify the effects of modifying the multipliers by varying the basic assumptions than rejecting the method completely.[7] Their conclusions suggest that much can be learned about the size distribution of wealth from analysis based on the estate/mortality

multipliers. Like most researchers, Atkinson and Harrison limit their
attentions to the position of the top 10 per cent of wealth-holders
because of the many data deficiencies which render detailed study
of the bottom 90 per cent a most difficult exercise. Finally, like the
Diamond Commission, Atkinson and Harrison separate their study
into periods before and after 1960, but they consider also the inter-
war years of 1923–38 separately from 1950–59, because of changes in
the form and coverage of the estate statistics.

Table 6.1. Cumulative (percentage) shares of personal wealth
owned by given quantile groups of the population, 1911–60

	Cumulative percentage share of personal wealth								
	England and Wales							Great Britain	
	1911–13	1924–30		1936–8		1954		1960	
Quantile group	a	a	b	a	b	a	b	a	b
Top 1%	69	62	58	56	54	43	44	42	34
5%	87	84	80	78	77	71	72	75	60
10%	92	91	87	88	86	79	—	83	72
Bottom 90%	8	9	13	12	14	21	—	17	28

SOURCES: The *a* estimates are from J. Revell, 'Changes in the Social
Distribution of Property in Britain During the Twentieth Century', Third
International Conference of Economic History, Munich, 1965. Revell's estimates
have been widely quoted and form Table 41 of the Diamond Commission,
Report No. 1, p. 97. The *b* estimates are from A. B. Atkinson and
A. J. Harrison, *Distribution of Personal Wealth in Britain*, Cambridge
University Press, 1978, Table 6.7, p. 165.

Table 6.1 summarizes the findings from various sources on the period
up to 1960. The two sets of estimates presented in the table have been
calculated differently,[8] but each tell virtually the same story. According
to both series, there was a considerable levelling down of wealth shares
from the very top of the distribution between 1911 and 1960, though the
relative decline for the top 10 per cent was considerably less than that
for the top 1 per cent in each case. In the case of Revell's estimates
(the *a* series), this relative difference was the result of a large fall in the
share of the top 1 per cent of wealth-holders being offset by an increase
in the share of the next 4 per cent of wealth-holders (by some 15·0
percentage points). From the table, the pattern emerging from the
estimates of Atkinson and Harrison looks very similar, though the
estimates diverge by several percentage points in certain years – in 1960
in particular. Given that the series is based on only a few observations,

Atkinson and Harrison admit the limitations of any conclusions which might be drawn and attempt a regression analysis to discover the real nature of the underlying trend. Their results suggest that, for the half-century between 1920 and 1970, the decline in the share of wealth enjoyed by the top 1 per cent of wealth-holders was at an approximate rate of 0·4 per cent per annum, though any trend in the share of the next 4 per cent is not readily apparent from their equations.

Table 6.2. Cumulative (percentage) shares of personal wealth owned by given quantile groups of the population, 1960–75

	Cumulative percentage share of personal wealth						
	Great Britain						U.K.
	1960		1965		1970		1975
Quantile group	a	b	a	b	a	b	c
Top 1%	38·2	34	33·0	33	29·0	30	23·2
5%	64·3	60	58·5	59	56·3	54	46·5
10%	76·7	72	73·3	72	70·1	69	62·4
Bottom 90%	23·3	28	26·7	28	29·9	31	37·6

SOURCES: The *a* estimates are taken from Table 45 of the Diamond Commision, Report No. 1. The figures relate to the total adult population (18 and over) and are adjusted for any of the deficiencies discussed earlier. The *b* estimates are from Atkinson and Harrison, *Distribution of Personal Wealth in Britain*, Table 67, p. 165. The *c* estimates relate to the United Kingdom and are taken from the Diamond Commission, Report No. 5, Table 33.

For the picture since 1960, Table 6.2 offers three sets of estimates. It would seem from these that the downward trend in the share of wealth enjoyed by the very top of the distribution has continued since 1960. Indeed, on the basis of the Inland Revenue estimates used by the Diamond Commission, the process of redistribution may have been greater after 1960 since the share of the 4 per cent quantile below the top 1 per cent fell significantly. This apparent trend is supported by the Gini coefficient, which stood at 81 in 1975 (for the United Kingdom) for the adult population aged 18 and over as opposed to 89 in 1960 (for Great Britain).[9] The estimates offered by Atkinson and Harrison show a similar pattern, with the decline in the share of the top 1 per cent continuing at a rate of 0·4 per cent per annum at least until 1970.

Possible reasons for the apparent redistribution of wealth over the course of this century are varied in nature, and some of the major causes, at least in theoretical terms, are discovered below. The deficiencies of data render supporting evidence for the varying hypotheses even more dubious than in the case of income distribution, but re-

The Concentration of Wealth 97

searchers have reached agreement on some of the causes. First, however, the trend picture is presented in Figure 6.1. Given the differing methods of calculation and data base used by the various studies, their results are not strictly comparable and interpreting a trend from the varying estimates may not be legitimate. However, since a similar pattern does emerge from each separate estimating exercise, a composite view can be offered of wealth distribution as it has altered during the course of the twentieth century. As can be seen from Figure 6.1, the fall in the share of the very top of the distribution has been striking, but the fall in the share of the quantiles immediately below the very top has been less spectacular, although substantial.

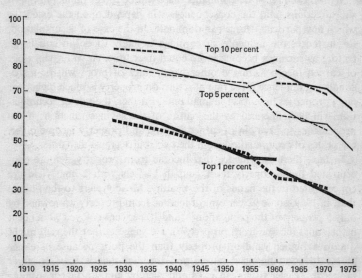

Figure 6.1. Trends in the distribution of wealth, 1911–75.

The Determinants of Concentration

A major reason why the rate of decline in wealth concentration has not been rapid, and why wealth remains more concentrated than income, is that many of the influences upon the distribution of wealth are long-term factors. The interplay of social, demographic and economic influences is part of a long and involved process working to determine the pattern of wealth concentration. A comprehensive account of this process is given by James Meade in his investigations into the causes of wealth concentration, Meade's analysis being aimed at an understanding of the workings of a 'property-owning democracy' where greater equality in the distribution of property mitigates against the forces of automation and their depressing effect upon labour's marginal product.[10] The three main sets of forces operating on the degree of wealth concentration are underlined by Meade as: (a) the forces of accumulation; (b) the patterns of mating and fertility; and (c) the mode of inheritance. Needless to say, the three sets of forces interact, but it is possible to go a considerable way towards an understanding of the determinants of wealth concentration by considering each one separately.

Within each set of determinants there will be forces pulling in opposite directions, and the consequences will depend upon the extent to which any particular force can dominate. In the case of accumulation, for instance, the influence of earnings is likely to be an equalizing factor: as earnings become more equal over time, so will savings out of earned income. On the other hand, rates of profit will be a disequalizing influence if the rate of return on property is much higher for large properties than it is for small ones. Further, the rate of accumulation will be influenced by the nature of the savings function: if the propensities to save out of earned income and property income differ, then rates of accumulation from the two sources must also differ.

In fact, there is evidence that income from property is more concentrated than property itself, and that assets with a high yield are concentrated in the hands of the wealthy. Meade refers to the finding that, in 1959, some 92 per cent of income from property was owned by only 5 per cent of the population[11] (and 10 per cent enjoyed 99 per cent of personal income from property[12]). He suggests that the rich might obtain a higher yield on property than the poor because of easier access to good financial advice and the fact that it is, with larger properties, easier to spread risks and thereby enjoy a higher average yield.[13] It must be true also that, if ownership of property spreads, the concentration of property incomes should be gradually broken down, other things remaining unchanged. Part of the explanation of the trend towards more equality in the concentration of wealth in the United Kingdom lies in the increase in the share of 'popular' assets – consumer durables, bank deposits, life policies and so forth – in the composition of total wealth, and the decline in the more narrowly held assets such as company shares. Quoting Lydall and Tipping,[14] the Diamond Commission points to estimates that company securities fell from 32 per cent of wealth holdings in 1936 to 22 per cent in 1954, while, during the same period, the share of cash and bank deposits rose from 12 to

19 per cent; and remarks that if the measure of wealth included all pension rights, the trend towards greater equality would be more apparent.[15]

It should be borne in mind also at this stage that the rate of accumulation out of property income can be subject to volatile changes if capital gains and losses are important determinants of the value of wealth. For example, considerable discussion has surrounded the effects of the 1973–4 fall in share prices. As pointed out by the Diamond Commission, the fall in share prices during 1974, of the order of 42 per cent, was much greater than in any previous year since 1960. Since the value of personal wealth in the aggregate changed little between 1973 and 1974, the Diamond Commission found it reasonable to attribute the fall in the share of the top 1 per cent of wealth-holders – from 27·6 to 23·9 per cent – to the fall in the prices of company securities.[16] The predictions of the regression model used by Atkinson and Harrison suggest that such a large fall in share prices would have an impact on the wealth share of the top 1 per cent of a size consistent with the estimates of the Diamond Commission.[17]

Some of the changes in the asset composition of wealth between 1960 and 1974 are shown in Figure 6.2. Those assets chosen for illustration demonstrate the growing relative importance of 'popular' wealth. Life policies and building society deposits both show a steady rise over the period, while the rise in the share attributed to dwellings is very marked. On the other hand, listed ordinary shares show a steady decline until 1972, followed by the rapid decline already referred to, while the fall in the share attributed to 'other financial assets' shows a marked decline after 1962. The overall shift in the relative importance of the two main types of asset is shown by the gradual convergence of the trends in the shares of physical assets (rising) and financial assets (declining).

But it is not just the form in which wealth is held which determines the rate of accumulation; the underlying savings function will also be a major factor. Meade has illustrated this point with a savings function which exhibits two main characteristics: first, the proportion of income saved rises as increases in real income occur; secondly, the proportion saved of any given income falls the larger is the property owned, since the need to accumulate is, for the person whose income derives from property, less than that of the individual who derives the same amount of income from earnings, despite the ability to save being the same in each case. Such a savings function has important implications for wealth accumulation. For example, comparing two individuals with equal incomes but unequal properties, the individual with the smaller

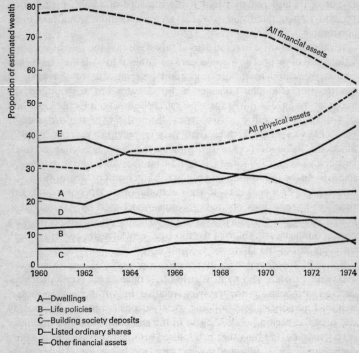

Figure 6.2. Selected changes in the asset composition of personal wealth, 1960–74.

A—Dwellings
B—Life policies
C—Building society deposits
D—Listed ordinary shares
E—Other financial assets

property has the higher earning power and therefore saves more – his property will be growing at a faster rate than the larger property. However, comparing two individuals with the same property but different incomes, the property of the individual with the higher income (higher earning power) will be growing more rapidly because he saves more. In other words,

... there will be exceptionally strong forces at work associating high properties with high earning power. This combination of forces will exaggerate the inequality in the distribution of total personal incomes.[18]

The real long-term nature of the influences upon the distribution of wealth is best appreciated, however, when social, biological and demographic factors are considered. It is impossible to provide even a brief summary of all the influences upon a person's potential wealth-holdings, since they are so many and varied. Only one or two key determinants will therefore be referred to. The complex set of relationships which ultimately determines a person's wealth begins to form even before birth to the extent that genetic endowments inherited from parents will be partly responsible for determining such things as earning power, ability to manage property and so on. After birth, genetic endowments mingle with material inheritance, educational opportunities, social environment, marital and other influences to produce an incredibly complex pattern of forces which operate to determine a person's share of the community's wealth. In later analysis of the causes of poverty, there will be some discussion of the 'balance-sheet' approach to the problem, but only a sample will be chosen of the many determinants of an individual's life-style.[19]

Three of the more obvious influences on the degree of wealth concentration are: (a) the degree of assortive mating; (b) the degree of differential fertility; and (c) the mode of inheritance. If mating were a random process, then the chances are high that individuals with large wealth-holdings would marry individuals with small ones. In fact, marriage tends to be strongly assortive, with rich marrying rich and poor marrying poor.[20] Differential fertility can work in either direction: if the rich had fewer children than the poor then concentration would increase and vice versa. Finally, the pattern of inheritance can influence greatly the degree of wealth concentration. For example, the custom of *primogeniture* – passing on property to the first-born or, more usually, the first-born son – is a strong factor working against the dispersion of property. Figure 6.3 presents a very simplified comparison of two modes of inheritance: one in which the first-born son is always the sole inheritor, and one in which wealth is always divided equally between son and daughter. The example assumes that, in each generation, every son and daughter has, in turn, a child of each sex. The pattern of inheritance begins with a married couple passing on £100. Equal splitting results in wealth being ever more dispersed while primogeniture maintains intact the original inheritance.

State Programmes to Break Up Concentration of Wealth

Of course, in reality the many processes working to influence the degree of wealth concentration are interrelated and examples such as that provided by Figure 6.3 are a gross over-simplification. Nevertheless, it should be clear that a more equal distribution of property can only be achieved over the very long term if the problem is left to some combination of social, demographic and economic forces. It would seem that a speedier break-up of wealth concentrations depends upon some exogenous influence being exerted, such as a state-designed and organized scheme of redistribution. Part of such a programme has been described already, since measures to redistribute incomes will influence earning potential and social environment in such a way that wealth will become more evenly shared. However, a real attack on concentration, to take effect in the short run, depends upon wealth shares being reduced from the top.

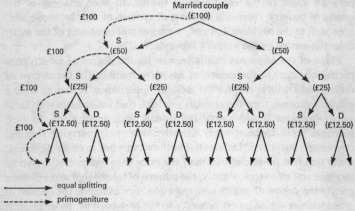

Figure 6.3. Contrasting patterns of inheritance and their effects on concentration of wealth.

The method of redistribution most favoured by Western democracies is some form of wealth tax. As far as the United Kingdom is concerned, for the period up to 1974, estate duty has been the main instrument of wealth redistribution. Unfortunately, estate duty was not a notable success in reducing inequalities, partly because it was never applied properly to discretionary trusts, and partly because the rules permitted exemption of gifts *inter vivos* unless such transfers took place within seven years prior to the donor's death. Perhaps, though, the greatest fault of estate duty as a means of reducing wealth inequality lay in the principle of taxing the value of an estate rather than the value of an inheritance. It is not large estates *per se* which perpetuate inequalities, but the fact that they are passed on as large inheritances and the most efficient way to promote equality by taxing wealth is to tax inherited receipts. Furthermore, taxing inheritances rather than estates offers an incentive to donors to disperse their wealth more widely than they would in the face of an estate duty, if the rates structure of the tax is progressive. For example a rates structure of 33⅓ per cent on the first £3,000 of wealth passed on and 50 per cent on the remainder reduces a £9,000 estate to £5,000 under an estates tax, whether there is one beneficiary or three; but under an inheritance tax with the same rates structure, the total tax bill is reduced to only £3,000 if the estate is shared by three beneficiaries, each receiving £2,000 net of tax.

If inheritance were not an important determinant of the degree of wealth concentration, then perhaps estate duty would have been a more acceptable form of tax. The available evidence suggests, however, that inheritance is one of two major factors in the self-perpetuating cycle of wealth determination, capital gains being the other. As two prominent writers in the field have put it recently:

The main sources of wealth are necessarily inheritance and capital gains, and most fortunes are the product of some combination of the two.[21]

Most of the evidence collected for the United Kingdom is found in the important work of C. D. Harbury and his collaborators. In 1962, Harbury published the results of an attempt to quantify the effect of inheritance on the distribution of wealth.[22] The attempt was based largely on an examination of the relationship between estates left by top wealth-holders and the estates left by their fathers, using a sample of large estates left in the years 1956 and 1957. Among other things, the study found that around two thirds of rich sons (estates over £100,000) had fathers who were in the top 0·25 per cent of wealth-holders, and that the 'self-made man' was in a small minority. In comparing Harbury's study with an earlier one undertaken by Wedgwood[23] for the years 1924–6, Atkinson finds that, in spite of social upheavals, inflation, estate duty and so on, there was no clear decline in the importance of inheritance during the first half of the twentieth century.[24] More recent empirical work by Harbury suggests that this view should be qualified somewhat, because inheritance *has* declined in importance since the earlier studies, but nevertheless the basic argument remains that inheritance is a prime factor in determining wealth. Thus Harbury and McMahon (1973) found that over 50 per cent of sons leaving over £100,000 had fathers who had done the same,[25] while Harbury and Hitchens (1976) found that some 58 per cent of those who died wealthy had themselves inherited large fortunes.[26]

An interesting tail-piece from the Diamond Commission can be added to the Harbury findings. Basing the analysis on a sample of 238 estates of £15,000 or more in 1973, the Diamond Commission tried to discover the extent to which the largest estates tended to remain intact across generations. The results suggest that the degree of fragmentation of estates increases with the size of the estate, which should, over the long run, work towards a more equal distribution of wealth.[27] However, this pattern of inheritance could also explain the fact that the decline in share of the top 1 per cent has been counter-balanced by the increased share of the next 2 to 5 per cent – the fragmentation of estates at the top works to the benefit of those nearly at the top![28]

The replacement of estate duty by the capital transfer tax (in 1974) will have an eventual effect on the pattern of inheritance, but the impact is unlikely to be as great as it might have been with further modifications. A big improvement over the estate duty is that capital transfer tax is levied on a cumulative basis not just on wealth at death but also on gifts and bequests *inter vivos*. In this way there can be no tax avoidance through gifts made prior to death. However, the capital transfer tax is still based on the estates principle and is not levied on receipts of transfer, and thus does not provide the additional incentive to disperse wealth that is offered by an inheritance tax. Because of this, several commentators have found the capital transfer tax to compare un-favourably with some form of *accessions tax*, which, being levied on receipts, would hit hardest at large transfers of wealth by gifts and bequests and encourage transfers at death to those who have received little in the form of gifts or bequests. This is certainly the view advanced by the Meade Committee, although it believes that 'the force of the argument can be overstated'.[29] The committee refers to the fact that, under an accessions tax, the tax bill is higher if an inheritance is passed on to someone who has already received substantial gifts and bequests than if the same estate is handed on to a recipient who has not benefited from prior gifts. But the committee also point to the fact that, under a capital transfer tax, this same estate passed on to a third generation will be taxed more at that stage if its second generation recipient has received prior gifts than if it is passed on to the third generation unaugmented by gifts received by the second. In other words, the capital transfer tax provides similar incentives to the accessions tax but one generation later. Thus, given the likelihood of 'fiscal myopia' – the relative attraction to the donor of an immediate tax saving under an accessions tax – the committee favour this wealth tax variant. Indeed, this immediate saving might prove to be the only relevant tax con-sideration, given the general uncertainty about the future and specific uncertainty surrounding the aims and abilities of recipients.

Of course, the whole case for any particular variant of wealth tax depends on more than its anticipated impact upon the distribution of property. Thus some form of annual net worth tax could well replace all existing taxes on the holding of wealth and the income deriving from it as a means of both redistribution and improvement in the tax system's ability to achieve the aims of horizontal equity and efficiency. Wealth, it is claimed, provides a better measure of 'ability to pay' than income – it offers security, power, and is self-perpetuating, even beyond the death of the owner, thus permitting his heirs to derive benefits. Further, if psychic rewards go untaxed, then absence of any tax on wealth may encourage the holding of wealth in 'non-productive' forms (such as old masters, antiques, stately homes). Finally, a wealth tax can be devised in such a way that it does not produce economic disincentives. For example, because a wealth tax is levied on the stock of assets and not on the flow of income from the stock, it cannot distort the trade-off between current income and leisure but, instead, produces a pure income effect (a smaller *net* stock produces a smaller flow of total income) which induces an increased consumption of income – that is, *work*. And replacing an income tax with a wealth tax will result in a substitution effect which encourages a higher level of savings: during working life income is untaxed, thus permitting more savings, and during the years of retirement, although the source of consumption is being taxed, the source will be much increased as a consequence of previous savings.[30]

In terms of achieving distributional objectives, however, the taxing of wealth *transfers* might result in short-term improvements leaving the difficult task of introducing a comprehensive tax on the *holdings* of wealth for the longer term policy package. But if the time factor is to be crucial, then other candidates for a policy of redistribution might be considered. Suppose, for example, that the state commandeers all property. Immediately there is a drastic alteration in the pattern of distribution, with the positions of the top wealth-holders being most severely diminished. The property so acquired can be employed by the state to help produce a social dividend in which each citizen has an equal share. The size of this (annual) share will be determined by the efficiency with which resources are allocated rather than by any pattern of distribution of resources. Such is the nature of 'market socialism', as advanced by Oskar Lange, in which the state owns all productive services, save labour, and enterprise managers are ordered to equate costs at the margin with prices dictated by the 'planning authority'.[31] But such a model is foreign to the type of mixed economy experienced by the United Kingdom and the initial redistribution so achieved would not square with any system of social values yet employed in UK politics. On the other hand, state acquisition of assets through the payment of compensatory contracts offering at least the equivalent of market prices for assets and the expected stream of net revenues from such assets does nothing to alter the distribution of wealth.[32]

Concluding Remarks

As with income, any conclusions about the distribution of wealth are ultimately dependent upon what the social welfare function specifies as a desirable pattern. The great upsurge of interest in the distribution problem has unearthed a mound of detail regarding the nature and causes of the pattern of wealth distribution. Several problems surround the interpretation of data based on estate duty returns, but it does seem clear from various sources that there has been a considerable re-distribution of property during the course of this century, and particu-larly since 1960. Yet the fact remains that wealth is much more con-centrated than income, and measures to disperse property holdings are being debated continually. Whether a switch to penalizing transfers, as opposed to estates, will eventually be introduced depends upon how concentrated wealth ranks in relation to other social problems dis-cussed in this book. Given that the redistribution has to date resulted from long-term changes in the social, demographic and economic structure of the United Kingdom, helped by estates taxation, and in the absence of either violent revolution or even large-scale nationalization of resources, it seems unlikely that a large-scale solution would now be adopted.

7. Income Maintenance (1):
Income Maintenance
and Social Insurance

In this section of study, covering some five chapters, the main area of inquiry is one which is usually described as 'social security'. This seems a good way to describe methods which are aimed to secure for everyone in a society the standard of income which is considered desirable by that society, as expressed through the social welfare function. However, the term 'social security' covers a variety of state activities which provide the mechanics behind two conceptually distinct objectives: first, to ensure that, as far as possible, individuals make some provision to offset the effects of expected events such as the onset of old age and of contingencies such as unemployment or sickness – the social insurance objective; and the relief of poverty by the provision of some kind of minimum income guarantee. To understand fully the rationale behind the present system of social security in Britain, and to avoid confusing the aims of the various components of the system, it is essential for us to make a sharp distinction between these two objectives.[1] We shall maintain the distinction by considering the scope and effects of social, or national, insurance in this chapter, while leaving a general discussion of the fight against poverty until the next.

The Case for State Intervention

There can be no guarantee that an economy will always operate with maximum efficiency, and that all individuals will always be properly catered for by the distribution of the rewards from the economic process. Is there, then, a role for the state to play in reducing the uncertainty surrounding the expected longer-term distribution of incomes?

In trying to answer this question, we must first consider the problems which are likely to face the individual who attempts to make his own provision for the future. If it is considered that these problems are too severe for the individual to overcome, then we may feel that the state is justified in giving some form of assistance. The justification for this would lie not only in the individual's own interest, but also in the interests of society since, assuming some degree of utility interdependence among individuals, the externalities from improvidence will encourage collective action. A good starting-point for this type of approach is to consider the case of provision for old age, since this involves decisions about some future standard of living during the years in which people are relatively unproductive in an economic sense. The problems surrounding such calculations are intensified by the lengthy time period involved between implementing the decisions and the eventual reaping of rewards.

Microeconomic theory depicts the individual as maximizing the satisfaction which he derives from consuming goods (including leisure) and services, according to his tastes and subject to various constraints. Since the rational individual is interested in lifetime utility, he will attach relative weights to present and future consumption levels according to his time-preference pattern of consumption and attempt to maximize satisfaction subject to both present and expected future constraints. Given that individuals do behave in this way, a state programme of compulsory provision for old age may distort the individual's 'optimal' (from the point of view of his own time-preference pattern) allocation of consumption between time periods. The individual with positive time preference is forced to increase his future consumption at the expense of the present; and even the individual who places a greater weight upon future consumption is only satisfied if the level of state provision accords with his own expectations and desires.[2]

The counter-argument is that the time preferences of most individuals are such that they make inadequate provision for old age for two main reasons: widespread myopia, intensified by the difficulties of decision-making which takes account of the distant future; and a lack of means by which to plan a consumption pattern over more than one time period. Even if the state could mitigate the latter part of the problem by providing those without means with a margin of saving over current consumption, this would only be fruitful if the first part of the problem could be solved.[3] Thus, given that individuals are improvident, or find the calculus of optimization concerning future income streams, investment yields, family circumstances, likelihood of employment and so forth beyond their mental powers, the state assumes a paternalistic role via the compulsory purchase of annuities so as to protect the individual from himself. If the individual does not want this protection – for example, if he has a very strong positive time preference for consumption – the state justifies its interference on the grounds of social costs. While utility interdependence might lead society to help the myopic and improvident, it does not prevent society from taking steps to ensure that the need for such aid is minimized – humanitarianism does not preclude cost minimization![4]

However, while a case might exist for compulsory insurance against future income loss, it is not immediately obvious why this requires the compulsory purchase of state annuities. Perhaps the case against the market is most easily appreciated if we consider first the problem of *temporary* loss of earnings as a result of ill-health or redundancy of market skills or other similar cause. Given the externalities that this creates, the most feasible short-run answer is to support the currently unemployed out of tax revenues provided by the currently employed. Now, it is reasonable to suppose that the currently employed will anticipate the need for such support recurring in the future and demand that steps be taken to minimize their contributions – that is, to also protect their own interests. One form that this protection might take is compulsory private insurance against contingencies. This solution, however, would be quite impossible in practice. It is too much to expect private companies to provide insurance against, say, sickness and unemployment. How could the risks be calculated? It is one task to estimate the likelihood of someone dying before a certain age (life insurance), but it is of quite a different order of difficulty to estimate the likelihood of someone contracting an illness which requires a rest from working. Even if such risks could be calculated, the premium structure would violate the 'ability to pay' principle. The risk/premium link would require those subject to the highest degree of risk to pay the highest premiums. In the case of sickness and unemployment, this would mean the lower income groups paying more for protection than the higher income groups. In contrast, a state-operated tax-transfer system can be organized on the basis of collective risk, each individual paying an average 'premium'.

Turning again to the problems created by those who make inadequate provision for their retirement years, the short-run solution here would be to support the retired population out of revenues collected from the working population. Now, it is reasonable to expect that the working population will wish to minimize the likelihood of *their children* having to support the retired population of some future date and demand that individuals be compelled to make proper provision for their retirement needs. Again, compulsory private insurance faces drawbacks. The risk problem disappears since old age is certain (for all who survive that long!), and the remaining degree of uncertainty – how much is required to finance the years of retirement – creates no problem in an inflation-free economy. But in a world of unstable prices, it is difficult for private companies to maintain a premium/pension link which safeguards against inflation. If the rate of inflation is underestimated, then collective transfers will be called for to maintain minimum income standards.

Furthermore, 'equal treatment of equals' relates to income (as a measure of ability to pay), and discrimination among workers according to the nature of their occupations (occupational pension schemes) offends this principle. But the issues here are by no means clear-cut ones.

Let us assume, at least for the time being, that the chosen form of collective action to protect the incomes of the aged is the compulsory purchase of state annuities. Should the state scheme be organized, as far as possible, on an insurance basis? The pension problem, and to some extent the contingency problem, is an inter-generation one. If we accept that the sole rationale for intervention is to protect a future generation of tax payers (the assumption we made above), then the state has a duty to organize its scheme on a funded basis, i.e. to ensure its actuarial soundness. As with a private scheme, the aim would be to set premiums which equalize the present expected values of both premiums and benefits. To protect current policy-holders against the possibility of receipts being less than adequate to cover benefit payments at some future date, a reserve fund would be accumulated on behalf of all insured persons. To create such a reserve, premiums would be set at a sufficiently high level; if the individual wants the promise of a higher level of benefit, or more comprehensive coverage than is allowed by his original contract, he must be prepared to pay a higher premium. In this way, then, a reserve is accumulated for each individual, and it follows that an increase in the number of people insured must mean an increase in total reserves.

However, if we modify the rationale of intervention to one of protecting all generations, including *current* taxpayers, then the state has no need to organize its scheme on a funded basis (even assuming it could do so), but can make use of its coercive powers to establish the programme on a 'pay-as-you-go' basis, whereby current beneficiaries are supported by current contributions. In other words, an 'acceptable' tax/transfer plan can be devised. This argument is based on two assumptions: (a) that the scheme is financed by compulsory contributions; and (b) that future governments maintain the compulsion. Given those conditions, we can view social 'insurance' as a form of social contract whereby the young are prepared to support the old on the guarantee that a future generation of taxpayers will do the same for them when they grow old.

This contract is acceptable because, under the right conditions, the value of benefits ultimately received on retirement will exceed the value of contributions made during working life. Assuming a growing population of constant age structure, there are more contributors than beneficiaries. 'Premiums' may be fixed at a level below that necessary to accumulate reserves, and each individual in later life receives a positive return on contributions made during his productive years. Moreover, this rate of return will approximate to the rate of growth of the economy as a result of the growth of the labour force and the general level of incomes. As long as national income and population grow proportionately, so that real income per head remains constant over time, then a pay-as-you-go tax/transfer scheme yields an implicit rate of return on contributions.

For example, assume two groups of equal size P. One group, L_1, consists of current workers; the other group, R_1, consists of retired workers. A proportional tax at rate t is levied on the earned income of each of the P workers in order to finance the support of the P retired persons who do not earn income and, we assume, do not have any un-earned income. Thus $Y^{R_1} = tY^{L_1}$ where Y^{R_1} is total income of the retired group and Y^{L_1} is total income of the workers. The average con-tribution from each worker is:

$$\frac{tY^{L_1}}{P}$$

Now consider this society twenty years on. There has been no price inflation, and wage rates have remained constant. R_1 have all died and L_1 have taken their place, to become R_2, the current generation of retired people. There is also a new generation, L_2, of N workers, where $N > P$. Thus total income of $R_2 = tY^{L_2}$, where:

$$Y^{L_2} = Y^{L_1} \cdot \frac{(N)}{P}$$

The average benefit payment to each retired person is:

$$\frac{tY^{L_2}}{P} = \frac{tY^{L_1} \cdot \frac{(N)}{P}}{P}$$

Hence, the average contribution of the L_1 workers yields an implicit rate of return equal to the rate of growth of population, $\frac{N}{P}$.

What we have described here is an extremely simplified version of Samuelson's famous model which predicts the 'general biological optimum interest rate'.[5] Of course, Samuelson's model is concerned with the social optimum and the search for the rate of interest which will bring about that happy state. In so doing, the model makes an important contribution to capital theory. But, at the same time, the optimum is also sought for in a world of perishable consumer goods (chocolates), and in the face of problems which this presents to the market mechanism, the optimum is achieved through a social compact which lays down the ground rules by which one generation is supported by another. We have abstracted from Samuelson's model a simple arithmetical illustration of how 'pay-as-you-go' can work, accepting that an optimum results and leaving the proof to Samuelson's rigorous essay. But, as a means of fixing the idea, and to hark back to one of our constant themes, consider this elegant statement of the proposition that ends may be served by differing means and that choosing among means, whether political, social or economic, is part of the search for social optima:

> Much as you and I may dislike government 'interferences' in economic life, we must face the positive fact that the motivations for higher living standards that a free market channels into Walrasian equilibrium when the special conditions for that pattern happen to be favourable – these same motivations often lead to social collusions and myriad uses of the apparatus of the state. For good or evil, these may not be aberrations from laissez faire, but theorems entailed by its intrinsic axioms.[6]

'Pay-as-You-Go' in Practice

Throughout the post-war period, the British people have enjoyed a comprehensive system of social insurance which provides benefit to: retired persons, widows and guardians, the sick and the unemployed; as well as providing a death grant, maternity benefit, disablement benefit, and compensation for industrial injury. Anyone experiencing need arising out of the categories covered by the scheme, but who is not eligible to receive benefit, can take refuge in a system of supplementary benefits which performs the task of a 'safety net' against poverty. This situation had its original conception in the Beveridge Report of 1942.[7]

Prior to this report, developments in the field of social insurance, and in the field of social security in general, had been somewhat piecemeal.[8] It was not until the beginning of the present century that the aim of poverty relief divorced itself from the penal system administered by the Poor Law authorities. This system had persevered since Elizabethan times, reaching its grand climax in the Poor Law Amendment Act of 1834, which was based primarily upon the 'Protestant ethic' – that poverty is testimony to personal failure. The erosion of this approach and its heavy reliance upon the workhouse 'solution' was gradually achieved by a change in attitude on the part of reformers and by the growing realization on the part of administrators that poverty is not always the result of personal failure, but more often a consequence of three primary causes: old age, sickness and unemployment.

This change in public opinion and approach had, by 1908, resulted in the establishment of non-contributory means-tested old-age pensions, and by 1912 compulsory insurance against sickness and unemployment was introduced, although coverage in this case was by no means universal. The inter-war period witnessed an extension of the coverage of these schemes, and in 1925 a national contributory pension plan was put into operation. Yet despite these advances, little attempt was made to integrate the various components into a comprehensive scheme, and such an uncoordinated programme inevitably spawned administrative complexities and gave rise to undesirable gaps in the coverage offered to the various categories of beneficiary. It was left to the Beveridge Report to try and correct this situation.

The recommendations of the Beveridge Report were aimed, primarily, at the alleviation of want, the main causes of which were seen to be the interruption of earnings or the cessation of earning-power as a result of sickness, unemployment, old age or the failure to relate earned income to family size. According to the report, any scheme of social security must have as its main feature a framework of social insurance against such risks. Since the plan was essentially one of 'insurance', it contained the outline of a system of flat-rate subsistence benefits, the primary aim of which was to give adequate support during time of need, while providing a basis for additional private supplementation. Finance for the scheme was to come from private citizens (employers and employees), who would make flat-rate contributions; and from the Exchequer. Hence, eligibility for benefit would be dependent upon the individual's contribution record. Such a scheme, unlike its predecessors, was to be administratively uniform and comprehensive with respect to coverage and needs.[9]

These principles have provided the salient features of postwar social security arrangements in Britain. Changes have been made, however, which have involved alterations to some of the mechanics of Beveridge's scheme. The year 1961 saw the introduction of a graduated pension, financed by a graduated contribution, a scheme which was extended to earnings-related supplements to unemployment benefit, sickness benefit and maternity allowance in 1966. Certain employees with occupational pension rights, considered 'adequate' by the authorities, were permitted to 'contract-out' of the graduated pensions scheme. Thus, by the end of the 1960s, the cost of benefits had risen very much in relation to the size of the potential 'tax base'. In consequence, from 1969 onwards, graduated contributions financed more and more of the flat-rate benefits until, in 1974/5, the bulk of the total benefits cost was being financed out of this source.[10] This method of finance was inevitable given the practical limits to raising the flat-rate contribution in a régime committed to helping the lower paid.

However, the major change is a recent one. In April 1975, the flat-rate and graduated scheme for employees ended and was replaced by one which was earnings related. From that date all contributions became earnings related and payable as a proportion of earnings (subject to upper and lower limits). The employer's contribution is calculated in the same way, but at a higher rate. The new arrangements extend the old graduated scheme, with some major changes to the liability rules being introduced. Further extensions to these structural changes came under the Social Security Pensions Act 1975 (which entered into force in April 1978). Under this Act, pensions for retirement, widowhood and invalidity consist of two parts: a basic, flat-rate, pension and an additional, earnings-related, pension. Those employees in occupational pension schemes which meet specific requirements may be contracted out of part of the state scheme, receiving a basic pension from the state but with their additional pension being provided by the occupational scheme. Those individuals who retired prior to the new scheme continue to receive flat-rate pensions under the old arrangements.

But the above changes affect the future. The major features of the postwar social insurance programme have their origins in legislation which is geared to the Beveridge principles. Thus, the aim in this chapter is to look at the financial and economic consequences of a policy[11] which has meant that, not only has there been increased coverage in terms of persons 'insured', but benefit expenditure has become an increasingly important feature of the national accounts. Table 7.1 gives an indication of this trend for the period 1950–75, during which expenditure on social insurance benefits steadily grew as a proportion of both GNP and current government expenditure. Over the twenty-five-year period spanned by Table 7.1, benefit expenditure rose to approximately 18 per cent of total government expenditure from a ratio of almost 9 per cent in 1950; while the ratio to GNP also doubled during the same period.

The post-Beveridge scheme of social insurance has operated on a virtual 'pay-as-you-go' basis since its inception. The finances of the scheme have been organized by the National Insurance Fund, Industrial Injuries Fund and the National Insurance (Reserve) Fund, the accounts of which show that the scheme has relied heavily for its finances upon

Table 7.1. **Expenditure on social insurance benefits, 1950–75 (selected years)**

Year	Total expenditure on benefits (£m)	Benefit expenditure as % GNP (factor cost)	Benefit expenditure as % total government expenditure
1950	389	3·33	8·89
1955	614	3·63	11·24
1960	992	4·35	15·00
1965	1,775	5·61	17·53
1970	2,715	6·17	15·14
1975	6,387	6·79	17·91

SOURCE: CSO, *National Income and Expenditure*, selected years.

current contributions and Exchequer assistance rather than investment income. Table 7.2 provides a comprehensive breakdown of the various sources of income to the funds during the post-war period. As the table illustrates, the bulk of current receipts have been in the form of contributions from insured persons and employers plus central government grants; interest income has never accounted for more than $7\frac{1}{2}$

Table 7.2. **Receipts of the national insurance funds, 1948–76 (selected years)**

1 Year	2 Total receipts to (£m)	3 Contributions from employers and employees (£m)	4 Grants from central govt. (£m)	5 Interest	6 3 as % 2	7 4 as %2	8 5 as % 2
1948	508	335	148	25	65·94	29·13	4·92
1950	626	440	153	33	70·29	24·44	5·27
1952	597	476	76	45	79·73	12·73	7·54
1954	660	532	79	49	80·61	11·97	7·42
1956	803	642	106	55	79·95	13·20	6·85
1958	969	760	149	60	78·43	15·38	6·19
1960	1,049	795	190	64	75·79	18·11	6·10
1962	1,303	1,030	201	68	79·05	15·43	5·22
1964	1,580	1,267	235	70	80·20	14·87	4·43
1966	2,002	1,609	306	76	80·37	15·28	3·80
1968	2,384	1,933	366	72	81·06	15·34	3·10
1970	2,885	2,378	426	65	82·43	14·76	2·25
1972	3,690	3,030	570	72	82·11	15·45	1·95
1974	5,594	4,688	769	112	83·76	13·80	1·99
1976	9,218	7,691	1,271	241	83·44	13·79	2·62

SOURCE: CSO, *National Income and Expenditure*, selected years.

per cent of total receipts, and since the late 1950s its contribution has gradually declined to less than 3 per cent. The relatively minor role accorded to interest receipts is reflected in the fact that the Funds' investments have been in safe, low-yield government securities, in direct contrast to privately funded schemes, which rely upon investments as a major source of finance.

Thus, reserve accumulation has not been a feature of British social insurance. Any annual surplus of receipts over payments has been left in the National Insurance Fund as a working balance. Despite its title, the National Insurance (Reserve) fund has never provided the scheme with a funded basis. Indeed, the amount held by the 'Reserve' Fund has remained static for long periods of time as the result of an annual transference of interest income to the National Insurance Fund.

In the absence of a funding scheme, current receipts have financed current payments. As shown in Figure 7.1, annual expenditures have been largely met by current contributions from private persons and central government grants.

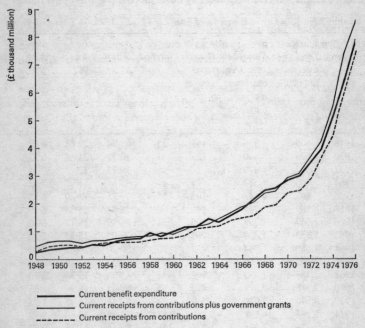

Current benefit expenditure
Current receipts from contributions plus government grants
Current receipts from contributions

Figure 7.1. Current expenditure and receipts (excluding interest receipts) of the National Insurance Funds, 1948–76.

Some Economic Effects of Social Insurance

The fact that the so-called 'national insurance' scheme operates as a tax/transfer mechanism raises the important issue of whether the nature of the taxes and the transfers fulfils the criteria for acceptability which are applied to other parts of the government revenue system. Unless it can be demonstrated that only an 'insurance' plan of the UK type can hope to achieve an optimum transfer of income across generations, doubts must be cast upon whether we are making the most of the means of socially financing short-term contingencies and long-term cessation of individual earnings streams. It may be that the same objectives can be achieved by replacing social insurance with a scheme of direct income transfers to such as the old, sick or unemployed, financed out of increased direct taxation. Lest even the possibility of such a change seems foreign to those who have lived with the postwar system of the United Kingdom (or, indeed, that of most Western European countries, or of the United States), let us consider the nature of the contribution/benefit framework as it has operated over the past thirty years.

A comprehensive scheme of social insurance is likely to have effects upon the economy at many levels of activity. For example, the extent to which the scheme's coverage alters the level of disposable income within the economy is likely to have consequences for government stabilization policy; the contribution/benefit structure might affect the supply of work effort; and so on. As we have seen, Britain's social insurance provisions have relied heavily upon a tripartite system of contributions, employers, employees and the Exchequer all contributing to the scheme. Before 1961, contributions from insured persons and their employers were flat-rate. After 1961, the flat-rate contribution existed alongside a graduated contribution for pensions, and this scheme extended to other benefits in 1966. Since 1978, an earnings-related pensions scheme has operated in place of the pensions flat-rate/graduated contribution framework for pensions. What has been the impact upon economic activity?

There are many gaps in our knowledge of the economic effects of social insurance, and while some empirical tests have been undertaken, we remain very much dependent upon theoretical analysis as a guide to how economic agents react to contributions and benefits. As far as employers and employees are concerned, the social insurance contribution is a tax. It might be argued that, unlike other direct taxes, an employee's social insurance contribution is assumed to be earmarked for the provision of some tangible benefit to the contributor, and to this extent resembles a subsidized fee. However, a compulsory deduction from income must be treated as a tax from the point of view of its economic consequences. Since an employer's contribution is proportional to the number of insured persons in his employment, it is a payroll tax; while the employee's flat-rate contribution is a lump-sum tax or 'poll tax'.

(a) *Incidence*

An important determinant of the effects of a tax is its incidence – who actually pays it! The answer to this question is still being sought, and although some agreement is emerging among empirical economists, the analysis of incidence is still very much at the conceptual stage. In the case of the employee's flat-rate contribution, the problem seems fairly straightforward. Being a lump-sum tax, the initial burden of the employees's contribution would seem to fall upon the workers themselves since the only way in which workers can pass on this burden is by successfully pressing for higher wages. Whether or not this will happen in practice depends upon the relative bargaining strengths of workers and employers, and also upon workers' perception of the social insurance contribution. There is, as yet, no clear evidence for the United Kingdom that trade unions use social insurance contributions as a lever to secure wage increases.

The case of the employer's contribution is somewhat more complex and must be analysed using a distinction between short and long-run effects. Neoclassical analysis tells us that, in the world of perfect competition, the burden of a payroll tax falls upon workers who receive a net wage which is equal to gross wage (marginal product) less any tax per unit of labour employed. The introduction of an employer's social insurance contribution (or an increase in the rate of an existing contribution) means an overall increase in the firm's wages bill. Thus, given competitive market conditions and assuming that the demand for labour is more elastic than supply, workers foot most of the tax bill – the demand curve for labour shifts leftwards until the price, which now absorbs the employer's contribution, falls to its previous level.[12] If we now assume that labour supply is completely inelastic, then all of the tax is borne by labour in the form of a wage reduction.

However, while the assumption of a completely inelastic supply of labour may initially appear to be reasonable for the régime of a universally applied payroll tax – labour has 'nowhere else to go' – it does overlook the intricacies of the work/leisure choice. How workers respond to a lower wage offer depends upon the relative strengths of income and substitution effects, and theory does not permit an unambiguous prediction. On the other hand, it might be argued that, when institutional arrangements do not permit variations in hours of work, discussion of income and substitution effects is no longer relevant. But if we accept the possibility of a varying supply of labour, then assessing the incidence of a payroll tax requires a general equilibrium model if we are to trace all the ramifications of the employment effect suffered by labourers, and the elasticity of substitution among factors of production becomes an important determinant of the final outcome. The only study to have attempted such an analysis still finds that, over a range of relative demand and supply elasticities (but always assuming a linear homogeneous production function), the burden of an employment tax is mainly borne by labour.[13]

As already mentioned, empirical evidence is scarce, but what there is does seem to provide a consensus that long-run incidence of payroll taxes falls mainly on labour. A major contribution in this area is the work of Brittain.[14] Assuming the CES production function and using regression analysis on US data, Brittain finds that,

firms treat their payroll tax like any other labour cost in setting output and price and in agreeing to the total compensation to be awarded a given degree of labour productivity. The long-run result appears to be that employers in the aggregate avoid the burden of their contribution via a trade off between the tax and real wages and salaries.[15]

This finding is endorsed, with some qualifications, by Vroman,[16] who assesses Brittain's analysis and, with the use of 'better' data, finds 'strong support' for Brittain's conclusion that capital's relative share in income is unaffected by payroll taxes. Both these studies, on the admission of the authors, fail to cover three important aspects of the incidence problem: the use of payroll tax receipts; the nature of the shift process; or the size of payroll tax rates in manufacturing relative to rates in other sectors. However, bearing in mind these qualifications, the degree of agreement over likely incidence of the payroll tax is striking. Final support for the argument comes from an earlier study by Weitenberg.[17] Based on a planning model used in the Dutch Central Planning Bureau, Weitenberg's analysis attempts to take more account of demand considerations than is allowed for by neoclassical theory, yet this does not qualify seriously the long-run effect, and it is estimated that the tax causes a 50 per cent reduction in the autonomous increase in nominal wage rates. This is a smaller effect than that produced by the other studies because some of the short-run price and employment effects still persist into the longer run according to Weitenberg's macro-view of the problem.

When analysing the short run, however, tracing the incidence of a payroll tax is somewhat more difficult because of the relative absence of competitive forces and the resultant breakdown of an important neo-classical assumption. One very important consequence of this is that 'forward shifting' of the tax (as opposed to the 'backward shifting' that we have discussed so far) must be considered since employers may try to raise their selling prices so as to avoid the burden of contributions. How successful they can be in this attempt, and what the consequences of price increases will be, depends upon the general state of the economy. Assuming the price rise is general, it is likely to result in a fall in effective demand, and hence in the level of employment. Without government measures to correct the situation, and in the absence of strong trade unions, the situation will worsen until wage rates fall to a level which permits the re-establishment of the pre-tax prices. Again the burden has been shifted backwards on to employees. But in a world in which government is committed to pursuing a policy of full employment, and in which trade unions prevent any fall in money wages, employers are likely to pass on the tax in higher prices and consumers will bear the ultimate burden. To the extent that wage-earners are also consumers, much of the burden must still rest with the employee.[18] Of course, if the government's short-term management of the economy also includes price controls as a means of fighting inflation, then profits will be forced to bear the burden of the payroll tax.

Support for the likelihood of such short-run effects emerging come again from Weitenberg's study,[19] which demonstrates that the nature of short-run consequences depends upon the initial state of the economy when the payroll measure is introduced. Taking a given level of unemployment as the starting-point, one of the conclusions of this Dutch experiment was that the 'process of shifting forward a payroll tax involves increasing prices and unemployment'.[20] As mentioned earlier, such effects may, to some degree, persist into the long run. However, the price effects must peter out eventually, unless there are favourable, exogenously induced changes in the state of the economy or improvements in the rate of growth of national income.

(b) Incentives

Closely related to the question of incidence is the problem of how economic incentives are affected by social insurance contributions, particularly the incentives to save and to work. A more thorough discussion of the incentive effects of certain parts of Britain's social security system is reserved for a later chapter, but some observations are called for in the present context. As far as savings are concerned, the introduction of compulsory social insurance creates a substitution effect away from private savings. On the other hand, the income effect may lead to an increase in savings. Again, the relative strengths of these two forces will determine the outcome. No study of these effects has been undertaken in the United Kingdom, and what evidence there is pertaining to other countries does not allow definite conclusions to be made. There is evidence from Cagan and Katona[21] that, as far as the United States is concerned, government pension provisions do not necessarily deter private saving, and savings may indeed increase. The arguments presented, at least by Cagan, would seem to appeal to an intuitive reasoning that low-income groups might regard saving as being worthwhile when it helps to build upon a guaranteed subsistence level of future consumption, but not worthwhile when the accumulated funds will not even guarantee subsistence.

On a wider view of the savings process, however, Feldstein[22] suggests that social security arrangements have a definite depressing effect upon saving. Feldstein uses the extended life-cycle model associated with Harrod[23] and Modigliani[24] to demonstrate that the impact of social security on private saving depends upon two opposing effects: (a) a *wealth replacement* effect; and (b) an *induced retirement* effect. The former reduces savings and stems from the fact that public pensions for the aged permit individual earners to reduce their savings and still plan to enjoy the same level of consumption during retirement. The second effect arises because social security benefits for the aged may induce more individuals to retire and therefore tend to increase aggregate saving. Taking a cross-sectional sample of several countries, Feldstein tests for these effects and finds that both do, in fact, operate, but that the wealth replacement effect is relatively stronger. In other words, the *net* effect of social security is to depress savings.

From the viewpoint of work effort, measured in terms of hours worked, the social insurance contribution in the UK system does not appear to have given rise to severe incentive effects. At least, this seems likely to have been the case with the flat-rate contribution. Since the contribution is a lump-sum tax, it will not affect a worker's decision concerning a marginal hour's work. Instead, the tax reduces disposable income by a fixed amount regardless of the number of hours worked. The only way in which an employee can avoid the tax is to give up paid employment, but such a drastic step is unlikely to follow the imposition of a social security tax (given that it does not absorb too large a slice of disposable income). This argument[25] is further substantiated if the worker regards the lump-sum reduction in disposable income, not as a tax in the normal sense, but as a contribution to a fund out of which he will receive appropriate benefits in the future.

This may consistute a reason why governments seem loath publicly to recognize the true nature of the 'pay-as-you-go' system and to finance benefits by an increase in direct taxation of income.

Of course, the bluff may be called when earnings-related contributions become an important component of social insurance financing. An earnings-related contribution is proportional to the amount of income earned, up to some chosen ceiling, by the individual over some period of time. As yet, the effect of the UK system on work incentives has not been tested, but we must be prepared for the possibility that, although we cannot yet predict whether a tax on income will lead to an increase or decrease in work effort, an earnings-related contribution will have a more significant effect upon marginal work/leisure decisions than will a flat-rate contribution.

To round off this brief discussion, we must consider the benefit side of the picture. While contributions affect most employees, benefits are aimed at alleviating hardship which arises from specific circumstances, and hence their economic effects may differ with respect to these circumstances. The payment most likely to give rise to consideration concerning work incentives is unemployment benefit. In the United Kingdom, the structure of the system of retirement benefits also gives rise to potential disincentives, but this is discussed more fully in the following chapter.

Since the unemployed individual receives from the state an income which is sufficient to live on, his idleness is subsidized. Furthermore, since receipt of benefit ceases when the individual is re-employed, the incentive to idleness is likely to be severe if income from working is not much above the level provided by benefit.[26] It therefore follows that, the higher the rate of benefit relative to the wage rate, the greater the possible disincentive effect. But while we cannot make *a priori* judgements on this issue, we may tentatively suggest two reasons why, up to 1966, flat-rate unemployment benefit in Britain was not a serious disincentive to effort. First, following on the Beveridge principle, benefits were geared to subsistence. Hence, for all but the lowly paid workers, income from work provided a higher standard of living than was provided by unemployment benefit. Furthermore, despite a system which provided benefits as of right, a social stigma still attached to those who preferred to live in a state of idleness. This factor, plus the mechanics of applying for (and maintaining eligibility for) benefit, provided sufficient incentive to most workers to remain in employment – the exceptions being those workers with only casual attachments to the labour force.[27]

However, since the introduction of an earnings-related supplement to unemployment benefit in October 1966, the situation may well have altered significantly. Recent empirical studies suggest that the rate of unemployment can be changed considerably by changes in the rate of unemployment benefit. The basis of this recent research has been a model advanced by Grubel and Maki,[28] which allows for utility maximizing reactions by individual workers to the reduced price of leisure and costs of job search which follows from an increase in the rate of unemployment benefit. Studies of Canada and the United States[29] suggest that changes in unemployment benefits do have a significant effect on the measured unemployment. A similar finding emerges from the work of Maki and Spindler. From their study of the British situation, Maki and Spindler have estimated that the elasticity of the unemployment rate with respect to the unemployment benefit/work income ratio was 0·62 for overall unemployment and 0·68 for male unemployment in the post-1966 period in Britain.[30] Their estimates further suggest that the introduction of the earnings-related supplement into Britain's insurance programme had a substantial effect on the benefit/income ratio; and that, on average, during the period 1967–72 the overall unemployment rate was 30 per cent higher, while that for male unemployment was 33 per cent higher than had been the case in the six-year period prior to 1967; and that much of this increase could be traced directly to the influence of the earnings-related supplement.[31] On the basis of this evidence, it would seem that government policy-makers cannot be complacent in their assumption regarding the effects of protective social measures.

(c) *Stabilization*

Finally, we may note that the impact of a social insurance programme is not confined to microeconomic effects. Unfortunately, the paucity of empirical findings is just as noticeable on macroeconomic issues as on the incentives question. In the absence of reserve accumulation, the contribution made by social insurance towards stabilizing the level of national income and employment would seem to depend upon the extent to which its compensatory effects are 'automatic'. Social insurance arrangements are often used to illustrate the concept of an automatic stabilizer, since benefit payments increase during times of recession and decrease during boom periods, without government intervention. This is not true of all benefits, of course – there seems little reason to expect pregnancies (and hence receipts of maternity benefit) to follow the path of the trade-cycle – but employment benefit, for example, would certainly follow this trend, and availability of jobs might influence the work/leisure decisions of retirement pensioners.

American sources seem agreed that social insurance, or at least unemployment insurance, can have a significant, stabilizing influence on the American economy.[32] However, a detailed British study[33] has suggested that it is possible to overestimate the automatic effect of social insurance arrangements in Britain. During the period from 1950/51 to 1964/5 the British unemployment insurance scheme made a positive contribution towards stabilizing the levels of income and employment, in nine pairs of years out of fourteen. In the remaining five pairs of years, the scheme contributed to stability in a negative fashion, i.e. fluctuations in income were accentuated by the scheme. Overall, the contribution of the scheme to stability was rather small, less than 2 per cent of the tendency of income to deviate from the trend being offset by the response of the unemployment insurance scheme.[34] The potential stabilizing influence of earnings-related benefits and contributions being introduced into the British scheme at an earlier date is difficult to assess. Earnings-related benefits and contributions would have strengthened the influence of the existing scheme during the years in which the latter produced a stabilizing effect. On the other hand, the influence of the existing scheme would also have been increased during the years in which this influence was destabilizing.[35] Coupled with the more general reservations which have been expressed about the efficacy of automatic stabilizers in the British economy,[36] these findings permit a tentative suggestion that the stabilizing influence of the social insurance programme has been neither strong nor constant.

Concluding Remarks

Researches into the economic effects of social security taxes have been lacking in the past, but current interests should ensure that more questions can be answered in the future. Britain's social insurance system has operated as a 'pay-as-you-go' tax/transfer mechanism, and as such it has affected the responses of economic agents to various problems. Our interpretation of these responses is still closely dependent upon the predictions of economic theory. What empirical evidence there is seems to suggest that the economic effects of the system have not been major ones, but such conclusions may reflect both the lack of proper research programmes and the fact that, until recently, social insurance contributions have not been fully recognized in their true guise as taxes. The right of the individual to an adequate pension is more likely to be recognized as dependent upon the nature of the tax/transfer system under the earnings-related schemes now in operation.

8. Income Maintenance (2):
The Concept of Poverty

The discussion of income distribution has usually assumed the bottom 30 per cent of the distribution to be the 'lower income groups'. No rationale has been provided for choosing this cut-off point, and there is no immediately apparent reason for why some other quantile grouping was not chosen. Who defines 'lower' – that is, who decides what is to be the yardstick of relativity?

Absolute v. Relative

A related problem to the above is how to identify 'the poor'. This difficulty is associated with the distribution discussion, since those who are defined as poor are necessarily to be found at the bottom of the distribution and the factors which determine the distribution of incomes have placed them there. But the problems are separated by those factors which determine the definition of 'poverty'. Conceptually, there exists a régime in which the top 10 per cent have annual incomes of £200,000 while each unit within the bottom 90 per cent, the 'lower income groups', has an income of only £20,000. The incomes of the bottom 90 per cent in this hypothetical example are much higher than the majority of incomes within countries of the developed world. Conceptually, there exists also a régime in which everyone receives the same amount of annual income, yet everyone is 'poor'. The essence of the problem is that the relativity yardstick is necessarily subjective since no means exist to measure poverty in an objective sense.

Of course, the idea of an absolute and objective measure of poverty is appealing. It permits a head-count of the poor, since all who do not possess the means to obtain and maintain the minimum standards as defined by the absolute definition can be classified as 'poor'. In this way, the magnitude of the poverty problem can be calculated without ambiguity. In addition, an absolute measure permits a check to be made over time so that the ongoing efficacy of social welfare policies can be monitored and regularly adjusted, whether organized by the state or through the institutions of private philanthropy.

In one sense, the fixing of an *absolute standard* automatically determines a *comparative standard*, since those units with incomes below the absolute must be in an income position which is *relatively* worse than that of units with incomes above the absolute. Yet, from the viewpoint of social policy, this involves more than a tautology, for the choice of the dependent variable in the relationship determines the type of policy which emerges. A philosophy which determines £x per annum as the absolute poverty line, where £x per annum just happens to be 30 per cent of average annual personal income in that society, differs significantly from one which chooses 30 per cent of average annual personal income as the definition of poverty. The issues involved in deciding how to define poverty are discussed more fully below, but first the relationship between absolute and relative standards must be appreciated.

The basic relationship referred to above emerges as a 'trade off' between the proportion of the population in poverty, determined by the absolute standard, and the *comparative* living standards of the poor.[1] Using the following notation:

m(£p.a.) – absolute poverty standard;
$\bar{y}$ (£p.a.) – median level of personal income;
k – number of income units with incomes below the poverty standard;
P – total number of income units in the population;

the relationship emerges:

$$k/P = f(m, \bar{y})$$

such that $\quad \dfrac{d(k/p)}{d(m/\bar{y})} > 0, \quad$ or $\quad \dfrac{d(P-k)}{d(\bar{y}-m)} > 0.$

What this relationship shows is that, for a given total income and a given pattern of distribution, a lowering of the absolute poverty standard leads to a smaller proportion of the population classified as 'poor', but the degree of poverty experienced by this group, measured by the difference between the absolute standard and the median income level, increases. Over time, however, changes in total income or changes in its distribution will make it possible for both the size of the proportion in poverty and the intensity of that poverty to change in the same direction.[2]

An absolute measure of poverty attempts to determine a minimum level of subsistence – that is, to define for the chosen unit (family, individual or household) that level and variety of real consumption considered to be essential to life. To count the number in poverty by such a definition requires the further definition of that level of command over resources which is sufficient to guarantee the minimum consumption requirements. The 'poor' are those whose command over resources falls short of the level so determined.

Now it takes but little thought to realize that defining absolute subsistence is both difficult and not very helpful in the formulation of policy. The requirements of clothing, shelter, nutrition and so forth vary with age and sex. Moreover, even assuming that separate standards could be established to allow for this, there is still the problem of persons within defined age and sex categories having a very heterogeneous set of requirements. A tall muscular person is more costly to clothe than a short, puny individual of the same age. A lumberjack requires a different calorie/protein balance from that, say, of a civil servant. Indeed, this latter comparison raises the further question of how the 'minimum' is to be defined (and who is to define it!). An important issue here is the nature of the prevailing conception of subsistence: whether or not it includes merely physical functioning without pain and undue respiratory discomfort; whether or not it extends to the total elimination of hunger and cold; whether or not the conception allows for 'adequate' functioning at play as well as at work; whether or not the conception remains invariant over time; and whether or not the conception varies across cultural boundaries. What many of these considerations underline is the observation that minimum living standards are, in large part, culturally determined and therefore contain a large *relative* component. An absolute standard is impossible if poverty can only be defined in relation to the prevailing social conventions and living standards of some given society at a given point in time. Applying an absolute standard from the Middle Ages in England to the same country in the 1970s would probably record no one as being poor while the income level associated with the prevailing minimum standard of living in the England of the 1970s would considerably enrich the material life-style of a Burundi native.

However, from the point of view of designing and pursuing social policies, defining relative poverty is more difficult than defining an absolute minimum standard since the factors influencing relativity are even more varied and numerous than those which establish the absolute. Presumably, a relative minimum guarantees some proportion of a higher income standard. But how high should be this standard? Does 'poverty' extend to whether or not an individual possesses the means of acquiring a television set, and if so, is the set to receive transmissions in colour or monochrome? Is an individual defined as 'deprived' if he does not own a car, or if he cannot afford at least one annual holiday away from home? Such questions encapsulate in very crude form the basic problem of defining 'relativity'.

Attempts to Construct a Conceptual Framework

Most writers on issues of social policy are aware of the difficulties outlined above,[3] and some are prepared to suggest means of arriving at acceptable definitions. Perhaps the most detailed attempt to define the structure of the poverty problem is that of Dudley Jackson, who suggests defining poverty in terms of a relative concept: 'adequate social functioning'.[4] While this might be accepted as a reasonable definition, it does no more by itself than suggest that any deprivation concept must be devised by the consensus within society since, by definition, 'adequate social functioning' must depend upon the prevailing culture. Thus, to help towards a more rigorous description of poverty's structure, Jackson underlines the distinction between stocks and flows – individuals must consume a minimum *flow* of goods and services if they are to survive in a physical sense, but the real nature of this survival, the quality of the prevailing life-style, is also determined by access to certain *stocks* of goods and services, such as clothing, housing and education. For any society, the emphasis placed upon such stocks tends to increase with the economic and social development of that society.

The distinction between stocks and flows is important to Jackson's scheme since it helps to furnish a distinction between *want* which is caused by the 'failure' of flows and *deprivation* which is caused by the 'failure' of stocks. 'Want' appears in this context to be synonymous with the term 'need', which is more favoured by social scientists who are not economists. It differs from the economists' 'want' (which refers to effective demand) in referring to a set of desires or drives which must be satisfied if a given 'standard of health' is to be maintained.[5] As such, the level of resources required to satisfy want for a unit of given size defines the minimum requirement or 'poverty line' for that unit. 'Deprivation', on the other hand, is more obviously determined by considerations of relativity – where the stocks owned by a given unit are small in relation to those of other units.

The importance of the distinction between stocks and flows is also seen in the dynamic view of the problem which stresses the self-perpetuating nature of poverty through the stock/flow cycle. Inadequate or inferior stocks of various forms of capital engender inferior flows of income and services which, in time, permit only inferior restocking and further impoverished income flows and so on.[6] Further, this dynamic cycle can be inter-generational, when poor stocks of housing, health-care, education and so on are inherited by children.

How useful is Jackson's framework for devising a pragmatic definition of poverty? First, there is an emphasis upon nutritional flows as the basic flows upon which all else rests. Thus, the minimum nutritional flow to sustain the chosen standard of health goes far towards establishing a minimum standard and the minimum level of income, per income unit, required to sustain it. But what of the point stressed earlier, that the minimum nutritional flow will vary from person to person? 'Social functioning' for the lumberjack is likely to be upset if his nutritional wants are based on those of the clerk. Further, there may be some, albeit small, trade-off between the various flows: warm clothing, for example, may to some extent be a substitute for the calorific value of food. Again, the possibility of such substitutes will depend at least upon the nature of stocks, upon occupational requirements and geographical location – that is, a variety of factors frustrate the establishment of a homogeneous standard even in the case of minimum physical requirements.

Similar problems pervade any attempt to define the standard of health which is used to determine minimum nutritional requirements. According to Jackson, this minimum flow can be measured approximately by life-expectancy, and failure to realize this has created a considerable amount of confused discussion over the problem of want. What counts as the minimum nutritional flow will vary among different countries at a given point in time and within a given country over a period of time. This argument (which partly relates to cultural differences) seems a reasonable one, but it does not establish the case for using life-expectancy as the yardstick. Life-expectancy is a function of prevailing standards of nutrition which may be 'wrong', and of many other social and economic variables which can change rapidly over time for a whole society, and may also differ widely across the social strata of a given society at any given time. A more logical approach would be to establish a *target* standard based on agreed aims about nutritional requirements related to some concept of a desired life-expectancy.

The second strand of Jackson's main argument concerns stocks. To isolate the determinants of this relative aspect of poverty, Jackson underlines the point that stocks which are inadequate or inferior can actually impair social functioning, basing his argument on a distinction between 'assets', which aid the social functioning of their owners, and 'liabilities', which are an impediment to social functioning. Thus an individual's 'net worth' determines social functioning and whether or not he is in a state of poverty.[7]

Unfortunately, this line of reasoning adopts a false analogy, though it does emphasize an important cog in the dynamics of the poverty cycle. It is true that an individual's stocks will determine his ability to function adequately in social life, but the accounting analogy used by Jackson is erroneous when applied beyond this basic observation. A possession cannot be both an asset and a liability in the accounting sense. What any individual unit can possess, however, is a stock of both good and bad assets. 'Liabilities' are *not* qualitatively inferior assets since the term merely applies to things used by the unit (and from which services are derived) but owned by someone else. What *is* important in measuring poverty is the comparison between qualitatively different asset structures: it is better to be warmly clad and to have a sound roof over one's head than to wear threadbare clothing and to shelter beneath a leaking roof; at the same time, threadbare clothes and a leaking roof are better than sleeping naked in the outdoors.

Thus, the net worth of individuals or households is determined in the normal accounting sense by recognizing that those units with a low net worth are suffering from ownership of assets which are inferior to those of units with a higher net worth. Within this comparison lies the essence of the relative component of poverty. What emerges from a correctly formulated balance-sheet approach to the problem of poverty is the importance of a unit's asset structure. Some units, through market transactions, inheritance (both material and genetic) and labour market rewards, accumulate assets which yield a high value of net worth and the consequent stream of net benefits. Other units, through the same set of forces, can be saddled with an asset structure which provides no more than a trickle of positive net benefits or even a negative flow. It seems that the short-run aim of social policies to fight poverty, whether operating through private agencies or state provisions, should be to lend support to social bankrupts; and that, over the longer run, the goal is to change and improve the asset structures of the lower income groups and hence those of their children.

The Search for an 'Index of Poverty'

It would seem from the arguments presented above that there are two main problems for society to resolve in trying to combat poverty. First, a decision must be reached on what level of real consumption should be offered to social bankrupts (and on how such provision should be made). Secondly, society must determine both the quantity and the quality of the stock of assets which, it is believed, ought to be available to every income unit (and what is the best method for securing everyone's access to such stocks).

These two problems require separate solutions, but they relate to each other in delineating the full nature of the poverty problem. A full answer to the first question, which concentrates on flows, requires detailed information about the social welfare function and, in particular, a knowledge of the prevailing consensus regarding the common hierarchy of wants, so that a minimum standard of living can be decided upon. Such a standard would be defined in relative terms to permit access to those goods and services which are deemed representative of the consumption norm for a particular society. The second question requires a set of similar definitions, but relating to stocks. It is on this question that there has been much disagreement among both academics and policy-makers, the problem of how to secure an efficient allocation of resources to the sectors of health care, education, housing and so forth, while simultaneously guaranteeing an equitable distribution of the products of these sectors, being among the most contentious issues in discussions of welfare policies.

One approach to the poverty problem which explicitly acknowledges these two difficulties is that which is usually referred to as 'behaviouristic', so described since it emphasizes behaviour as exhibited through spending patterns. This approach emphasizes the relative aspect of poverty and uses a very wide definition of deprivation indicators – two points of emphasis which have been adopted in this chapter. Perhaps the leading exponent of the approach in the United Kingdom in recent years has been Professor Peter Townsend, who believes that it is possible to define poverty 'objectively and . . . constantly only in terms of the concept of relative deprivation'.[8] Townsend's view of the problem accepts a similar line to that of Jackson's idea of 'adequate social functioning', by placing emphasis on the concept of a 'style of living' which widens the definition of poverty to embrace, not just diet, but also participation in those activities and access to the 'living conditions and amenities which are customary, or at least widely encouraged or approved, in the societies to which they belong'.[9]

Townsend's reasons for advancing such a relative approach to the problem follow the arguments outlined earlier in this chapter, and without making the point explicit, stress the importance of stocks as well as flows in the determination of poverty. However, his efforts to widen the concept of poverty underline a serious dilemma for the social policy-maker, since the full range of factors which can influence the extent to which an individual, family or household is relatively deprived underlines the limitations of attempts to date to measure the extent of poverty while simultaneously rendering impossible a foolproof universal poverty yardstick.

In terms of the self-imposed tasks of the social scientist, Townsend argues for a switch of emphasis away from *feelings* of deprivation, the conventional interpretation of the concept, towards *conditions* of deprivation, so that such conditions might be specified and measured, both these tasks having been avoided in most recent works on poverty.[10] By emphasizing conditions of deprivation, attention is concentrated upon the numerous social and economic influences which determine 'needs'. Such needs vary among different social groupings within any society, and they change over time at different rates and in different directions according to the social pressures of the immediate group to which the reference unit belongs. It is important, therefore, to distinguish between,

the resources which are made available by society to individuals and families and the style of life with which they are expected or to which they feel prompted to conform. This is the set of customs and activities which they are expected to share or in which they are expected to join.[11]

Moreoever, besides accounting for such influences on the extent of needs, a programme to combat poverty must allow for the fact that in any social rankings based on a criterion of inequality, cash income is an inadequate indicator, given the many sources of income in kind made available through the various institutions which influence lifestyles. As Townsend points out:

Living standards depend on the total contribution of not one but several systems distributing resources to individuals, families, work groups and communities. To concentrate on cash incomes is to ignore the subtle ways developed in both modern and traditional societies for conferring and redistributing benefits.[12]

However, while accepting that 'social functioning' or 'style of living' are conceptually superior concepts to 'consumption' as poverty indicators, they are at the same time much less pragmatic. This is clearly demonstrated by the index referred to by Townsend and used in a national survey carried out in the United Kingdom in 1968–9.[13]

A deprivation index
This is graded according to the percentage of a sample population which:

1. Has not had a week's holiday away from home in the previous twelve months: 53·6
2. *Adults only*. Has not had a relative or friend to the home for a meal or snack in the past few weeks: 33·4

3. *Adults only.* Has not been out in the past few weeks to a relative or friend for a meal or snack: 45·1

4. *Children only* (under 15). Has not had a friend to play or to tea in past four weeks: 36·3

5. *Children only.* Did not have a party on last birthday: 56·6

6. Has not had an afternoon or evening out for entertainment in the past two weeks: 47·0

7. Does not have fresh meat (including meals out) as many as four days a week: 19·3

8. Has gone through one or more days in the past fortnight without a cooked meal: 7·0

9. Has not had a cooked breakfast most days of the week: 67·3

10. Household does not have a refrigerator: 45·1

11. Household does not usually have a Sunday joint (3 in 4 times):   25·9

12. Household does not have sole use of four amenities indoors (flush WC; sink or wash-basin and cold-water tap; fixed bath or shower; and gas or electric cooker):   21·4

Points 1–12 in the index underline two important observations about poverty. First, there is partial as well as total poverty in that an individual may be deprived (relatively) in some areas of life-style but not necessarily in others. Secondly, life-cycle effects are extremely important in that many individuals may experience poverty at some stage in their lifetime and yet may be relatively affluent at the point in time of a particular poverty survey. Both these observations must cast doubts on attempts to measure the extent of poverty by relying solely on an indicator of monetary income which relates to a given point in time. The first observation suggests that such measurements will always understate the true extent of poverty, while the second may either understate or overstate the nature of *trends* in poverty.

It is for reasons such as the above that this type of index should be employed. On the other hand, as the sole guide to the extent of poverty, such an index is highly ambiguous, largely because of the reasons for which it is constructed. Since the relative life-style of any unit is influenced by such factors as customs, education or propaganda, the very items which are important to one unit may be unimportant (or even carry a negative weighting) to some other unit in constructing a list of the determinants of an adequate life-style. When this factor is coupled with the forces of temporary circumstances (sickness in children, baby-sitters on holiday, adult limbs fractured as a result of a riding accident and so on), the actual number in poverty, as calculated by such an index as that referred to by Townsend, can be totally misleading. Indeed, as prisoners of tastes, the present author's household is relatively deprived (poor) on points 5, 7, 8, 9 and 11 of the above index, and from time to time is impoverished on several of the other counts when circumstances so prevail.

Similar problems face any attempt to devise an operational rule for measuring the extent of poverty by concentrating on the main characteristics of the spending patterns of the poor. One such pattern, the famous 'Engel's Law', emerged from early budget studies which found consistently that the poor spent a substantially higher proportion of their income on necessities (and, in particular, on food) compared with the non-poor. But to define as 'poor' those households with such an expenditure pattern is to court the same problems as those facing the deprivation index already described, and in particular the factor of tastes. Some evidence that such difficulties will present themselves is provided in the NIESR study referred to earlier.[14] In an attempt to discover further evidence of Engel's Law, the NIESR study compares the expenditure patterns of various percentiles in the income distribution for the United Kingdom over the period 1953/4 to 1971. It seems apparent from the comparisons that the expenditure patterns are not sufficiently and consistently different to warrant using such a method to identify the poor. Furthermore, possible explanations of the pattern point largely to changing tastes in a world of rapid cultural change under the onslaught of consumer education programmes and product advertising, and rapid changes in household technology, both features which are likely to render inoperative a poverty index based on expenditure patterns.

The NIESR study does find some evidence to support Engel's Law in that, over the period considered, although the proportion of expenditure allocated to necessities – fuel, housing, light and power and food – declined for all income groups, the fall for households in the lowest fifth and tenth percentiles was less than for the median household, and by 1971 the fifth percentile was still devoting 64 per cent of expenditure to necessities, compared with 48 per cent by the median household.[15] However, within this general pattern there emerge certain features of specific expenditure which are likely to confound attempts to draft a consistent poverty index. For example, in the case of 'necessity' the authors of the study are moved to comment that a need exists 'to reconsider the traditional view that, as a single item at least, clothing should be regarded as a necessity; for most of the population it may also be regarded as an item of affluence'. Presumably the qualitative changes wrought by product differentiation are an important agent in this change. But, even on the most basic item, food, the spending of the poor on specific items is no longer so obviously different from that of higher income groups. While the NIESR study confirms that consumption by the poor of very basic foods, such as bread, margarine, lard and tea, remains relatively high, it finds also that expenditure by this group on meat, fresh fish, milk, butter, cheese, eggs and fresh vegetables is not far below that of the median household.[16] Further down the scale of requirements the pattern varies: expenditure on domestic leisure aids such as newspapers, radio and television is not very different between poor and non-poor, while the poor spend some 30 per cent less than the median on costly leisure pursuits such as meals out, cinemas, holidays or private motoring.[17]

Clearly, the lack of a definite distinction between patterns of specific expenditures is a force against the construction of an unambiguous index of poverty. Nor can such an index be built on a clear divergence in general expenditure. The NIESR study is unable to distinguish between 'poor' and 'non-poor' on the basis of a discrete change in expenditure behaviour as income changes:

... despite the fairly consistent picture which emerges of changes in expenditure patterns over the income range, it does not appear ... that any line can be drawn between percentiles on the basis of a significant and comparatively abrupt change in consumption patterns.[18]

Reference standards and actual empirical studies

No doubt a growing awareness of the problems posed by trying to formulate a fully comprehensive and unambiguous index of poverty has been one of the reasons why researchers have increasingly resorted to the 'official' poverty line adopted by the policy-makers when looking for a yardstick with which to measure the extent of poverty among the population. The search for the yardstick itself has continued ever since the pioneering studies by Booth[19] and Rowntree[20] at the turn of the century. The Rowntree exercise was particularly important since it was the first attempt to approach the problem 'scientifically' – to attempt definitions and to quantify on the basis of these definitions – and it was twice repeated at later stages.[21] Rowntree's definition of poverty, however, is subject to criticisms, made earlier in this chapter, of an absolute standard, since it attempts to delineate a level of income which permits access to necessities, things which permit a minimal (physical) existence. The method involved in all three Rowntree surveys involved estimating needs for families of given size and translating such needs into money terms, the minimum amount so calculated being then compared with actual family earnings levels to determine whether or not shortfalls existed.

The methods employed by Beveridge in preparing his report,[22] which formed the basis of the post-war system of social security in Britain,

were similar to those of Rowntree in that attempts were made to prescribe minimum standards. Such standards had to be established since
Beveridge's proposed national insurance benefits were intended to
provide a subsistence standard of living and this had to be defined.
Drawing on several sources, including the Rowntree surveys,[23] Beveridge
estimated minimum requirements, or 'necessary expenditure', in terms
of clothing, food, light and fuel, rent and household sundries. The
minimum scales which actually emerged in the 1948 implementation
of Beveridge's scheme were based on similar criteria, though adjustments were made for various-sized household units in a manner which is
difficult to comprehend. Furthermore, in terms of the state minimum
since 1948 there has been no major overhaul of the basic criteria which
determine standards. Instead, the minimum rates have apparently
risen in accordance with the predilections of the prevailing government,
tempered by the constraints imposed by the economic climate, even
though provisions were introduced under the National Insurance Act
of 1974 for the minimum state transfer (supplementary benefit) to rise
in line with prices.

The deficiencies of the absolute standard, combined with the desire
to maintain a consistent yardstick, have resulted in most of the major
post-war studies adopting the state's minimum standard when trying to
measure the full extent of poverty in the United Kingdom. This was
certainly the case in three very important studies published during the
1960s.[24] An additional and important argument advanced for using
this reference standard concerns the desire to test the efficacy of government policies in fighting poverty: in the words of Atkinson, 'the success of Government policy is being judged in the light of its own minimum standards'.[25] Within the framework of a parliamentary democracy,
this approach seems to be the only possible way in which self-imposed
standards, and therefore the consensus view on relative life styles, might
be judged in terms of success in limiting the numbers falling below
these standards. Nevertheless, there remains the problem that the
initial establishment of the standard is faced by the many difficulties
discussed earlier in this chapter, and comparisons with this standard
over time, while helping to judge success in achieving a self-imposed
target, do not guarantee that the target is correctly defined.

Concluding Remarks

'Poverty' as a concept, descriptive of a standard of living, cannot
be defined in absolutes. The need for a clear conceptual definition is
required for two reasons: (a) to help discover the number of people

living at such a standard, and (b) to judge the success of government policies in fighting poverty with a view to suggesting improvements – and in each case the need for a relative standard is paramount.

Yet allowing for a measure of relativity is to risk the dangers of subjectivity which can emerge from either the direction of the researcher or that of his sample population. In a world of rapid cultural change, in which the tastes, ideas and habits of one class can be quickly transmitted to and aped by another, and in which technology hastens this process, a comprehensive and objective index is not feasible as a tool to guide the policy-maker. Nevertheless, such an index does serve to remind observers that the standards adopted by state tax/transfer programmes can be equally subjective and are usually somewhat narrow. Such standards that are adopted by state welfare programmes provide the most consistent test of the strength of society's commitment to eradicating poverty as well as the success of the programmes themselves. Used in a cautionary manner, perhaps against the backcloth of a wider index like that referred to earlier in this chapter, such a yardstick should be a useful guide to future policy requirements.

9. Income Maintenance (3): Poverty and Market Solutions

Introduction

This chapter falls into two distinct sections. Part A discusses the theory of charitable behaviour and takes a brief look at the system of controlling private charities operative in the United Kingdom. Part B discusses minimum wage legislation as a method for resolving poverty, particular attention being given to the British system of wages councils. Yet a common link between these areas of study permits their being grouped within the same chapter. This link is provided by the fact that both these areas are concerned with the market as a means of solving the problem of poverty.

Charities are, on the one hand, a vehicle by which individuals can transfer some of their resources to other individuals who are considered to be in some state of need. The Welfare State has assumed responsibility for several of the objectives traditionally pursued by voluntary organizations, and it is interesting to consider whether or not private bodies could be more relied upon as in earlier times. What we find is that private charities have in-built drawbacks which the state is able to avoid. There is, however, a strong case for the coexistence of public and private sectors with respect to charitable activity.

On the other hand, minimum wage legislation does not leave the problem wholly in the market-place; rather, it constitutes an attempt at altering market solutions without completely supplanting the basic mechanism. The main intention is to guarantee the supply side of the labour market a minimum return for labour services. Unfortunately, as is often the case, the market proves a difficult institution to counteract, and the results of minimum wage legislation have not been very impressive. In this sphere of activity, the case for a comprehensive state alternative may be fairly strong.

Part A: Private Charity

One oft-praised feature of the market system is that it 'fills in the gaps'. When needs arise, they become expressed as wants through the forces of demand, thus inducing a supply response; and ultimately they are satisfied at a clearing price by the combined forces of supply and demand. But, as we saw in Chapter 2, the ability of the market to respond in this manner depends upon certain conditions first being satisfied. Sometimes these conditions are not met and the market 'fails' in some sense – a problem which dogs the effective redistribution of income through the market mechanism as much as it hinders the efficient allocation of resources.

Historically, the problem of poverty relied heavily for its solution upon voluntary aid or 'charity'. Why has this reliance diminished in the sphere of income maintenance, at least within the domestic sphere (voluntary aid being still of prime importance in the area of international income redistribution)? To understand fully the conceptual problems for the economist and the practical problems for the policy-makers in the area of voluntary income transfers it is necessary to make a further excursion into the analysis of Chapters 1 and 2. There we saw two, conceptually separate, justifications for income redistribution. One approach is to formulate a social welfare function defined in terms of independent utility functions. With such a formulation, it is possible to say that some income redistribution benefits society even though some individuals are made worse off. The major problem here is that defining the social welfare function requires interpersonal comparisons of utility to be made, a problem we have discussed previously at some length.

The second approach is through interdependent utility functions whereby each individual's utility is affected by the behaviour of other individuals. Adopting this framework, poverty becomes a problem within the general set of problems previously described as 'externalities'.[1] It is this approach which seems the more natural for the analysis of voluntary income redistribution, though, as we shall see, many conceptual difficulties remain.

Recalling the analysis of Chapter 2, we are able to contrast a trading equilibrium for the two-commodity world, wherein the marginal rates of substitution between one commodity and the numéraire good are equalized for all individuals, with a transfer equilibrium derived in the following manner.

Representing the two commodities by y and x and introducing two individuals α and β, we can represent α as charitable and β as neutral (for simplicity) by:

$$U^\alpha = U^\alpha(x^\alpha, y^\alpha, x^\beta) \tag{1}$$

$$U^\beta = U^\beta(x^\beta, y^\beta) \tag{2}$$

where U represents utility.

Now, if β's consumption of x at the margin yields a positive utility gain to α, a *marginal* externality exists, denoted as (3):

$$\frac{\partial U^\alpha/\partial x^\beta}{\partial U^\alpha/\partial y^\alpha} > 0 \tag{3}$$

However, condition (3) tells us little except that a small increase in β's activities in consumption affects α's utility. A stronger condition, one more likely to evoke response from α is given by (4):

$$\frac{\partial U^\alpha/\partial x^\beta}{\partial U^\alpha/\partial y^\alpha} > \frac{\partial U^\alpha/\partial x^\alpha}{\partial U^\alpha/\partial y^\alpha} \tag{4}$$

Condition (4) denotes a *Pareto-relevant* marginal externality, and is, as such, still insufficient to guarantee that α will transfer some of his income to β. Whether such a transfer takes place depends upon the relative costs of alternative methods of increasing β's consumption. If modifying β's behaviour in some other way – for example, by educating β to want to consume more x or coercing him to consume more – is cheaper from α's point of view than a direct transfer, then the transfer will not be effected. But if the direct transfer proves the least costly method, then condition (4) ensures that α will adopt this method. α will give to β until there obtains a transfer equilibrium[2] where:

$$\frac{\partial U^x/\partial x^\beta}{\partial U^\alpha/\partial y^x} = \frac{\partial U^\alpha/\partial x^\alpha}{\partial U^\alpha/\partial y^\alpha} \tag{5}$$

In the n-person case, of course, α's options are wider. Even condition (4) is an insufficient deterrent to α acting as a 'free-rider'. If some other person is the agent of β's increase in consumption, then α can still enjoy the resultant externality. In this world, where an income transfer yields benefits to all potential givers, optimality is achieved when Samuelson's public good condition (as discussed in Chapter 2) is satisfied. Adopting the notation used in conditions (1) to (5), this optimality requires:

$$\sum_{\text{all } \alpha's} \frac{\partial U^\alpha/\partial x^\beta}{\partial U^\alpha/\partial y^\alpha} + \frac{\partial U^\beta/\partial x^\beta}{\partial U^\beta/\partial y^\beta} = \frac{fx}{fy} \qquad (6)$$

where fx/fy is the marginal rate of transformation between x and y.

As a description of real-world possibilities, the above model works well in the small group case – the family, the street or the village – where there is perfect information regarding the requirements and the location of the needy. Even the free-rider diminishes as he becomes easier to identify and is forced to respond to social pressures. But as group size increases, information becomes less than perfect and the free-rider finds it increasingly easier to dodge the pressures of social disapproval. It is in these circumstances that the charitable 'firm' appears by which co-operative effort helps to reduce the search costs so prohibitive of individual action by collecting and distributing information on the circumstances and the whereabouts of those in need. Cooperative enterprise can also yield economies in the raising of donations and the dispensing of aid. We must now consider, therefore, the likely behaviour of such an enterprise if we are to see whether or not it can be relied upon to fulfil the wants of the prevailing social welfare function.

The aims of private charities, of course, can differ widely, but the problems they face in maintaining efficiency are common to all, and we can remain, as a means of general illustration, with the example of an enterprise which aims to redistribute income. The two activities to be undertaken by such a charity are (a) the raising of donations and (b) the transfer of aid; and we can assume that the objective is to maximize the amount of aid which is finally transferred to recipients. This enables us to analyse the firm's behaviour with the use of marginalist analysis, defining potential aid as the difference between the amount of donations (the 'revenue' equivalent) and the total costs of collecting and dispensing. It would seem, then, that the problem of raising donations is analogous to the sales problem of the firm in neoclassical microeconomics. But what does the private charity sell to potential donors? Presumably, the firm offers a set of opportunities by which charitable acts might be undertaken, the number and rate of opportunities being a function of the type and scope of appeals campaigns and the distribution of the means of collection – arrangements for postal donations, issues of savings boxes, frequency of street collections and so forth.

There seems no reason why the functions in such a model should not be 'normally' shaped. Fund-raising activities are likely to meet eventually increasing costs and the rate at which donations accumulate is likely to diminish as a function of the opportunities offered to potential donors. Figure 9.1 presents a familiar picture. Representing the number

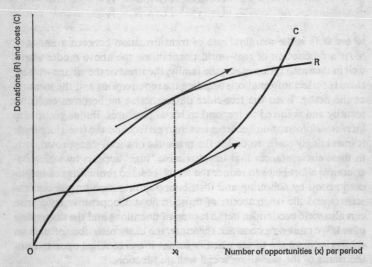

Figure 9.1.

of opportunities to do charitable acts by x, total donations by R and total costs by C, maximum (net) aid is obtained when $\frac{dR}{dx} = \frac{dC}{dx}$, which occurs at Ox_1 opportunities. But what are the guarantees that the charity firm will always seek to maximize aid in this way? The model depicted by Figure 9.1 is akin to that of the owner-managed firm, where the aims of the 'owners' and the decision-makers coincide. The decision-maker tries, in this case, to maintain costs as low as possible, and the opportunity cost of his own services is low because he derives much of his return in psychic income which is an increasing function of the amount of aid transferred to the needy.

There are, however, other models for the charity firm to follow, each one as likely as the above example. For example, suppose that the decision-maker aims to cover his monetary opportunity earnings. This leads to either one of two possibilities. In one case, the wishes of decision-maker and owners diverge since, while the aim of maximizing net aid can still be pursued, the cost of the charity's operations are increased and, other things being equal, the scale of operations will be reduced. The other possibility, preferable from the owners' point of view, is where other things do not remain equal because the money income maximizer making the decisions is a professional fund-raiser and he promotes a shift in the donations curve relative to the cost increase.

Another model for the charity firm to follow, and the one which seems most likely, given the nature of the problem, is that which seems to combine features of both 'X-inefficiency' and sales-maximizing behaviour.[3] In the absence of market checks, such as operate under conditions of competition, the efficiency of any firm depends upon how closely the decision-maker's actions are monitored. But, in the case of a private charity, such vigilance may be absent as a consequence of the peculiar nature of the charitable donor. The truly charitable donor derives utility from the act of giving rather than receiving and may be relatively unconcerned about the objects of any charity, remaining content to offer his contribution wherever he is informed of need. Thus donors behave like passive shareholders and are really not interested in the activities of the organization to which they have transferred income. In this situation, the charity's operating costs may rise because of organizational slackness, and intensive advertising could expand the scale of operations beyond the point which maximizes the amount of aid available to the needy – maximizing donations becomes the overriding aim.

A curious aspect of the above situation is that the divorce of ownership from control can lead to Pareto improvements. For example, suppose that donor A gives cash to charity B which has publicized its aim to help those of a given need, C. However, B's decision-makers spend A's money on a dinner party, the result being that A feels better off (by virtue of making the gift), B's decision-makers are better off, and those in C are no worse off. It should be stressed that this peculiar result is not based on imperfect information in the usual sense. Since the donor's primary motive is *giving*, he acts on the belief that information given to him by the charity firm is reliable. Nor does he receive new information from the 'product'. The purchaser of a private good normally expects consumption benefits about which he has previously been informed. If his information proves to be misleading, he will not purchase the commodity again. But the charitable donor does not receive any such property right when he makes his contribution because in such a 'market' such rights do not exist, there is no need for them, and therefore he does not automatically discover how unreliable is his information.

Historically, these control problems have been one reason why the state has become involved in charitable activity and why there still exists a need for machinery to monitor the activities of those charities which currently operate alongside the régime of the Welfare State. This co-existence is encouraged because, although private charities proved incapable of coping with the magnitude of social problems created by the Industrial Revolution and the forces of the trade cycle, they are more flexible than state activity and can make a quick response to new areas of need. This latter characteristic was recognized by the Nathan Report,[4] which was instrumental in the formulation of the Charities Act of 1960, the governing statute on private charities. Both the report and the Act gave recognition to the interdependence between state and voluntary private action and to the idea that the role of private charities is to *pioneer*.

The Act of 1960 made other provisions, including the important step of ensuring that adequate records are kept of private charities' activities and establishing a Central Register of Charities with most charities compelled to register. One result of the Act, then, has been a comprehensive check on the growth in numbers and types of charities. By 1975, there were approximately 115,000 charities registered and some 2,800 charities being added annually.[5] Another important feature of the Act from the viewpoint of our present purpose is the Constitution of the Charity Commissioners, the governing and registration body for private charities. The Act defined the Commissioners' general function as being the

promoting of the effective use of charitable resources: – (a) by encouraging the development of better methods of administration, (b) by giving Charity trustees information or advice on any matter affecting the charity, and (c) by investigating and checking abuses.[6]

It would appear that, in principle at least, the Charity Commissioners possess powers to correct any inefficiencies of the type suggested earlier by our models. In practice, however, these powers have not been exercised with much vigour. For example, the commissioners do not reject many applicants for registration – in the first decade after the Act, only 2·5 per cent of total applications were rejected. One major reason for this is the fact that the law does not operate a precise definition of 'charity'. The yardstick employed to guide the commissioners is that laid down by Lord Macnaghton in 1891: a trust is charitable if it exists for (a) the relief of poverty, (b) the advancement of education or religion, or (c) other purposes beneficial to the community. Given such a broad guideline, it is difficult to appreciate how the commissioners manage to refuse registration to any organization!

Another important point to note about the commissioners' powers in practice is that, although they recognize that running costs will vary according to different charitable objects and that new charities may face high threshold costs, they do not lay down any efficiency guidelines for established charities with the same objective. In fact, the main way in which the commissioners collect information on the running of private charities is from the voluntary bodies themselves when they request advice on trust management. The main reason for this lack of power is that the Act prevents the commissioners from acting in the administration of a charity so that any donor who *is* dissatisfied with the organization of a charity must seek redress from the charity itself. Apparently, the major concern of the commissioners is not efficiency but to ensure that the purpose of an organization, as set out in its governing instrument, is charitable in law.[7]

Legislation also appears to hamper the powers of the commissioners in cases where there is a duplication of effort among charities which pursue similar objectives. This is one area where there might be scope for cost savings through the economies of scale which could result from the pooling of information and the sharing of fund raising and aid distribution. But the Act does not permit the commissioners to decline registration of any organization simply because it is likely to overlap or even duplicate the work of existing charities. There is a vehicle by which the commissioners can try to minimize duplication and outmoded methods – the *scheme*, which is an instrument made by the commissioners, *on the application of trustees*, to alter the existing purposes of a charity or number of charities. By this method it should be possible for charitable objects to keep abreast of social and economic change, and for the small incomes of several charities to be pooled into a more effective supply of resources. Unfortunately, the main channel by which requests for scheme-making arise is the *local review*, and here the record has been somewhat disappointing. The aim of a review is to survey the charitable organizations within a particular locality to ensure that they are giving the most effective available aid to those in need but unable to receive help from the statutory services and to prevent duplication of effort among voluntary organizations. However, the commissioners do not possess the power to enforce a local authority to conduct a review, and participation in a review is on a voluntary basis. Furthermore, even if a charity is found to be outmoded in its objects, or when a merger seems the sensible course of action, the commissioners have no powers of compulsion.

A final reason for doubting the efficacy of the UK system of private charities is that voluntary bodies are not permitted to be politically active. Charities must not act as pressure groups or lobbies since to do so goes beyond their declared purposes. In this case, paradoxically, the commissioners do possess some power – to compel by law a miscreant organization to recoup any of the funds which have been spent to further ends outside its purpose. It would seem that voluntary organizations are to pioneer, to find new areas where state action might be called for, but they are not permitted to apply pressure on the authorities to this end – like the gun dog, they must point but not disturb.

Our conclusion, from UK experience, must be that we cannot properly judge the efficiency of private voluntary organizations. The Charity Commissioners do not operate any defined measure of efficiency, and the law does not permit the necessary powers to promote improvements where they might be perceived, or to experiment in areas where there is apparent room for improvement. Therefore, there has, as yet, been no formal test of the models outlined earlier. Nevertheless, our discussion calls for caution in relying upon the market as the means of redistributing income. Not only does theory suggest that charitable intermediaries can fail to pursue those ends which induce contributions from donors, but practice shows the difficulties of legislating for control of these institutions. While accepting that overt checks by the state may stifle the higher motivations of the human spirit, a more tolerant alternative may lead to abuse, mismanagement or a general misallocation of charitable resources. Historically, the state has supplanted private charity in the provision of minimum standards for all in the satisfaction of basic wants. While the Protestant ethic helped to keep charity on a parochial basis throughout most of the eighteenth and nineteenth centuries, it was clear by the beginning of the twentieth century that voluntary agencies could not cope with the magnitude of the social problems facing the industrialized urban society. Both the basic structure of the charitable intermediary and the pervasiveness of the free-rider call for collective action in the face of a need for a massive programme of income redistribution. It may be that the pioneering role of charity has always been its comparative advantage, and that a collective takeover of traditional charitable ends had to await the combination of eroded religious prejudice and the dawn of mass communication before the state was called upon to assume the role of charitable intermediary on a massive scale. As the Nathan Report states, 'historically, state action is voluntary action crystallized and made universal'.[8]

Part B: Minimum Wage Legislation

A statutory, binding, minimum wage is a direct interference with the forces at work in the market for labour. However, we are classifying this discussion under 'market solutions' because, in spirit, this policy seems closer to the market mechanism than, say, the alternative of a state minimum (social dividend) which completely by-passes the market process. A statutory minimum wage is aimed to protect those who depend upon the labour market for their livelihood and who face the prospect of rewards determined by conditions of demand for the products which they help to make. The demand for some products will be low relative to the demands for others, and in some industries the monopoly power of employers goes unchallenged through ignorance and/or the costs of organizing labour into a countervailing force at the bargaining table. Such conditions breed low pay, levels of remuneration below that considered by society to be 'acceptable'.

The statutory minimum may be either nationally applied – a guaranteed minimum rate for labour services, regardless of skill or industry – or it may vary from industry to industry and among grades within any given industry. Ramifications of the two systems will differ both at the micro and macro levels of economic activity. However, so far as employers are concerned, if the minimum is established above the market clearing rate, then they face an unambiguous increase in their wages bills if the same number of workers continue in employment after the minimum comes into force. This can be a major drawback to the use of minimum wages as a device for fighting poverty since the policy can lead to unemployment, a prediction which follows from the simple neoclassical view of the labour market. Figure 9.2 illustrates the problem, and depicts the market situation for a particular type of labour.[9] D_0 represents the employers' demand curve for labour and S the supply curve of labour to the employers. If allowed freely to adjust, this market would settle at an equilibrium wage rate of OW_0 and an employment rate of ON_0.

If a minimum wage of OW_1 is established for this market, we can predict that $ON_0 - ON_1$ workers will be released from employment and the total excess supply of labour will be $ON_2 - ON_1$. Thus the establishment of a minimum wage rate benefits those workers who remain in employment after the rate has been fixed but at the expense of those who are thrown out of work.

Two qualifications must be made to the above argument. First, the amount of unemployment created by the minimum wage will depend upon (among other things) the price elasticity of demand for labour – the more inelastic the demand (with a given supply curve) the less will be

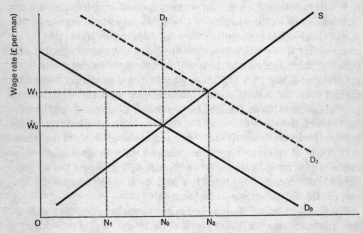

Figure 9.2.

the unemployment effects. Figure 9.2 shows the limiting case of D_1 where the employers' demand response is perfectly inelastic, in which case the employers bear the burden of the statutory minimum through an increase in their wages bills rather than by any adjustments in their labour force.

Secondly, if the higher wage creates a productivity increase (for example, because workers are now better fed or they have experienced a morale boost), then unemployment may not follow upon the establishment of a minimum wage. Figure 9.2 also shows this possibility. The higher wage induces a productivity increase which, being a parametric change, shifts the demand curve for labour to the right. If the productivity increase is sufficient to shift the demand curve to D_2, then no unemployment results. Indeed, the whole of the excess supply of labour at wage rate OW_0 is mopped up by the demand shift.

The above predictions and qualifications are the standard arguments used to explain the likely effects of minimum wage legislation. To discover whether or not the analysis bears out reality, we must rely mainly on US experience since the British model operates rather differently from the theoretical case just outlined and there are no data as yet collected for the United Kingdom which would permit the predictions to be tested.[10] Being a statutory minimum set on a national basis, the United States' system has provided the raw material for several empirical tests from which there emerges a consensus that it is, indeed, likely for a minimum wage to result in some unemployment and so, to that extent at least, such a device might be self-defeating.

Some twenty years ago, John M. Peterson re-examined studies undertaken by the Department of Labor in the United States which government officials had accepted as demonstrating that employment changes are not inversely related to changes in minimum wages.[11] Peterson did not claim that a rigorous test of the neoclassical model could be made with the cross-section data then available, but he was prepared to postulate, as an empirically testable hypothesis, that there would be an inverse relationship between employment changes and alterations in minimum wages among firms making a very similar product for the same market. Taking the three lowest wage industries studied by the Department of Labor in 1949–50, Peterson's study was able to lend support for this hypothesis, contrary to the conclusions of the Department of Labor. Shortly after Peterson's study appeared, Douty published the results of his inquiry into the effect of the 1956 rise in the US national minimum wage from 75 cents to $1.00.[12] This increase in the minimum rate led to a sharp rise in wage levels in low-wage industries, and there was, in consequence, unemployment. Douty found that in all except one of the manufacturing industries studied, employment declined between the period preceding and the period immediately following the date of the higher minimum wage rate, and that, more importantly, even one year after the imposition of the higher rate, employment was lower than in the 75 cents' period in all except two of the industries studied, the declines ranging from 3·2 per cent to more than 15 per cent.

Other studies, considering the problem from differing angles, have usually supported the unemployment argument. Examining the effects of *state* minimum wage laws on unemployment, Campbell and Campbell found that the unemployment rate in major labour market areas without state minimum wage laws was, on average, lower than in those areas with such laws over a period of sixteen years.[13] Furthermore, of the twenty-three increases in minimum wage rates studied by the

Campbells, fourteen were followed by higher relative rates of unemployment. In a study of the teenage labour market, Brozen was able to substantiate earlier findings by both himself and other researchers.[14] According to this study, a definite employment effect did result from the bunching of national minimum wage increases during the 1960s, and the extension of the Fair Labor Standards Act during the same period left fewer alternatives for those unable to find jobs in 'covered employment'. A close examination of teenage unemployment rates in the month before an increase in the statutory minimum and in the month when the increase became effective indicated that the market for teenagers was competitive and that each time an increase in minimum rates occurred there was a consequent increase in teenage unemployment. Strong support for Brozen's conclusions also came from a study undertaken by Kosters and Welch, who concentrated on the *distribution* of employment and how such distribution changes over the course of the trade-cycle.[15] They found that increases in the effective minimum wage over the period 1954–68 had a significant impact on employment patterns, tending to decrease the share of normal employment and increasing vulnerability to cyclical changes in employment for the group most 'marginal' to the work force – teenagers.[16]

The British Example

The history of minimum wage legislation in Britain is not one of consistent aims, and chronological developments have coincided with evolution of purpose. Yet one common thread does run through the historical developments: the assumption that low wages are normally the result of the inadequate collective organization of labour. Britain's answer to such inadequacy has been 'to erect, for each trade it thus seems indicated, a synthetic similitude of the bargaining, conciliatory and arbitration procedures of more organized industries; to specify what is expected of these artificial bodies or what powers they possess; and to give their decisions on legal enforcement'.[17]

The original drive to establish the system came from a growing, intense distaste for 'sweating', the organization of production by which large numbers were employed in very poor working conditions, at wage rates below those prevailing in the primary industrial sectors of the economy and where organized resistance to the power of market forces was frustrated by the prevalence of sub-contracted home working. By the end of the nineteenth century, the plight of sweated labour was being greatly publicized by social researchers such as Charles Booth and Seebohm Rowntree, and by the vociferous demands of the National Anti-Sweating League. A constant theme emerging from the research was that, given the structure of the sweated trades, the crippling grip of market forces upon sweated labour could only be broken by state action, and in 1909 the Trade Boards Act provided a positive response to the pleas of the reformers.

This initial experiment concentrated on four trades where 'homework sweating' was the dominant form of enterprise: ready-made and wholesale bespoke tailoring; chain-making; paper and cardboard box making; and the mending of machine-made lace and net. The criteria by which trades boards were to assess eligibility for a minimum wage to be legally set were 'that the rate of wages prevailing in any branch of the trade is exceptionally low, as compared with that in other employments, and that the other circumstances of the trade are such as to render the application of this Act to the trade expedient'.[18] In 1917, legal minimum wages were extended to agriculture, but the great extension into the small manufacturing industries occurred under the second major piece of legislation, the Trade Boards Act of 1918.

The 1918 Act was based on the recommendations of the Whitley Committee, the latter having been concerned with the idea of trade boards as forerunners of a collective bargaining system. In consequence, the rather vague criteria of the earlier legislation were replaced by a more definite instruction that collective wage fixing by wages boards be carried out whenever there was an absence of any machinery to promote voluntary negotiations. The assumption was that the need for boards in such circumstances would disappear over the long run as wage-bargaining arrangements became established in these trades.

A third stage in the development of minimum wage legislation awaited the final years of the Second World War when the Catering Wages Act of 1943 and the Wages Councils Act of 1945 came into force. Both pieces of legislation were coloured by the long-running concern over inadequate arrangements for voluntary collective bargaining, the special conditions of the catering industry warranting separate legislation in the opinion of Ernest Bevin, then Minister of Labour. Thus it was that legislative machinery finally became divorced from the primary concern of maintaining adequate living standards. Indeed, the rationale of market interference through the establishment of wages councils (to replace trade boards) was extended to the protection of voluntary collective bargaining against the effects of cyclical movements of the economic system.[19] Following on from this Act, the next two decades saw existing legislation extended to embrace many areas outside manufacturing to the extent of offering protection to nearly all workers not covered by normal trade-union bargaining. In 1959, another Wages

Councils Act consolidated the various pieces of legislation put into force from 1943 onwards.

Finally, in this context, some reference must be made to the Employment Protection Act of 1976. Under Section 11 of this Act, workers may seek redress through the Industrial Court if their employer is offering wages below those obtained under collective agreements established in other firms. But, to approach the court, workers must first belong to a trade union or else be working on a government contract so that appeal can be made under the Fair Wages Clause which compels government contractors to pay wages comparable with those determined under collective agreements. The importance of Section 11 is that it forces workers to join unions to gain wage increases, whereas under the wages councils orders there was no compulsion. It therefore seems likely that unions will permit wages councils to become moribund and thereby exploit the Employment Protection Act. In so doing they will be emulating the local government trade unions which used the Comparable Industrial Disputes Order 1376 during the 1950s to enlarge their memberships.

It seems from this brief summary that two main arguments for legislation have evolved. First came the objective of protecting the living standards of low paid workers; and secondly came the objective of promoting voluntary collective bargaining. The current situation reflects the results of a slow dwindling in the numbers of wages councils over the past thirty years, and a recent estimate suggests that there are still some three million workers covered by wages council rates.[20] How successfully has the British system tackled its objectives? We consider first the primary aim of protecting the earnings of the low paid.

Protecting the Low Paid

We can state at the outset that workers covered by wages councils are among the lowest paid. This is not to say that low pay is peculiar to the wages council sector since there are many workers covered by collective agreements who also receive weekly earnings well below the average for their industrial grouping. But, as we consider levels of earnings ever more removed from the average, the predominance of the wages council sector begins to emerge. Figure 9.3 presents for 1977 a pictorial ranking, showing the bottom fifteen industries for men and the bottom ten for women, ranked from low to high in terms of the proportion of workers receiving earnings within each of the chosen ranges below the average level of earnings for the sample (full-time male manual and full-time female manual workers). In 1977, the average gross weekly earnings for full-time male manual workers were £71.50, and for full-time female manual workers, average gross weekly earnings were £42.20.

Figure 9.3 shows that earnings determined by wages boards or councils in 1977 feature prominently in the rankings of low-earnings levels for all the chosen ranges of earnings, but tend to bunch more around the lowest levels of the ranking as earnings ranges well below the average are considered. For the lowest range of men covered by the *New Earnings Survey* (less than £40 a week), wages council earnings hold the bottom five positions – that is, the proportion of men with gross weekly earnings of less than £40 in 1977 was highest in five wages council industries: (a) licensed residential establishments and restaurants; (b)

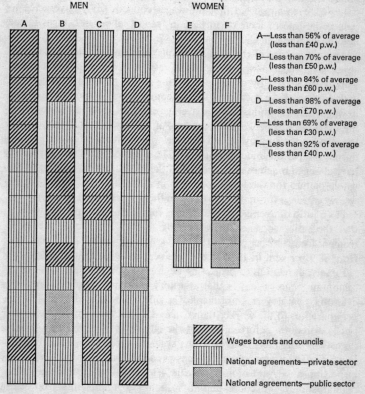

MEN · WOMEN

A · B · C · D · E · F

A—Less than 56% of average (less than £40 p.w.)

B—Less than 70% of average (less than £50 p.w.)

C—Less than 84% of average (less than £60 p.w.)

D—Less than 98% of average (less than £70 p.w.)

E—Less than 69% of average (less than £30 p.w.)

F—Less than 92% of average (less than £40 p.w.)

Wages boards and councils

National agreements—private sector

National agreements—public sector

Figure 9.3. The ranking in 1977 of industries (low to high) in below-average earnings ranges.

retail drapery, outfitting and footwear; (c) retail furnishing and allied trades; (d) agriculture – England and Wales; and (e) retail food – England and Wales. Thus it would seem that the wages councils figure prominently where low earnings are concerned, but even more prominently when the problem is one of very low earnings. This situation is not new, nor has it changed much over the post-war period.[21] Of course, these observations do not necessarily imply criticism of wages councils since there may have been fundamental market forces at work to undermine a council's influence – it is difficult to raise an industry into a higher earnings league if demand for the industry's product is in the throes of a long-term irrevocable decline. Nevertheless, the wages councils have been criticized on their record of improving remunerations to the low paid (and not solely by private researchers[22]). One critic has even suggested that the wages councils 'may have acted to reduce the rate of increase in pay, in face of labour shortages in the hotel trade and elsewhere'.[23]

Another feature of the wages councils' performance that has caused concern has been a worsening of the *relative* earnings position of the workers protected by councils. Looking at the period 1968–72, Field and Winyard have measured the difference between the lowest decile in wages councils industries and average earnings in all industries, finding that 'the gap between the rewards of the lowest paid 10 per cent of Wages Council employees and average wages widened for each group during the period under scrutiny'.[24] The situation does not appear to have changed much over the period of the 1970s. Indeed, looking at the whole picture for the lowest-paid group and taking the average gross weekly earnings for manual workers in the wages council sector expressed as a ratio of average gross earnings for all manual workers, we find that the ratio worsened between 1972 and 1977 for both men and women: from 88·7 per cent in 1972 to 84·9 per cent in 1977 for men; and from 88·9 per cent in 1972 to 84·7 per cent in 1977 for women.

Finally, in relation to protecting the low paid, a problem within any minimum wage system is that statutory procedures do not preclude evasion by employers. In principle, the rule of law should offer a stronger guarantee to the worker than can ever be the case with the market, but laws require enforcement and the efficiency of monitoring procedures will ultimately determine the system's success in protecting the low paid. The wages councils do possess appropriate powers – of entry, inspection and imposition of arrears – to be called forth as part of a regular survey procedure and in response to complaints from employees. However, the story has in reality not been one to allay the fears of the critics completely. In a mid-1960s' study of wages councils in

Birmingham, E. G. A. Armstrong found that wide variations in under-payment can occur at the local level – even in times of relatively full employment.[25] Enforcement is likely to be most difficult in the case of small establishments, and this was suggested by Armstrong's findings: small firms (each employing less than eleven workers) accounted for 60 per cent of underpaid workers and 63 per cent of arrears paid. Looking at the broader view, Field and Winyard have estimated that about one in ten establishments inspected between 1968 and 1972 were regularly paying less than the legal minimum.[26]

Collective Bargaining

Turning to the other major objective of the wages council system – the encouragement of collective bargaining – we see again a fairly unim-pressive record. The rate of decrease in the number of wages councils has been slow and abolitions have been sporadic. In the first fifteen years after the Second World War, only eight councils were abolished, and the next fifteen years, up to 1977, saw the abolition of a further thirteen councils.

One reason for the slow rate of decline in wages councils is that some employers have expressed a preference for the wages councils system since it ensures uniformity of rates and so helps the fight against foreign competition (cutlery employers in 1969[27]); and because the system as a whole ensures impartiality and therefore provides means of conciliation and arbitration (employers in the hair, bass and fibre industry, 1961[28]). But the major reason for the slow development of collective bargaining procedures in wages council industries is the prohibitive costs of orga-nization among a greatly dispersed labour force. Where the problem *has* been overcome, earnings have greatly improved, as in the cases of road haulage (still covered by a wages council) and milk distribution (wages council abolished in 1975). In both these cases, strong organiza-tions developed on both sides of the bargaining process.[29] It could seem that industrial structure, an influence underlined by Marquand in 1967,[30] remains an important variable in the determination of low pay and one which has not been overcome consistently by wages councils. In those wages council industries where minimum earnings have re-mained low, the average-sized firm is very small – licensed residential establishments and restaurants, retail trading and agriculture being prime examples – while workers are greatly dispersed and organizing costs are very high.

Despite an earlier statement to the contrary, the preceding summary may have conveyed the impression that low pay features only in wages council industries. This is not the case. The sector merely epitomizes the features of any industry in which earnings are low: non-existent or ineffectual collective bargaining procedures, mainly because of the high proportion of small firms; a high proportion of female and/or aged workers; and a high proportion of unskilled workers. If we add to this list the features of those industries which are contracting, then we have a comprehensive guide to the main causes of low pay, whether or not minimum rates are set by wages councils. This list of characteristics was clearly identified in Marquand's study, but it is no less relevant to the current labour market. Taking a range of gross earnings less than 70 per cent of the weekly average for manual workers in 1977, we find that the motor vehicle retail and repair industry had the second highest percentage of labour earning this low level of remuneration – not a wages council industry, but one which underlines the problems of collective bargaining among small, dispersed firms. Other industries which have a relatively high proportion of the labour force earning much less than the weekly average for manual workers include: the retail grocery trade; textile bleaching, dyeing and finishing; cotton spinning and weaving; woollen and worsted spinning and weaving; and footwear – all industries which rely heavily on female and unskilled labour, and several of which are in a state of decline through falling demand for the final product.

Finally, we have not mentioned employment and price effects in the context of experience with the wages councils. As was pointed out earlier, the data collected by the Department of Employment do not permit the predictions of the competitive model to be tested for Britain. It is possible, however, to glean a little evidence from various studies which have been attempted. Studies of the early Trades Boards by Tawney[31] suggest that the setting of minimum wages resulted in some employers dismissing workers and/or raising their hiring standards. It has been suggested that these adverse effects would have been more serious but for the upward trend in market demand.[32] Other evidence of wage rigidity and unemployment as a result of statutory rates is present in the Report of the Cave Committee (1922).[33] Regarding the price effect, evidence collected by the National Board for Prices and Incomes suggests that minimum wages have led to higher prices in both the laundry and road-haulage industries.[34]

Concluding Remarks

While admitting that, on British experience, the case against minimum wages is somewhat flimsy, we must note also that there is no clear evidence to contradict neoclassical economic theory, and, coupling this fact with the evidence from the United States, the neoclassical predictions begin to look near the mark. In addition, we have observed that the record of the wages councils falls short of achieving the system's objectives. There is, on the other hand, a further dimension to the problem, relating to the use of minimum wages as a device to combat poverty. Minimum wages can at best offer only a small degree of protection against the impact of market forces upon the price of labour; they cannot be expected to offer workers a comprehensive system of income maintenance. Yet the social implications of low pay extend beyond the mere fact that a worker might receive much less remuneration than the average for his industry in any given week. Regular low pay determines a life-style which is relatively deprived. Fringe benefits, work conditions, holidays and occupational pensions are all likely to be less generous in the low-pay sector; the unskilled worker runs a higher risk of unemployment than the skilled worker;[35] and irregular employment is not conducive to effective planning of lifetime consumption patterns, nor does it permit ready access to the finance market. Atkinson has ably demonstrated that low pay at any one time in a person's life may well be a factor leading to poverty later in life.[36] Low weekly earnings may mean that adequate health precautions cannot be taken and diets may be deficient, such risks extending to dependants if earnings are the sole source of household income.

Coupling the above observations with the fact that minimum wages do not provide help for individuals who are in poverty but are outside the labour force – for example, the aged and the sick – and a case begins to emerge for a comprehensive state scheme of income maintenance whereby everyone is guaranteed some agreed minimum standard of consumption, regardless of occupational category or income class. In this way, the market is allowed to allocate resources without hindrance while the consequences for income distribution are taken account of by another mechanism. The UK social security programme falls short of this suggestion, despite an extension of income maintenance to full-time members of the labour force through the Family Income Supplement. But we leave the detailed discussion of state income maintenance measures until the following chapter, noting that both sections of the present discussion have encountered reasons for no more than a cautious reliance upon market solutions to the problem of poverty.

10. Income Maintenance (4): State Programmes and the UK Experience in the Post-War Period

Chapter 8 was concerned with methodology and the search for a definition of poverty which is not only normatively acceptable but also permits ready measurement by available statistics. While accepting the conclusion reached there – that there is no perfect measure of poverty – the analysis now continues by adopting the statutory yardstick (currently the Supplementary Benefit scales) for reasons previously outlined.

The past thirty years have constituted an important period in the battle against poverty. Post-war developments have reflected not only changes in the global distribution of political and economic power but also changes in governmental commitments, anti-poverty measures having become an intrinsic part of the domestic policy programmes of many of the countries fortunate enough to enjoy a share in the fruits of economic growth. The United Kingdom has been a pioneer in policies to fight poverty, with the post-war legislation having its foundations in the radical proposals advanced in the Beveridge Report.[1]

Prior to Beveridge, alleviation of poverty relied upon a piecemeal system of state aid which provided help under a number of separate insurance schemes covering sickness, industrial injury, unemployment and old age, but which did not extend the arm of support to all the circumstances in which poverty might arise. The aim of Beveridge was to supplant this system by a programme to eradicate want, no matter where its origins might lie – maternity, unemployment, sickness, old age and death ('from the cradle to the grave', in the romantic phrasing of socialist hopes). The front line of attack was to be provided by a comprehensive social insurance programme of flat-rate benefits financed by the weekly contributions of those covered by the scheme, supported by Family Allowances payable to all children except the first, at varying rates dependent upon the age of the child. But in case this juggernaut failed, a safety-net National Assistance programme was proposed to catch those by-passed by the insurance programme. Finally, this plan was to be augmented within a wider framework of state provision: health services were to be universally available free of user charge, and maintenance of full employment was to be a government priority.

The insurance provisions were discussed in an earlier chapter, but the security or income maintenance aspects of the programme were then neglected. The comprehensive nature of the programme, coupled with the income guarantees which it proposed, gave rise to considerable optimism regarding the future prospects of the poor. National Insurance benefits were to be sufficient to guarantee subsistence, and the role of National Assistance, the provision of means-tested benefits financed by the Exchequer, was anticipated to be minimal. Family Allowances were to provide for the subsistence needs of children, but were not made available for the first child on the assumption that, in a fully employed economy, wages inadequate for the support of a one-child family unit would be a rarity.

Much of the scheme became legislation, although, as we shall see, not all of the Beveridge principles were adhered to, and full employment coupled with the rising living standards from eventual post-war economic recovery lulled the policy-maker into believing, by the beginning of the 1960s, that the battle against poverty had been won. But the illusion was sorely disturbed by the work of Abel-Smith and Townsend, which demonstrated, among other things, that in 1960 two million people had incomes below the (then) National Assistance scale, with nearly half a million people surviving at 20 per cent below the National Assistance scale and nearly a million at 10 per cent below the scale.[2] Shock waves from these findings spawned further inquiries by both private researchers and government departments, and by the end of the 1970s we were able to look back on two decades which had seen the documentation of the poor and their problems at an unprecedented pitch.[3]

What is the picture that emerged? Table 10.1 summarizes the findings of the more comprehensive inquiries. Without reiterating our earlier discussion regarding data variations and measurement problems, we must remind ourselves that the calculations presented in the table have different bases. The data sources used by Gough and Stark combine CSO calculations with Inland Revenue returns, while the other sources rely upon the *Family Expenditure Survey*. Among the important differences resulting from these varied sources is the point that income estimates also vary, Inland Revenue data reflecting annual incomes as defined for income tax purposes (and thus excluding social security payments); CSO estimates being adjusted to include both social security benefits and incomes below the effective tax exemption limit; and *Family Expenditure Survey* estimates relying on household budget samples based on a given week and using reported 'normal' take-home earnings. Another difference to note is that, while Gough and Stark and Atkinson adopt a (similar) calculation of *average* rent, Abel-Smith and

Townsend and the NIESR study use *actual* rent. However, these differences are not believed to be sufficiently important to shake our faith in the 'large gain of truth' contained in the comparisons, though they may explain some of the differences in the rates of change in poverty as observed by varying studies.

Table 10.1.

Year	Source	Percentage of population in poverty (with income less than the National Assistance or Supplementary Benefit Scales)	
1953/4	Abel-Smith and Townsend[a]	1·2	
	Gough and Stark[b]	12·3	
	NIESR[c]	4·8	(22·5*)
1960	Abel-Smith and Townsend	3·8	
1963	Gough and Stark	9·4	
	NIESR		(9·4*)
1967	Atkinson[d]	3·5	
	NIESR		(5·5*)
1969	Atkinson[e]	3·4	
1971	NIESR	4·9	

SOURCES: [a] *The Poor and the Poorest.*
[b] *Manchester School.*
[c] *Poverty and Progress in Britain 1958–73.*
[d] *Poverty in Britain and the Reform of Social Security in Britain.*
[e] *Conflicts in Policy Objective.*
For full references, see page 235, ns. 2 and 3.

The significant feature to emerge from the comparisons in Table 10.1 is that, no matter which figure we take to be most accurate for 1953/4,[4] the proportion of the population in poverty in given years, measured in terms of the 'official' poverty line for each given year, remained high after twenty years of economic progress. Perhaps most significant is the fact that, despite the renewed concern over poverty which characterized social research in the 1960s, the rate of fall in the proportion of the population in poverty over the decade 1960–70 was disappointingly low. Indeed, if we compare the combined estimates for 1960–70 with the NIESR estimate for 1971, the rate of fall may have reached zero or even become negative by the end of the decade. A somewhat brighter picture is offered by the NIESR estimates based upon an absolute poverty standard which involves applying the 1971 Supplementary Benefit Scales (held constant in real terms) to the twenty-year time-stream – the resulting estimates being given by the asterisked figures in Table 10.1. This method of calculation may provide a useful comparison with figures based on current statutory poverty scales since it avoids the problem of measuring poverty when standards dictated by legislation change over time.[5] According to this standard, individual poverty has declined over the two decades by a factor of (approximately) four, but again we should note that the rate of decline is much slower in the second decade.[6]

Why has want not been eradicated on the scale envisaged by Beveridge? Reasons stem from the nature of the scheme itself, and also from the interpretation of its philosophy by successive post-war governments. So large a scheme, covering so many categories of want in a discretionary manner, is likely to be slow to adapt to changes in the social and economic structure of society. The post-war period has seen many demographic changes, the most obvious being proportional increases in the dependent sectors of the population – old people and young children – as well as changes in the incidence of unemployment, and in the occupational wage structure. A depressing result of these many changes has been the heavy dependency upon the role of National Assistance and Supplementary Benefit (as it is now termed) in the social security programme. The Beveridge intention that the safety net would play a minimal role has not been realized, a fact which has been compounded by governments' refusals to ensure that National Insurance benefits be at least equal to subsistence requirements as recommended by Beveridge. This has been a major factor in explaining the numbers of old people falling below the poverty line, a problem we shall turn to presently.

Another area where the Beveridge assumptions have failed is that of family poverty. Population growth has resulted in many children being placed at economic risk, a risk which has not been alleviated by family allowances. This particular social security benefit has remained static in value for very long periods, the longest being twelve years, from 1956 to 1968. Furthermore, the expectation that earnings from market employment would suffice to support a one-child family has not been borne out, giving rise to a need for a state scheme which caters for families in poverty even when the wage-earner is in full-time employment.

Finally, there has been, throughout the era of the Welfare State, the persistent problem of 'take-up'. When social security benefits are means-tested and must be claimed for, ignorance and/or a fear of social stigma can result in many potential recipients of state aid failing to declare their eligibility. This problem has been prevalent among the old and has blunted recent attempts to deal with the problem of family poverty. Let us now take a closer look at these two areas of poverty.

Poverty among the Aged

Poverty among old people is not a new feature of society, but its importance as a contributor to the total domestic poverty problem has been growing alarmingly over the course of this century. The justly famous results of Rowntree on this subject are worth repeating: his original survey of York in 1899 found that old age was the major factor causing poverty in less than 5 per cent of the households living within his definition of poverty, but in his third survey of 1951, old age was the culprit in about two thirds of poor households.[7]

Rowntree's explanations of this change included the increase in the relative size of the aged population and the increasing tendency for the aged to live alone rather than with children or in an institution. The proportional growth in the aged population has continued unabated since Rowntree's studies, with the result that over the first seven decades of this century the proportion of the population having reached retirement age (65 for men and 60 for women) grew from 6·2 per cent to 16 per cent, and was expected to reach 17 per cent by the end of the 1970s.[8] Numerically, this trend resulted in the numbers of retirement pensioners reaching over eight million (2·8 million men and 5·3 million women) by 1975.

Income sources for the aged differ from those of the young in that while the old may still rely to some extent upon market earnings, they are more likely to be dependent upon financial aid from relatives or private charities, upon the product of accumulated savings, including private pension schemes, and upon the state retirement pension. Access to income from these alternative sources will determine whether or not an individual of retirement age will fall into poverty. Bearing this in mind, we can briefly summarize an interesting attempt by the NIESR study already referred to[9] to calculate both the *risk* of poverty as a consequence of the life-cycle (the proportion of elderly households which are poor) and the *accountability* of the elderly characteristic (the number of poor households which are old as a proportion of total households in poverty).

Using the *Family Expenditure Survey*, the NIESR study calculated, for 1971, a 17 per cent risk of poverty for the elderly compared with only 4 per cent for children and 2½ per cent for other adults.[10] The risk facing the elderly who lived in households comprising one man and one woman was also 17 per cent, while the old living alone faced a risk as high as 30 per cent. The low-risk elderly, as calculated by the NIESR team, lived in households comprising three or four adults – that is, a sharing arrangement – but even here the risk of poverty remained as high as 7 per cent, which is between two and three times the average risk for this size of household. In total, elderly households accounted for approximately 42 per cent of the poverty among the 1971 sample.[11]

From the meagre evidence available, it would seem that the aged in Britain are heavily dependent upon the state retirement pension for their main source of income. The importance of market earnings has been dwindling over the past sixty years. Taking activity rates as an indicator of the importance of the market as a source of income for the pensioner household, for men over 65 years of age, the rate had declined from 58·9 in 1921 to 31·1 in 1951, and by 1971 had fallen to 19·4.[12] Presumably, such a trend is to be expected in the régime of a state retirement pension supported by an increasing number of occupational pension schemes, but before making any definite conclusions, we should first take a brief look at the mechanics of the UK retirement pension.

The most important element in the system is a flat-rate pension payable to men on reaching age 65 and women on reaching 60. Although a graduated pension (supported by earnings-related contributions) was introduced in 1961, the UK scheme is still based on the original Beveridge intention. In our present context, the important point to note is that the pension, at least during the first five years of retirement, is not an 'old-age pension' but a retirement pension: following the Beveridge recommendations, the state pension is aimed to help replace earnings when they cease at the end of a working life. To help enforce this retirement principle, the UK authorities introduced, along with the pension, an earnings test whereby, during the first five years of retirement, an individual's pension is reduced if earnings exceed a given threshold. Encouragement to continue in paid employment after minimum retirement age is provided by increments to the flat-rate pension (on eventual retirement at 70 for men and 65 for women) to those deferring retirement and continuing to pay social security contributions.

More detail about the earnings rule and a discussion of its possible effects is provided in the next chapter. Meanwhile, we should note that the retirement condition seems meant to support an insurance principle: the pension is to offset the loss of earning power. Given this objective, an earnings rule, as operated in the United Kingdom, would make sense if the state insurance scheme were actuarily based, but, as we saw in Chapter 7, the UK programme has been 'pay-as-you-go' ever since its inception. The case for this special tax on pensioner earnings is far from clear.

The number of pensioners having their pension either reduced or extinguished by the operation of the earnings rule is not great, and the proportion has been falling over time: the proportion of pensioners

subject to the earnings rule and actually having their pensions reduced
or extinguished was 4·8 per cent for men and 2·5 per cent for women
in 1956, and had fallen to 0·8 per cent for men and 0·3 per cent for
women by 1975.[13] Of course, it is not possible to attribute the reason
for these low proportions directly to the discouragements imposed by
the 'earnings rule', but, as we shall see later, a potential work disincentive does exist. As far as the effect on actual earnings is concerned, we
have no recent information, the main factual guide being an inquiry by
the (then) Ministry of Pensions and National Insurance published in
1966, which reported that, in 1965, 25·6 per cent of married pensioner
couples relied on net earnings to supplement their incomes, the proportions for single men and single women being 11·4 per cent and 13·2
per cent respectively.[14]

According to the 1965 inquiry, net earnings came second in importance as a source of income, the most important source being occupational pensions.[15] Again, however, the proportion of pensioners in
receipt of occupational pensions is, as yet, much too low to rely upon
this source of income significantly to alleviate poverty among old
people.[16] A similar picture emerges from other sources of income
supplement – increased pensions from deferred retirement and graduated pensions have not as yet made a very significant contribution
towards the fight against poverty among the aged.

But what about the flat-rate retirement pension itself – why has this
programme failed to remove old people from the rigours of poverty?
There seem to be two major reasons, one resulting from Beveridge's
recommendations being ignored, the other a factor not foreseen by
Beveridge. Despite the intention of Beveridge, the retirement pension
has not been a subsistence allowance. Thus, even a long-established
pension system was unable to prevent the 1965 inquiry from finding
that 40 per cent of single men, 62 per cent of single women and 34 per
cent of married couples had, at that time, incomes (excluding National
Assistance) which were below the National Assistance Scale.[17] This
denial of Beveridge by successive governments has been decried by
many social commentators,[18] and yet the situation remained unchanged
by the end of the 1970s, the pension paid to either a single person or a
married couple being slightly below the basic supplementary benefit
level for these categories of beneficiary and considerably below the full
supplementary benefit allowance which takes account of rent requirements.

Another factor not foreseen by Beveridge, but an indirect consequence of the scheme rather than the result of government policy, is
the problem of low 'take-up' of supplementary benefit by retirement

pensioners. This point was underlined in detail by the 1965 inquiry, which found that a third of pensioners were ignorant of the availability of National Assistance, while 30 per cent of married couples and 20 per cent of single men and women indicated that pride prevented them from applying for this supplementary aid.[19] Low take-up of National Assistance by pensioners was also noted by Abel-Smith and Townsend,[20] as well as by a survey undertaken in 1959–60 by Cole and Utting.[21] As Atkinson puts it, 'despite the formal abolition of the Poor Law in the Act of 1948, National Assistance retained sufficient stigma for people still to prefer to live below the National Assistance scale rather than apply.'[22]

Poverty and the Family

Life-cycle effects are not confined to old age, and much attention has been devoted by researchers to the effects of poverty on children and the extent to which children are one of the causes of poverty. This latter relationship has undergone significant change over the past fifty years. It is clear that, for any given household, children place demands on scarce household resources, and they may constrain the use made by parents (or at least one of the parents) of market earnings opportunities. However, whether these effects will place a family in poverty depends upon the total resource flow available to the family. From the time of Rowntree's inquiries in 1859 to the Beveridge Report, there was an assumption, based on a certain amount of fact, that a large number of children is a basic cause of family poverty.

Beveridge's proposed solution to the problem of poverty caused by 'large families' was Family Allowances payable to *all* families with two or more children, regardless of means. This universal family benefit was therefore aimed at raising the net income of all families, even those where the father was in full-time employment. The allowance was not to be payable to one-child families, or on behalf of the first child in families comprising two or more children, in the belief that market wages would suffice to provide for the one-child family.[23] There have been some recent modifications to the Family Allowance system, but until 1976 its eligibility structure was that proposed by Beveridge, and the reasons why this system has failed to solve the problem of family poverty demand some attention.

Before considering the reasons why family poverty has remained with us, despite Beveridge, we might first note that the number of children in a family, as a basic cause of poverty, has declined in post-war years. Using information collected by the Ministry of Social

Security,[24] Atkinson has classified, for 1966, poor families according to the number of children in the family. Not surprisingly, a much higher proportion of large families fell below the poverty line in 1966 than was the case with small families – while only 1 per cent of families with two children had income below the (1966) National Assistance scale, 14 per cent of families with six children or more had incomes below the scale.[25] But, while risk of poverty was apparently high among large families, accountability, the extent to which large families accounted for the amount of poverty in 1966, was not particularly great: families with two and three children accounted, together, for over half the numbers falling into poverty in 1966, and these families accounted for nearly 40 per cent of the total number of children living in families with income below the National Assistance Scale.[26] The evidence on the numbers of children in poverty largely substantiated similar findings in the earlier study by Abel-Smith and Townsend.[27] The NIESR study has also attempted risk and accountability calculations in relation to the number of children in families as the cause of poverty, and has arrived at similar conclusions to the above: 'although the risk of poverty for households with large numbers of children (five or more) may be high, the numerical importance of such poverty is now even less significant'.[28]

The point we are trying to emphasize here is not that poverty among children is insignificant. Quite the contrary – the absolute number of children in poverty (children in some 70,000 families) is, according to the 1966 inquiry, alarming but substantiated by the NIESR inquiry, which estimates that children account for 24 per cent of all individuals in poverty (600,000 in all)[29] – but also that poverty *may exist even when the family size is small*. An obvious candidate to single out as the cause of poverty among families with a small number of children is low earnings – the Beveridge assumption may have been too optimistic. But before taking a close look at this explanation, we should consider the role of Family Allowances in the post-war social security structure. Why therefore has poverty among children persisted when a universal system of benefit payable to all but the first child has been so long a part of the Welfare State?

Family allowances

It cannot be denied that without Family Allowances, the plight of poor families with children would have been much worse in the post-war period. Using the results of the Ministry of Social Security inquiry of 1966, Atkinson has estimated that, without Family Allowances, twice as many families would have fallen below the National Assistance scale[30] – 5 per cent instead of 2½ per cent. Yet this record would have been much improved if Family Allowance had been paid at rates advised by Beveridge. The Beveridge proposal was that such allowances should suffice to cover subsistence for children of varying ages, and that the rates should be set at least equal to the subsistence rate used in the National Assistance scale; but this proposal has never been implemented. Family Allowance rates have never varied according to the age of the children in the family (except for a small differentiation between first and subsequent eligible children), and the flat rate payable has never even reached the lowest rate payable for dependent children under supplementary social security arrangements. In 1948, the Family Allowance of 25p (the original 1945 rate) was only two thirds of the National Assistance rate for a child under 5 years of age, and just under one half of the rate payable for a child aged between 11 and 15.

By 1977, this relationship had worsened considerably – taking the Family Allowance of £1.50 for the second child, this represented approximately 42 per cent of the Supplementary Benefit rate for a child under 5; 28 per cent of the rate for an 11-year-old; and a mere 14 per cent of rate payable for a child of 16. Furthermore, the real value of Family Allowances declined considerably from the scheme's inception. In spite of price inflation, the rate payable to the first eligible child was raised only twice between 1945 and 1975! Using a price base of 1963 = 100, Maynard has calculated that the real value of family allowances declined by 22 per cent during the period 1948–67, and that, despite an increase in allowance in 1968, there was a reduction of 23 per cent during the period 1967–72.[31]

Thus, by the 1970s, considerable pressure was being placed upon policy-makers to modify the system of Family Allowances and to move it more into line with the Beveridge intentions. But the proposed policy changes have not been confined to Family Allowances. As well as direct benefit payable to families with children, the state has long provided help in the form of child tax allowances whereby deductions are allowed from income for tax purposes at rates which vary according to the age of the child. While such allowances do provide indirect help to families with children, the distributional consequences differ from those of direct benefits. After 1968, Family Allowances were classified as taxable income and recouped by the Inland Revenue (the famous 'claw-back' principle). Hence, the value of Family Allowances rose as family income fell. On the other hand, child tax allowances, in a progressive income tax rates structure, increase in value as family income rises. This means that families with income so low as to be unaffected by the income tax do not receive any benefit from the tax allowances (a problem we return to in the following chapter), and the indirect benefits enjoyed by tax-payers are favoured towards the higher income groups. Both effects are undesirable, given the social welfare function we have adopted, and changes have been advocated.

Eventually the UK government paid heed to the various criticisms and family allowances were replaced in April 1977 by a system of 'child benefits' payable directly to the family unit, the rate of benefit payable to rise over time as part of a programme (commenced in tax year 1978/9) to phase out child tax allowances.

Low earnings and state aid to families

Like that of the retirement pension, the record of the system of family allowances has suffered not only from successive governments ignoring the Beveridge proposals, but also from misleading assumptions made by Beveridge. As we saw earlier, some 40 per cent of families in poverty in 1966 had only two or three children, which suggests that low earnings has been a factor creating poverty. It would seem that Beveridge's assumption about earnings has not been borne out. Atkinson has estimated that, in 1968, the proportion of adult men working for low *hourly* earnings (taken to be 37·5p per hour for 1968) was as high as 14·4 per cent.[32] Calculating the proportion receiving low hourly earnings counteracts the claim that low weekly earnings are simply a result of working shorter hours. Reasons for low earnings include ill-health and the nature of the industry in which the earner works, a factor we considered in a previous chapter when we discussed minimum wage legislation.

Recognizing that Family Allowances have not sufficed to help families in poverty with the 'breadwinner' in full-time employment, the UK government introduced in 1971 a scheme of direct state aid to such families. This new benefit carried the label 'Family Income Supplement' and was introduced in a flourish of expectancy and hope.[33] The full details of this measure are given in a later discussion of means-tested benefits, but we can note two points at this stage. First, the term 'supplement' is operative – the benefit paid to eligible families does not raise family income to the amount prescribed by the state as adequate for that family, but fills in only 50 per cent of the gap between this amount and actual family income (inclusive of family allowance). Secondly, the take-up of the scheme has fallen short of expectations – even in its first year of operation, the year of maximum publicity, 60 per cent of those eligible for the supplement did not claim it.[34] This take-up problem seems to be the bugbear of means-tested schemes, and we shall return to the problem presently.

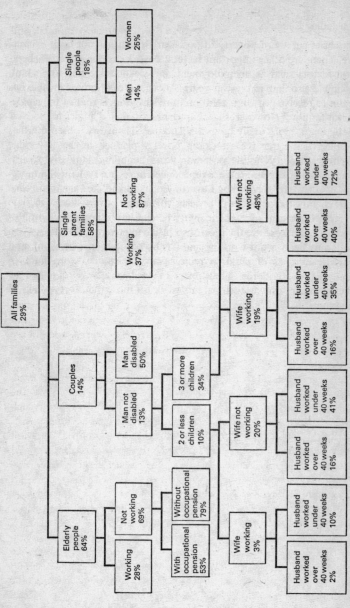

Figure 10.1. Percentage of families in each category having household income below 140 per cent of supplementary benefit.

Concluding Remarks

This brief survey of poverty in post-war Britain has not been exhaustive. There are other important factors at work causing poverty: short-term factors such as unemployment and sickness are still important, though less so than in pre-war years. Another area of poverty which has begun to receive growing attention in recent years is that of the single-parent family.[35] However, this chapter has attempted a fairly close view of the main, more easily quantifiable, areas of poverty, observing that in spite of the massive attack on poverty planned in the Beveridge Report, the story of the post-war years contains many disappointments. As a postscript, there is reproduced in Figure 10.1 the illuminating 'poverty tree' devised by Layard, Piachaud and Stewart as a means of tracing the major causes of poverty.[36] Taking a poverty line of income below 140 per cent of supplementary benefit level, the tree re-emphasizes that old people are the most susceptible to poverty (especially when the family head is not working and has no occupational pension), and that the number of children remains an important determinant of family living standards. The impact of each variable is qualified by whether or not one or both parents work for more than forty weeks of the year.

11. Income Maintenance (5):
State Programmes
and the Alternatives to Beveridge

Because of the problems outlined in the previous chapters some observers have recommended the adoption of a 'cure-all' named *negative taxation*. This term has been used to describe various social security plans over the past fifteen years or so, and yet its use is still taken to be suggestive of a brand-new scheme of things. Because of this belief, and also because 'negative taxation' covers a wide variety of different schemes, the term can sometimes mislead. A rigorous analysis of any of the plans advanced as alterations to the Beveridge programme may reveal something radical about the generosity of the welfare payments involved and/or the nature of the required administrative changes, but not about the basic principles governing receipts of benefits and payments of taxes. A wider recognition of the generality of these principles should serve to temper the ongoing debate on how to tackle the problem of poverty.

All the means-tested benefits previously discussed in our survey of the social security system in the United Kingdom are examples of negative tax schemes in the sense that principles governing receipt of benefit include elements of tax as well as welfare payment. These separable elements emerge from both the direction of the *total* resource flow involved and the nature of the impact at the *margin* of economic activity.[1] Taking the case of a family unit of given size, we can demonstrate this point by assuming eligibility for weekly benefit to be determined by the amount of weekly income earned by the unit from other sources – say, from earned income. Thus, at the margin, the net flow of resources is from the private sector to the government, the family unit, in other words, being *taxed* on additional earnings; but the total flow of resources remains in the opposite direction to that of a tax since the net overall effect of the scheme is a supplement to the income of the family unit. Representing net income of the family unit, from all sources, by Yn, earned income by Ye, and social security benefit by B, we can summarize the situation as follows:

$$Yn = Ye + B$$
$$B > 0$$

$$\frac{dYn}{dYe} > 0$$

$$\frac{dB}{dYe} < 0$$

We may also note at this stage that the structure of means-tested benefits, as in this example, usually bears the other hallmarks of a taxation scheme. Benefit is paid to, or withheld from, a defined tax unit (say, head of household plus dependants); is determined by reference to a defined base (say, earned income); and the benefit payable in any period depends on income received by the tax unit from the base source during that same period. There is, however, one feature of means-tested social security benefits which does set them apart from usual tax conventions: the marginal rate of tax applied to low levels of income is often very high; indeed, it can be often 100 per cent. This effect at the margin arises from the assumption that state supplements to income are a *substitute* for a lack of income from other sources within the tax base: as other income rises, the supplement is withdrawn. The rationale for this may lie in the philosophy behind the system – only those who have a genuine need for state help can receive it – and/or a lack of resources in society to permit a more generous redistribution of resources towards the lower income groups. Whatever the reason for such high marginal rates of tax, they pose a potential threat to incentives for the tax unit to gain income from sources other than the state. However, this question of disincentives is not clear-cut and we shall return to it presently.

Let us now illustrate the above observations with reference to two schemes operative within the United Kingdom framework of social security: the Family Income Supplement (FIS) and the state retirement pension.

Family Income Supplement

To repeat earlier remarks, this scheme was introduced into the United Kingdom's system in 1971 with the aim of helping low-income families where the family head is in full-time employment. The scheme's target for each family is termed the 'prescribed amount', and the prescription varies according to the structure of the family (number of children being the main variable). Supplement is then payable to any eligible unit whose total amount of resources (husband's gross earnings plus wife's earnings plus family allowances) is less then the prescribed amount. The amount of supplement is half the difference between resources and prescribed amount. Representing gross family resources by Yg; the prescribed amount by Y^*; and net disposable family income by Yn; the FIS scheme can be shown by a simple diagram, as in Figure 11.1.

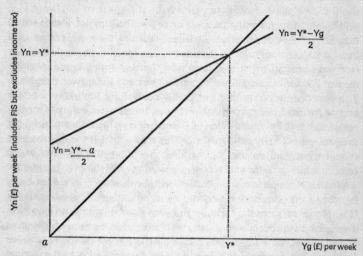

Figure 11.1.

Along the 45° line in Figure 11.1, net disposable family income is equivalent to gross family income (as defined for purposes of the scheme). The actual path followed by net income as gross income rises is shown by the line $Yn = (Y^* - Yg)/2$. When gross family income is α, net disposable income is equal to $Y^* - \alpha/2$; but as gross income approaches Y^*, the two become equal at Y^* (the 'prescribed amount'). Thus every marginal increase in gross family income is effectively taxed at 50 per cent: for every £1 increase to gross income 50p less is received from the state as FIS – that is, net disposable income rises by only 50p. Note, however, that for income levels below Y^* the net flow of resources is still from the state to the family unit.

The Retirement Pension

The retirement pension is classified as taxable income by the revenue authorities of the United Kingdom, but it is not this fact which we are to consider here. Rather, it is the negative tax element of the system to which we are to refer as a further illustration of an earlier point.

(It is true, of course, that any resultant tax rates may be compounded by the pension's treatment under the income tax system.)

We noted in the previous chapter that, despite initial intentions, neither the financing of the UK pensions scheme, nor the rules determining the receipt of benefit, have been in the spirit of an 'insurance principle'. Indeed, for the pension to be awarded on *retirement* rather than be an 'old-age pension', the rules governing the receipt of pension include an 'earnings rule' which results in a reduction in pension benefit received during the first five years of retirement (minimum age 65 for men and 60 for women) if market earnings exceed some given threshold. This rule operates to reduce the weekly pension by 50p in every £1 for every £1 earned in employment within an initial narrow earnings band per week, and by £1 for every £1 of earnings above that band until the pension is finally extinguished. This means that the social security system is imposing an effective marginal rate of tax of 50 per cent over a certain earnings range and 100 per cent on earnings above this range.[2]

We can demonstrate the effect of the above rate on net disposable income to the pensioner household by using a diagram such as Figure 11.1. However, since the earnings rule imposes a direct tax on earnings, it might be appropriate to illustrate its operation by using the market opportunities, or budget, line faced by the representative pensioner. Figure 11.2 attempts to do this and refers, for simplicity, to the case of a single retirement pensioner, entitled to receipt of pension according to the 'insurance' rules operated within the social security system.

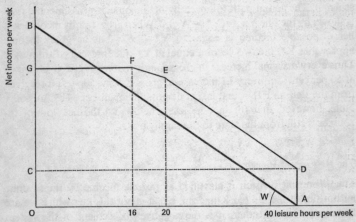

Figure 11.2.

In the absence of a state benefit income, opportunities for the pensioner are assumed to be determined by work in the labour market at a wage rate of w per hour. The representative pensioner is assumed to be prepared to work no more than forty hours a week. Further, he is assumed to be eligible to receive the full retirement pension for a single individual of OC per week.

Market earnings opportunities are shown by the line AB – by foregoing leisure, the pensioner can gain income from the market at a rate of w per hour. However, the picture changes with the introduction of a flat-rate retirement pension of OC since this income is guaranteed even if the pensioner opts for forty hours of leisure per week – the opportunities line is raised from A to D. If the pensioner decides to follow market opportunities, he moves along DE, being rewarded at the wage rate w until he is working twenty hours a week. At this work rate his market income becomes sufficient to invoke the first of the earnings rule penalties, and on his marginal hours of work he forfeits 50p for every £1 earned in the market-place, moving along the segment EF. Should the pensioner continue working up to and beyond twenty-four hours a week he will become subject to the 100 per cent marginal reduction in pension and opportunities will be presented by the segment FG.

Thus, overall, the net opportunities line when the state pension is introduced becomes ADEFG. The breaks of slope in this budget line clearly show the effects of the tax element in the system, but it should be noted that if the pensioner chooses some point to the right of G on the budget line, the total resource flow within the pension scheme remains in the direction of the pensioner and away from the state. Again, we are considering a negative tax type of welfare scheme.

Larger Scale Plans

The above illustrations represent only a small sample of the many means-tested benefit arrangements which operate as negative tax schemes. Much of the social security system in the United Kingdom (and in other countries) has operated on these principles since the Second World War. Why, then, does the term 'negative taxation' give rise to such debate? A major reason is that the term has been applied to various plans, advanced over the past decade or so, which are meant to supplant large parts, if not all (including insurance benefits), of the existing social security system by a simple extension of the *tax system*. Taking income, as the most often suggested base, a negative income tax scheme would combine both social security benefits and positive tax payments into a single system of redistribution, centrally administered by the revenue authorities. Those who dislike this idea tend to have a general mistrust of negative tax schemes because of the high marginal tax rates involved, or else they consider the existing arrangement of earmarked social security benefits to have merits not possessed by a generalized negative income tax. Let us now consider the various forms that a negative income tax might take in order to appreciate the advantages and disadvantages of such a scheme.

There are two major variants of negative income taxation: *negative rates taxation* and *social dividend taxation*. Both are variations on the scheme outlined above, individuals being compelled to transfer resources to the state when their incomes lie above some defined level and the state transferring resources to individuals when their incomes fall below this level. Both variants can be rendered identical by the choice of values attaching to the variables involved, the latter being the same for each variant. However, the emphasis within each variant differs, and for this reason they are usually discussed separately.

Negative rates taxation involves a very simple extension of the income tax structure along the lines already outlined, and is less radical in its proposed redistribution of income. On the other hand, social dividend taxation represents a more radical restructuring of the existing state of income distribution since it aims to provide a guaranteed minimum income for *all*, regardless of need. In other words, the social dividend approach is 'universal' in contrast to the more 'selective' approach of negative rates taxation. Both schemes, however, contain the same three basic variables: a guaranteed minimum level of income which varies with family size and composition; a tax rate, or rates, applied to a defined tax base; and a break-even level of income where tax liability equals guaranteed advance. As we shall see, the different choice of dependent variable is the distinguishing feature of the schemes.[3] Figure 11.3 provides a summary of how either plan would work.

The situation depicted in this figure is a very simple one in which a single tax rate (positive and negative) is applied in proportion to gross income. This proportional rate of tax is t. Both the tax unit (say, the family), and the tax base (say, income as defined under the existing income tax) have been defined, and the horizontal axis measures the tax unit's gross income for the given tax period while the vertical axis measures the tax unit's income after taxes have been paid or transfers received. Along O A, disposable income is equivalent to gross income, while the line BC shows the path that income actually follows as gross income is modified by the tax system. As can be seen, actual disposable income and actual gross income are equal when the latter reaches OD: above this break-even level the tax unit pays taxes in the normal way, while below it the tax unit receives from the state amounts equal to t times the difference between OE (= OD) and actual gross income. Thus, when gross income for the tax unit is zero, disposable income stands at a guaranteed level of OB (= t.OE), and as actual gross income rises above zero, actual disposable income rises at a rate of 1 − t.

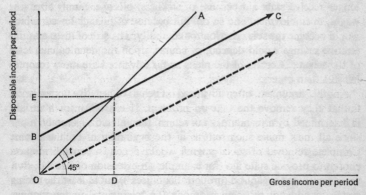

Figure 11.3.

The difference between the two variants lies in the choice of dependent variable. Negative rates taxation permits the break-even level of income (Y_b) to combine with the tax rate (t), and thus determine the minimum guaranteed level of income (Y_g): $R \cdot t = Y_g$. Social dividend taxation determines the break-even level of income by a combination of the minimum income guarantee and the tax rate: $Y_g/t = R$. Clearly, $R = Y_g/t$ in each case and will have the same value if the variables Y_g and t also have the same values. In terms of Figure 11.3, given the same tax rate t and break-even level OD(= OE), each scheme results in a guaranteed minimum income of OB. But it should be noted that, in the social dividend scheme, the break-even level of income is the dependent variable, while in negative rates taxation it is the minimum income guarantee. For this reason, the *level* of the minimum income guarantee varies considerably among different negative tax proposals. We shall return to this point presently.

Pros and Cons

Administratively, either of the above plans should be an improvement on the social security arrangements as they currently exist in the United Kingdom. An extended Inland Revenue which 'pays out' as well as 'takes in' should, in principle, be a net saving in administrative resources in comparison with a system involving so many departments dealing with so many categories of recipient. Individuals would no longer receive state aid because of sickness, old age, family size, low wages, unemployment and so on, but because of financial need, which would become the sole criterion for eligibility. The size of these administrative savings would depend, of course, upon the detailed character of the scheme. Certain of the plans so far advanced are more comprehensive than others.

Another argument, often advanced on behalf of negative tax schemes, is that they remove the take-up problem. If eligibility for state aid is determined by a mandatory tax return, then all citizens are on a par since all must make such returns at the beginning of each tax year. Complete removal of social stigma would depend upon the method chosen to provide state aid (for example, an extension of PAYE, or a voucher scheme organized through 'tax offices'), but at least the claims system would not distinguish among the 'claimants' in the manner applied by the existing social security system. Presumably the likelihood of any sort of social stigma would be less under a social dividend scheme than under a negative rates plan since the dividend is universal. However, as long as the chosen scheme is mandatory, either plan should do much to alleviate the take-up problem which has dogged means-tested benefit schemes.

Counter-balancing the advantages of negative tax schemes, there are at least two major problems to be surmounted. First, there is the choice of the tax period. Existing tax arrangements assess liability for the forthcoming tax *year*, and the simplest method of extending existing arrangements into a negative tax plan would be to continue with annual returns and perhaps make negative tax benefits from the state to the individual tax unit payable on a monthly, or weekly, basis. However, while any delay in tax code adjustment, following an unexpected change in circumstances during the course of the tax year, might not cause too great a hardship for a middle- to high- income taxpayer, it could prove disastrous to a low-income family dependent upon receipt of negative tax benefit. In other words, any adopted scheme would require maximum flexibility in adjusting to unforseen change in financial circumstances experienced by the tax unit. This could prove impossible to administer without the help of supplementary agencies to deal with short-run problems, an arrangement which would increase the running costs of the scheme and might resurrect the problem of low take-up.

A second major problem to solve is the choice of break-even income level. If the aim of the policy is to remove poverty, then the guaranteed minimum allowance must equal the poverty line. But this might mean marginal rates of tax so high that the incentive to seek alternative forms of income from, say market earnings, might be extremely weak for the low-income groups. Yet the alternative of applying lower rates might mean a guaranteed minimum which is less than the poverty line, and an extra 'safety net' might be required, with all the attendant difficulties as experienced by the supplementary benefit scheme. This problem of incentives has received more attention than other features of negative taxation.

It does not seem possible in a world of scarce resources for a negative income tax scheme to provide a guaranteed subsistence minimum for all without the attendant high marginal rates of tax. Presently we shall consider the features of certain plans which have been proposed, but let us first take a closer look at the potential disincentives operating within the principle of such schemes.

In terms of effort, reactions to a negative tax scheme by those who participate in it will depend, as usual, upon the relative strengths of income and substitution effects. As we have seen, those who benefit from the negative tax programme are faced with a negative average rate of tax while the marginal tax rate remains positive. The income/ leisure choice therefore depends upon the combined results of a lump-sum income transfer (the guaranteed minimum), on the one hand, and, on the other, a tax rate which induces a price change by altering the relative prices of leisure and income. A lump-sum income transfer has a money-income effect which favours leisure relative to work if leisure is a 'normal good'. Furthermore, the price change produced by the operation of the tax, as income from sources other than the state rises, lowers the tax unit's net return at the margin, thus reducing the price of leisure, relative to income, and involving a substitution of leisure for income. However, the tax-induced reduction in net earnings for a given amount of effort also produces a 'pure' income effect which encourages more effort to regain income which is lost as a result of the tax rate.

Which of the above forces will be decisive? It seems clear that the 'pure' income effect will be smaller than the (opposite) income effect exacted by the transfer, and the greater the transfer (the higher the guaranteed minimum level of income), the more the lump-sum income effect will tend to outweigh the 'pure' income effect associated with the tax rate. The total net effect would seem to work towards a reduction in work effort if leisure is a normal good.

We can summarize the operation of the negative tax type of income maintenance programme and its potential effect upon the supply of effort by use of the following symbols:

(a) Y_i^n is the net (of all taxes and transfers) income of the representative tax unit i (for simplicity, assumed to be a single individual).

(b) Y_i^g is the guaranteed minimum level of income offered by the state to individual i.

(c) Y_i^b is the 'break-even' level of income for i.

(d) w is the market wage rate and wages are assumed to be the sole alternative source of income for i.

(e) L_i is the maximum number of hours per period that i is prepared to work in the market-place.

(f) t is the negative income tax rate.

Hence: $$Y_i^n = wLi + t (Y_i^b - wLi), \text{ if } Y_i^b > wLi \tag{1}$$

and: $$Y_i^n = wLi, \text{ if } Y_i^b < wLi \tag{2}$$

The total amount of negative tax payment (N) may be written as:

$$N = t(Y_i^b - wLi), \text{ where } Y_i^b > wLi$$

And equation (1) may then be rewritten as:

$$Y_i^n = wLi + N \tag{3}$$

or: $$Y_i^n = Y_i^g + wLi (1 - t) \tag{4}$$

To find the break-even level of income, Y_i^b, we simply equate the budget constraint without negative income tax with the constraint operating under the negative tax system:

$$Y_i^b = wLi = Y_i^g + wLi (1 - t) \tag{5}$$

Hence: $Y_i^b - wLi (1 - t) = Y_i^g$

or: $$Y_i^b - Y_i^b (1 - t) = Y_i^g \tag{6}$$

$$\therefore t_i^Y = Y_i^g/t \tag{7}$$

Which is the formula used at the beginning of our discussion.

We can now find the income and substitution effects operating within such a scheme. The income effect is found by simply subtracting the budget constraint without a negative tax plan from the constraint resulting from such a plan:

$$Y_i^n = Y_i^g + wLi \, (1 - t) - wLi \tag{8}$$

$$Y_i^n = Y_i^g - t \, wLi \tag{9}$$

Given condition (9), Y_i^n is greater than zero when $wLi < Y_i^b$. If the tax unit reduces work effect as a result of this disincentive, the amount of state transfer increases and so does the income effect.

Representing the number of hours devoted to leisure by α_i (where α_i equals the difference between L_i, and the total number of hours available to i), we can now compare the substitution effect of the above tax/transfer plan with the no-transfer marginal rate of substitution between leisure and income:

$$(-) \, \frac{\partial Y_i^n}{\partial \alpha_i} = w.$$

Under the negative income tax scheme the marginal rate of substitution is calculated as follows:

$$Y_i^n = Y_i^g + wLi \, (1 - t) = w\alpha_i \, (1 - t) \tag{10}$$

$$(-) \, \frac{\partial Y_i^n}{\partial \alpha_i} = (-) \, w + tw \tag{11}$$

$$= w(1 - t)$$

Now, since t is a constant and independent of α_i and the t value lies between zero and unity, the cost of leisure has fallen below the no-transfer opportunity cost w, and thus leisure is a more attractive element within the budget opportunities.

Whether or not the potential disincentive within a negative income tax scheme would actually lead to a reduction of effort can only be decided by real-world tests. Our knowledge of the work reactions by recipients of means-tested social security benefits is very meagre, and though there have been more thorough attempts to measure the impact of the (positive) income tax, the evidence so far collected is no more definite than the theoretical prediction.[4] It would appear that individuals faced with a (progressive) tax on work income are as likely to supply more effort in order to maintain their achieved income levels as they are to reduce the supply of effort in response to the reduced opportunity cost of leisure. Such is the impression gained from interview studies of employees, while the predictions of econometric studies on cross-section data have created some confusion regarding the sign of the substitution effect, though more recent analysis does lend support to a positive substitution elasticity which is stronger than the negative income elasticity.[5] Similarly, there is as yet no clear-cut picture emerging from the experiments with negative income taxation undertaken in several areas of the United States.[6]

We should note here that the degree of concern over this question will depend upon the variables within the social welfare function. It can be argued that the true measure of income, particularly when used as a proxy for 'welfare', must include leisure. Using such a definition would require that improvements in the income levels of the poor include increased opportunities for leisure consumption. What is the trade-off between money income and leisure that a society would accept as part of its income redistribution plan? This question can only be answered in the context of the social, political and cultural background of the society to which the question is put. As far as the United Kingdom is concerned, social attitudes would seem to reflect an emphasis upon work income rather than leisure. A. J. Culyer has underlined this important point in his observation that concern about negative tax disincentives arises 'for the odd and Puritan reason that the nature of the externality is that it is all right to raise the real income of the poor so long as they do not take their real incomes in the form of leisure'.[7]

A Selection of Schemes

It is now time to consider a sample of the various specific programmes which have been suggested as solutions to the problem of income maintenance. The sample has been chosen on the basis of potential application within the UK social security system, some of the plans having been advanced with this possibility in mind.

Friedman's plan

An early suggestion for a negative rates plan which has received much attention was that of Milton Friedman.[8] Income tax systems, as adopted by Western Europe and the United States, take account of the personal income commitments of the tax unit and grant certain allowances and reliefs when assessing ability to pay, that is, liability for income tax. In this way (as we saw in an earlier chapter), the income tax system has a potential for income redistribution. This potential can only be realized, however, when all tax units can take full advantage of all their allowances and reliefs. A tax unit with income which is less than the total value of allowances and reliefs cannot take full advantage of the system and is, in a sense, being discriminated against. Friedman's scheme acknowledges this point and suggests an alternative which does provide positive help, through the income tax system, to poor families. The basic idea of a Friedman type of plan is to transfer to tax units with income below the break-even level some proportion of the difference between gross income (adjusted in accordance with any other reliefs permitted by the income tax system) and the permitted exemption level of income as determined by the value of personal allowances.

Let us demonstrate how such a scheme would operate by assuming it to adopt the personal allowances operating under the income tax system of the United Kingdom in 1977. For simplicity, we further assume a standard (negative and positive) tax rate of 50 per cent, recognizing that any real-world schemes would probably require a lower positive rate. The case to be considered is that of a tax unit comprising a husband, who is also the sole earner; a wife; and three children aged 7 years, 12 years and 17 years (the 17-year-old is assumed to be receiving full-time education). The only form of income received by the tax unit (other than the negative tax supplement) is the market earnings of the husband. Combining the married person's allowance with the three child allowances yields total tax allowances of £1,913. Thus income possibilities, net of tax, for this tax unit are shown in Figure 11.4.

As can be seen from the figure, maximum benefit from the scheme for

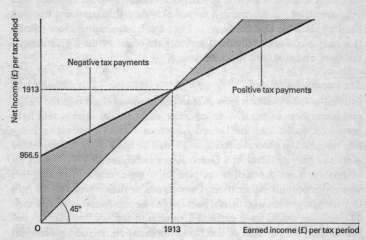

Figure 11.4.

the chosen tax unit is a negative tax payment of £956.5, which equals 50 per cent of the difference between zero earned income and the total allowance level of £1,913. As earned income rises, the 50 per cent marginal reduction in benefit from the state comes into operation until the break-even level of £1,913 is reached.

The direct help given to families with children by such a scheme is a distinct improvement on the system of reliance upon tax allowances. An important advantage of the scheme is the simple administrative procedure involved. In terms of benefiting the poor, such a scheme should guarantee take-up since it is based on a mandatory income tax return, an 'acceptable' means test. For these reasons, the scheme has attracted much attention, and a novel variation on the theme was advanced in 1967 by Lees as a substitute for family allowances.[9]

Unfortunately, however, this type of scheme suffers from its piecemeal application. Since the plan does not provide a guaranteed minimum income which is at least equal to subsistence level, it can only be used as a separate part of a still complicated social security system, and Lee's idea of replacing only one part of the existing arrangements is an example of this. The opportunity to reap further economies of administration is thus neglected. It is for this reason, of course, that the scheme is able to apply marginal rates of tax which are much less than the rates operative under existing social security schemes. If the scheme is expanded to replace a larger part of the social security system, the negative tax payment would have to be established at a higher level and therefore the reduction in marginal tax rates would be much less. Proponents of the scheme can presumably turn this argument upon its head by claiming that the benefits from a subsistence guarantee scheme (for example, a social dividend variant) are offset by the high marginal tax rates and resultant disincentives.

The tax credits scheme

Interest in the Friedman type of plan has been sustained into the 1970s, and some form of negative income tax along similar lines would have been introduced into the United Kingdom if the Conservative Party had not lost the general election in 1974. The basis of the Conservative plan was fully outlined in a Green Paper published in 1972.[10] As a set of proposals for a negative tax plan by a government in power, this was an important publication. Once again, a major aim was to help low-income groups who do not gain the full benefit from tax allowances. The scheme would have granted a minimum income coverage to approximately 90 per cent of the British population, including National Insurance beneficiaries (old, unemployed, sick and other categories) and all those earning in excess of 25 per cent of national average earnings (in 1972, this average was approximately £32 per week).[11] Existing arrangements to be replaced by the scheme included family allowances, family income supplement and the main personal tax allowances. These arrangements would give way to a system of weekly tax credits payable to all covered by the new scheme – a feature which makes this plan a variant of the social dividend approach. Administration of the scheme was to be along the lines of existing tax and social security arrangements in that the tax credit would be paid to the individual by his employer (an extension of the PAYE system), who would, in turn account for such payments in his final returns to the Inland Revenue. Anyone receiving sickness or unemployment benefit for a period of six weeks or more would have his 'credit card' transferred from employer to social security office so that payment of credits might continue.

As an income maintenance scheme, this plan could have been very simple indeed, and one to be readily understood by the participants. Representing credits by C, earned income by Y^e and tax rate by t, then if $C > tY^e$, the tax unit would be a net beneficiary, and if $C < tY^e$, the tax unit would be a net contributor. As an illustration, consider a two-child family in which the husband is the sole earner, earning £25 per week. Tax credits are £6 for a married couple and £2 per child (as suggested in the 1972 proposals); and the marginal tax rate, positive and negative, is 30 per cent (also suggested in the proposals). Tax liability for this household would be £7.5 per week, to be set against an allowed credits total of £14 per week, leaving a shortfall of £6.5 per week to be paid through the employer. Thus income net of all taxes and transfers would be £31.5 per week for this particular tax unit.

By referring to the negative tax formula used earlier in our discussions, we readily see how the above system acknowledges the ability-to-pay principle in giving more favourable treatment to larger families. The formula $Y^g/t = R$ yields break-even levels of £20 for a childless couple, £33.33 for a family comprising two adults and two children – this unit would receive the value of average earnings for 1972; and £46.66 for a four-child family. Figure 11.5 shows the net income path that would be followed by these three cases, assuming market earnings to be the sole alternative source of income.

The immediate attraction of the tax credits proposal for the policy-maker is the administrative simplicity of the scheme. Adopting a single rate of tax for most taxpayers, and maintaining this rate in both the positive and negative payments part of the plan, means that liability is easily calculated and understood by the participants. Unfortunately, the scheme does not permit the full economies of scale in administration of a comprehensive social dividend plan because separate social security arrangements must be maintained to cater for the needs of the 10 per cent of the population not covered by the scheme and those taxpayers who need a further supplement to their income. This latter requirement results from the fact that the minimum income guarantee is not (and was not intended to be by the Green Paper) a subsistence guarantee. In this sense, the proposal is less radical than it appears at first sight.

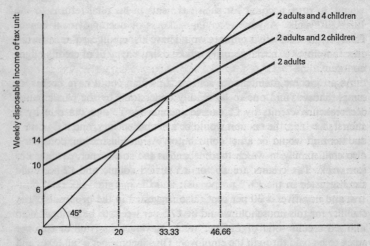

Figure 11.5.

A major advantage of this type of scheme is that the take-up problem is reduced and immediate beneficiaries would include those families eligible for family income supplement who do not claim it and those retirement pensioners who do not take up supplementary benefit despite their eligibility. Again, this advantage is somewhat qualified by the fact that take-up may remain a problem among those not covered by the scheme and requiring further income assistance to supplement their income guarantee. Related to these problems is the further observation that any reduction in disincentives, resulting from the reduced marginal rate of tax, may not apply to those who are dependent on the supplementary (means-tested) arrangements where high rates of tax at the margin may still operate.

As a step towards a general overhaul of the income tax system, the tax credits scheme would adopt a more comprehensive tax base since social security benefits would be included. But whether the overall scheme would lead to improvements is difficult to judge as the published proposals did not pay as much attention to the problems of financing the scheme as they did to the operation of the tax credits. This question is also important in the context of who benefits from the scheme. As Atkinson has shown, the extent to which any group would benefit from tax credits must depend on the method of finance which is chosen.[12]

Social dividends

The concern over an 'adequate' minimum income guarantee is a real one. If we are to minimize most of the thorny problems mentioned so far – providing access to a subsistence minimum; low take-up; poverty through low earnings; bureaucratic administration, among others – it seems that we must work towards a unified system which is sufficiently comprehensive to give an income guarantee which provides at least subsistence living and supplants most, if not all, of the separate income maintenance arrangements which seem to have decorated the plans discussed so far. The likeliest contender to fit this bill seems to be some form of social dividend scheme which produces (at least) a basic subsistence minimum.

A stepping-stone in this direction is suggested by the 'reverse income tax' scheme advanced by the Institute of Economic Affairs (IEA).[13] This scheme takes its major aim to be the provision of a minimum income guarantee – at least equal to supplementary benefit level – to everyone. It differs from the other schemes discussed so far in that no one receives net benefit when income from alternative sources is greater than the basic minimum. In other words, those tax units with earnings less than the basic minimum would receive an income subsidy equal to 100 per cent of the deficiency, while those with earnings above the minimum would pay proportional tax on those earnings, the tax rate being determined to yield the necessary finance for subsidizing incomes below the minimum. The drawback should be apparent: with a marginal rate of tax of 100 per cent operating on incomes below the minimum, the 'poverty trap' remains.

The alternative to the IEA scheme which would still fit our specification might therefore be some form of social dividend along the lines outlined earlier.[14] Again, the subsistence guarantee would be provided for all, but the break-even level of income would lie above this – tax units could continue to benefit when earned income rises, as we saw in Figure 11.3. But if this type of scheme is so attractive, why has there been a reluctance by government to implement such an idea? The answer would seem to lie in the cost of the scheme. A recent estimate by Professor James Meade[15] suggests a standard rate of tax of 53 per cent to finance what he labels the 'unmodified' social dividend. However, in the same publication, Meade proposes a 'modified' social dividend which might offer more hope.[16] The modification combines the social dividend payment with a lump-sum tax of 100 per cent on the first slice of earnings, this first slice being less than the social dividend. This so-called 'flat-rate levy' means that, while everyone is guaranteed the basic minimum living standard, those tax units with income in excess of this pay back some of their dividend because of the levy, the remaining finance for the social dividend being raised by a proportional tax on all earnings net of the flat-rate levy. In Meade's estimation, this would significantly reduce the cost of the social dividend scheme to the middle-income taxpayer, but would nevertheless require a standard rate of income tax of 43 per cent, which is much higher than taxpayers are currently facing in the United Kingdom.

These ideas are developed further in the report prepared by the committee chaired by Professor Meade and sponsored by the Institute for Fiscal Studies.[17] In particular, modification to the social dividend concept is offered in the guise of a 'two-tier social dividend' which attempts to relate payments to market status. This relationship is established through a scheme which offers two levels of benefit: first, a lower, unconditional, rate paid to all families regardless of needs or unemployment situation; and secondly, a higher, conditional rate paid only to those who are prevented from earning a full-time wage through old age, involuntary unemployment, sickness and so on. To take a simple example of such a scheme, assume a conditional rate of 40 per cent and an unconditional rate of 20 per cent, and suppose that one third of the population receives conditional benefit. Further, assume that a tax rate of 15 per cent is required to finance other public expenditure. Thus, total cost of the scheme is $33\frac{1}{3}$ per cent of 40 per cent, *plus* $66\frac{2}{3}$ per cent of 20 per cent, *plus* 15 per cent, equals a required tax revenue of 42 per cent of total income. Any individual out of work receives the full (conditional) social dividend of 40 per cent of average income, but if he is in work he retains only 58 per cent of his earnings. Such a scheme is preferred to the modified social dividend plan since it avoids the severe marginal disincentive effects at the lower end of the income scale. However, such a plan could prove to be a disincentive to entering the labour force since a conditional credit is offered and, the lower the level of potential earnings, the greater the disincentive. This problem is similar to the one facing the development of an unemployment benefit scheme along Beveridge lines.

Concluding Remarks

Where does the above survey leave us? The existing social security system in the United Kingdom is unnecessarily cumbersome and relies too heavily on unpopular means tests since several of the benefit schemes have failed to maintain the income standards recommended by Beveridge. To return to the Beveridge principle would represent an improvement in terms of benefit standards, but it would not do enough for a rationalization of the payments system.

Nevertheless, such an idea has found favour with some writers on income maintenance, including Atkinson and members of the Meade committee.[18] The machinery for the tax/transfer mechanism to work is already in operation, and the Beveridge principles, if adhered to, could protect against poverty if additional arrangements were made to protect low earners. Needless to say, the burden on taxpayers financing these principles would increase, but probably less so than in the case of a (more generous) social dividend proposal.

Of all the negative tax types of plan, the social dividend would seem to offer most hope in terms of streamlining administration while guaranteeing 'adequate' minimum standards. Unfortunately, such a plan might involve high marginal rates of tax: on the poor as they attempt to supplement state income by market earnings; and on the rich so as to finance income transfers to the poor. Therefore we seem to return to a more basic question: what sort of society do we want? It would seem that any solution must involve a trade-off between objectives – either total costs are kept low and tax rates high, or tax rates are lowered at the expense of an increase in total costs. We must discover the degree of income equality which is politically acceptable besides being economically feasible. Neoclassical (neutral) economic man is unlikely to provide the answer to this question. But neither can we rely upon the 'other regarding' principle as being the norm. The interdependent utility functions assumed in an earlier chapter permitted a Pareto optimal redistribution of income, but only because we assumed that the benefits to givers outweighed the costs. The social dividend redistribution requires a degree of benevolence in terms of both monetary contributions and in attitudes towards defining real income to include leisure which has not as yet been evidenced by a majority of voters in the United Kingdom.

12. Women in the Mixed Economy

In earlier chapters on income distribution and poverty, there were references to some problem areas which concerned women in relation to both their position in the labour market and in the home. The role of women as wives and mothers is an essential aspect of any study concerned with the social and economic development of a society. But the history of women in the developed world is also one of labour undertaken outside the domestic environment. The case for devoting a whole chapter to such a development is two-fold: first, the implications for family formation and the rearing of children; and secondly, the equity of the treatment given to females by the labour market. The past fifteen years have seen a groundswell of female dissatisfaction grow into a movement which has been instrumental in the formation of a welter of legislation designed to protect the female worker and, to a lesser extent, her position as wife and mother. In a study of how economics can contribute to an understanding of social problems, the problems associated with women cannot be ignored. The following survey attempts to cover most of the points at issue by splitting into three sections: women at home (marriage and children); women in the market-place (wages and opportunities relative to those of men); and women and taxation.

Women at Home

Throughout most of its historical development, microeconomic theory has distinguished between households and firms in terms of the ends they seek – households consume and firms produce. Within the model of the household, the role of women is relegated to that of other household members – as a mere agent of consumption. Indeed, all individuals within the household surrender their identity to that of some aggregate: *household* consumption, as desired and exhibited through a *household* preference function, set against the constraint of *household* disposable income. The microeconomics of household decision-making has concentrated for the most part on predicting the consumption patterns likely to emerge from various scenarios of this type.

Household production and children

But even a casual observation of the real world suggests that households produce as well as consume. Furthermore, viewing the household purely as a consumption unit does not answer all the questions surrounding consumption patterns, and in particular does little to explain the allocation among household activities of that most precious of resources – time. Without considering time allocation, it proves difficult to fully explain such things as fertility patterns among the different income groups or rates of female participation in labour markets. One might push the point even further to observe that viewing the household as no more than a consumption unit renders several of the arguments advanced by feminists to be nothing except an outcome of clashes in tastes. In the case of children in particular, there must be several factors at work determining the outcome of choices since in many cases, if not in most, the number of children, the timing of their births and the quality of their upbringing result from joint decisions arrived at between two parents.

The model which has done most to shed light upon the conceptual nature of household decision-making is that advanced by Gary Becker of the University of Chicago. In a seminal paper, Becker was able to derive a household production function, using time as a main independent variable, to predict household reactions to changes in the market prices of both goods and labour services.[1] In a later extension of the model, Becker was to develop a theory of marriage and family formation.[2]

The Becker analysis emphasises an important observation usually overlooked in the conventional approach to consumer behaviour: that households often do not consume at the exact moment of purchase. While there are several occasions when 'purchase' and 'consumption' are virtually synonymous – for example, ice-cream on a hot day, restaurant meals, or theatre visits – there are many others when household purchases are undertaken with a view to consumption at a later date, after the items so acquired have been processed in some way. In other words, market goods and services become inputs into a process, a production function, which produces some 'final' commodity. Utility or satisfaction to the household remains a function of consuming goods and services, but of final commodities and not market goods.

Using Z for final commodities, $t_{1 \ldots n}$ for different kinds of time, $x_{1 \ldots n}$ for market goods and services and X for other variables, we can represent the household utility function (U) as:

$$U = U(Z_{1 \ldots n}) \tag{1}$$

and the production function determining any quantity of Z_i as:

$$Z_i = f_i(x_1 \ldots {}_n; t_1 \ldots {}_n; X) \tag{2}$$

The constraints operating upon this production function are already suggested by the inputs: household money income is matched against the market prices $(p_1 \ldots {}_n)$ of $x_1 \ldots {}_n$ and the prices of household time. Thus it is possible to write:

$$Y^m = \sum_{i=1}^{n} p_i x_i \tag{3}$$

which equates money income to money expenditures on market goods and services. Total time available, T, may be divided between market work, t_w, and other pursuits, $t_1 \ldots {}_n$. Any time not spent at work (including time spent sleeping) is treated as an input into the production of some final commodity. Hence:

$$T = \sum_{i=1}^{n} t_i + t_w \tag{4}$$

Time spent at market work is transformed into money returns through the market wage rate, w, and combines with other sources of money income, such as rents, dividends or interest, to make up total household money income:

$$Y^m = w \cdot t_w + V = \sum_{i=1}^{n} p_i x_i \tag{5}$$

Thus (5) summarizes all the constraints operating upon the household's choices of market purchase – the amount of potential expenditure on market goods and services is limited by the sum of the money value of time spent at work and the total money value of other forms of income. If the value of time devoted to collecting and processing goods bought in the market place is added now to the monetary constraints summarized in (5), an expression can be found to represent final or 'full' income, Y^f. This value of time is a shadow price measured by the opportunity cost of market work time forgone at the margin – the wage rate. The final expression is:

$$Y^f = \sum_{i=1}^{n} p_i x_i + \sum_{i=1}^{n} w \cdot t_w = w \cdot tw + V \tag{6}$$

Expression (6) summarizes some of the points made earlier – final income is 'spent' partly on market goods and services and partly on time devoted to household production (financed by forgone earnings).[3] By separating the goods and time components, the expression indicates also some of the likely trade-offs in household decision-making. For example, an increase in the relative price of Z_1 would reduce the amount of it consumed by the household, and if the increased cost of Z_1 results from a rise in the wage rate, then a relatively higher proportion of the increase would fall on those final goods which rely heavily on time inputs into the production function. Indeed, the Becker analysis can go further than this to suggest that an increase in the wage rate, compensated by a decline in property income, would not affect total household opportunities but would produce two substitution effects: goods would be substituted for time in the production of final commodities, and goods-intensive commodities would be substituted for time-intensive commodities in consumption.

The above predictions offer a variation on the alternative that a rise in the wage rate induces a substitution effect towards work and away from 'leisure'. Becker's analysis shows how the rise in the wage rate leads to trade-offs within the household's patterns of production and consumption. It would seem, therefore, that Becker's framework can be linked with that of Lancaster on goods characteristics.[4] As wages rise and the household switches into goods-intensive commodities and away from time-intensive ones, the household will be switching simultaneously from one set of commodity characteristics to another. Taking the example of a dinner, the household might trade a characteristic like 'flavour' or 'texture', to be found in, say, fresh meat and vegetables, for one like 'convenience', to be found in prepackaged or frozen foods. This switch results not from any change in the relative prices of characteristics, but from a change in tastes induced by the alteration in time costs: other things being equal, a rise in wages makes 'convenience' relatively more attractive than, say, 'flavour'.

For present purposes, however, the more interesting predictions concern the relationship between male and female roles within marriage[5] and the important influences upon family formation. At the general level, the theory would seem to predict that a rise in the male wage rate,[6] other things (including the market rate for female labour) remaining unchanged, will induce both single male households and marital households in which each spouse engages in market work to increase production and consumption of goods-intensive final commodities. In households where only the husband is gainfully employed, such a switch will be less obvious since female time, now relatively cheaper, will be substituted for male time. Where no substitution is possible – where spouses have very different household skills – an increase in goods-intensive commodity consumption will be observed.

At more specific levels, the Becker analysis has important consequences for the study of family formation. A household utility function, at least to the extent that it is also a parental utility function, will include among the independent variables a set of commodities relating to 'child services', defined to cover both the quantity and the quality of children within the household. Children demand both goods and time, requiring an allocation of these inputs between child services and other goods. Two points to bear in mind from the start are that children are relatively time-intensive in their early years, becoming more goods-intensive with age, and they have traditionally been more demanding of the wife's time than the husband's. Hence the importance of the implication of the basic model: if the husband's wage rate rises relative to other 'leisure' opportunity costs, alternative inputs, including the wife's time, will be substituted for his time in the production of final commodities, including child services.[7]

Clearly, the Becker analysis offers many insights into the problems of choice for women in relation to the choice between market and home, number of children and so on. The model's predictions have to be fully tested yet for the United Kingdom, but several empirical studies have been undertaken in the United States and elsewhere, mainly by economists of the Chicago persuasion.[8] The overriding questions to be answered relate to a world of increasing educational and job opportunities for both men and women. Overall, the impact of rising real incomes upon household or family formation, as in so many choice decisions, depends upon the relative strengths of income and substitution effects. Higher parental earnings increase *total* household consumption opportunities while they also invoke a substitution effect away from time-intensive child services through the increased opportunity cost of rearing children. Some evidence that the substitution effect is the stronger of these two forces (in the United States) has been offered by Willis from the tests of a model which depicts three main dependent variables: quantity of children; quality of the same; and other sources of household utility.[9]

But the effects of child-rearing on women's use of time and goods is perhaps more interesting from the present point of view. The fact that child-rearing is indeed relatively intensive in mothers' time is reflected in several studies (for various countries) which have found evidence of a negative association between the wife's market wage-rate and the number of children in the family.[10] Equally significant is the relation between *opportunities* for higher earnings and the consumption of child services. In this respect education becomes important since it not only influences the relative wage rates of spouses but also alters the relative prices of other household inputs and permits the income effect to be realized in the *quality* of children. Education raises the market potential of parents, changes their relative preferences among quality and quantity of children and other sources of utility, and also lowers the price of quality relatively to quantity.[11]

However, the empirical tests of the relationships between parental education and consumption of child services are not unambiguously conclusive. Certainly the link between wife's education and quantity of children is clear cut – empirical studies bear out the basic model's prediction of a negative relationship between the two. But the relationship between number of children and husband's education is not so definite. Gardner has found for the United States (rural families in North Carolina) that both the husband's wage rate and education are negatively related to family size,[12] while for the same country (national sample) Michael finds that, although husband's education is generally negatively related with quantity of children, the effect is smaller in magnitude and more erratic than the relationship between quantity and wife's education.[13] Ben-Porath's evidence (pertaining to Israel) suggests that the relationship between husband's education and number of children is ambiguous,[14] while Hashimoto (for Japan) finds that both male earnings and education have a *positive* effect but are less significant relative to female variables.[15]

More difficult to define and less rigorously tested to date are the links between parental education and the quality of child services. However, a model advanced by Becker and Lewis suggests that education can increase the efficiency with which quality in children can be produced since there is a positive relationship between the shadow price of the *quantity* and the level of quality of child services, and also a positive relationship between the shadow price of the *quality* of children and the quantity of child services.[16] Furthermore, an empirical test by De Tray lends support to this hypothesis in the finding that an increase in female education raises the efficiency with which child quality can be produced.[17]

Clearly the Chicago model makes some fascinating predictions, some of which appear to be supported by empirical findings, particularly in the work of American economists. So far as the United Kingdom is concerned, the model has not been tested rigorously. There are on the surface some observations which advise caution rather than an unqualified acceptance of the Chicago predictions. For example, over most of the post-war period, neither female earnings nor female job opportunities have risen relatively to those of men, yet the same period has seen a very significant increase in the number of married women in market employment.

One possible explanation of this, not allowed for in the Chicago model, is the influence of tastes. The search for a more varied lifestyle, possibly fuelled by the dictates of fashion, may have induced a distaste for housework. Additionally, changes in tastes could explain any positive associations between education and market work, and negative associations between education and number of children – as women have consumed more education, so domestic work has been downgraded in terms of 'net advantages'. Some evidence to support these possibilities is offered by a Ministry of Labour survey undertaken in the mid 1960s.[18] This survey covered a national sample of 10,000 households, and tried to contact all women between the ages of 16 and 64 (inclusive) within these households. On the question of the attractions of market employment, the survey found that, while the financial attraction was the most frequently named, it accounted for less than half the total of attractions named.[19] Furthermore, the small number of students covered by the survey were more likely to name non-financial attractions (to escape boredom, to have independence, to use skills or qualifications).[20] The survey found also that working married women

were more likely than others to mention the attraction of dispelling boredom. Non-manual workers were more likely than manual workers to give this answer (31 per cent compared with 24 per cent). Younger non-working women were less preoccupied with the financial attractions and more concerned with the 'social' attractions than were older workers.[21]

Finally, working mothers were keen to rationalize their choice of market employment in terms of wider benefits to their children:

An overwhelming majority of working mothers believed their children benefited through their mothers going out to work: they emphasized material benefits but also referred to greater independence and improved mother-child relationships.[22]

There is also room for some doubt about the substitution of quality for quantity in the production and consumption of child-services. The post-war demographic pattern does not seem to fit neatly into the Becker hypothesis. For example, marital fertility rose between 1955 and 1965 and has fallen since that time. The overall pattern which has emerged is one of couples having fewer children at longer intervals than was the case prior to, say, 1955. However, within this general pattern lies the interesting fact that the wives of non-manual workers, and especially the wives of the upper income groups, have shown higher fertility. Comparing wives of similar age and married for the same length of time (to avoid the difficulties inherent in comparing different age structures – different career and recruitment patterns, etc.), there is evidence of just such a pattern for 1956. For example, Noble has found: farmers' wives married later than the wives of agricultural workers, but had larger families after five years of marriage; and among the middle-class groups, families were largest among the independent professionals (group 3) – larger than most manual workers' families; while junior non-manual workers (group 6) had the smallest families of all.[23] Further, according to Noble, 'studies of anticipated family size suggest that this pattern persisted at least until the later 1960s'.[24] He concludes that,

fertility is neither a simple function of prosperity and poverty nor a direct product of market situation. Undeniably these factors constrain people's lives, but the general attitudes and values that each particular couple have also entered into their family planning decisions.[25]

To underline attitudes is to stress an important variable which is largely ignored by the Chicago school. It might be said also that the costs and/or the efficiency of contraceptive techniques has also been underplayed. Improved birth-control technology, cheaply available, has increased the range of choices open to all social classes, but particularly the lower income groups. This newly found ability among manual workers to control family size must surely have lessened the strength of the income effect relative to that of the substitution effect.

Marriage

At the heart of such questions as to what determines the attitudes of spouses to work and leisure and household choices of the quantity and quality of children is the reason why people marry. Finding an answer to this question is more than a theoretical challenge – it is essential to the formulation of suitable policies to protect the incomes of families in a way compatible with the wants of household members and the efficient rearing of children. An anthropological and somewhat descriptive approach to the study of marriage has long been advanced by sociologists, but in terms of the wider economic and social questions raised in this chapter, the basic question of why people marry is more important and remains unanswered by the anthropological approach. Rather, there may be more hope for an answer provided in Becker's extension of his own model of time allocation, combined with the neo-classical trade model to the analysis of a 'marriage market' in which participants form associations to their mutual gain on the basis of comparative advantage.[26] Marital partners are assumed to maximize utility from 'final' commodities produced within the household itself, subject to the constraints imposed by a constant returns-to-scale production function in which the main inputs are market commodities and the time of household members. Within this framework, gains from trade accrue from the production of own children since, even with constant returns to scale, the time inputs of spouses are not perfect substitutes, either for each other or for market goods. In other words, small-scale (single-person) replication of the optimal (marital) household is not possible. The potential gains from trade are at a maximum in an association between two individuals with similar tastes but different endowments of skills.

The implications of the neoclassical model of marriage are too numerous to be discussed in detail here. They range from the strength and direction of association between personal traits; the frequency and incidence of divorce, in relation to the costs both of acquiring information before marriage and of a legal termination of the marriage; and the rationale behind different marital systems – monogamy results from diminishing returns to adding spouses to the household while polygamy occurs when there are surplus females or when females differ in productivity. Such implications should provide an impetus to essential future research into many of the problems raised in this chapter.

Research work, based on the marriage model, has already commenced in the United States. For example, some aspects of Becker's model have been supported by Frieden, whose test of the US marriage market finds that the proportion of females who are married is positively related to the ratio of the sexes; that there is some evidence of the incidence of marriage rising as divorce becomes easier; and that, taking age factors into account, there is a suggestion that the elasticity of marriage with respect to the cost of divorce declines monotonically with age.[27] On the gains from marriage, there has been an interesting study by Benham which seems to lend support to some of the arguments advanced by feminists and which is relevant to the suggestion of a 'housewife's wage' (discussed later in this chapter). Benham assumes that the effective stock of human capital for each partner in a marriage is a positive function of the individual stock of human capital of each spouse within the household, and the model is used to examine the relationship between the market productivity of the husband and both spouses' capital stock.[28] The study produces results apparently consistent with the likelihood that the labour market benefits for men are associated with their marrying well-educated women. Overall, a wife's education is found to provide benefits to the family beyond the increments to her own earnings, and hence both the private and the social returns to women's education may be higher than is generally believed.

Women in the Labour Market

One striking feature of the post-war labour market has been the increasing importance of women as a source of labour. A major feature within this trend has been the growth in the number of *married* women in market employment.[29] Table 12.1 presents the broad picture for the

Table 12.1. Female Composition of the Labour Force, G.B. 1950–86

Year	Females as Percentage of Total Labour Force	Married Females as Percentage of Female Labour Force
1951	31	39
1961	32	51
1971	37	63
1976	39	67
1986 (1975-based projection)	40	69

SOURCE: CSO, *Social Trends*, 1977, Table 5.2, p. 81. (The figures in the table have been rounded up to the nearest percentage point.)

two and a half decades after 1950, and includes a projection for the mid 1980s. It shows a steady increase in the proportion of females in the labour force over the post-war period, from 31 per cent in 1951 to almost 40 per cent by the middle of the 1970s. According to the 1975-based projection, this trend will slow down somewhat in the 1980s, though the proportion will continue to rise. In terms of the proportion of married women in the female labour force, however, the increase is quite spectacular, as reflected in a jump of some 30 percentage points between 1951 and 1976, from 39 per cent to 67 per cent. This latter increase is also reflected in the participation rates for married women: 49 per cent of all married women were employed in the market-place in 1976, compared with only 22 per cent in 1951 (and the 1975-based projection for 1986 is a figure of 55 per cent).[30]

The needs of the British economy throughout the Second World War were responsible for many women gaining their first experience of employment outside the household, and the continuing demand for female labour during the post-war reconstruction helped to establish market work as a natural alternative to housework for women. Thus the inside story of this pattern, as illustrated by Table 12.1, is an interesting one since it involves both demand and supply factors. Particularly significant is the possible influence of tastes. While there has been a longstanding assumption that men will operate as 'breadwinners', the idea of the market as a real alternative to the home for female job-seekers is a comparatively recent one. The issues raised by this alternative have united feminists on the question of the role of woman as mother, wife and worker, and on the question of the methods of child care sanctioned and encouraged by society. Such questions inevitably provoke further debate about the role of income maintenance programmes, personal income taxation and related topics, all discussed at various points in the present study.

Of the many issues raised by the increased participation of females in the labour force, perhaps those which have created most debate have concerned equal pay and discrimination. The Equal Pay Act of 1970, the Sex Discrimination Act of 1975 and the Employment Protection Act of 1975 are important landmarks in the history of the struggle for women's rights and were introduced to combat a situation which, it was believed, would not be resolved at a speed to satisfy the feminist lobby if left to normal social and economic forces.

One of the major factors leading to the Equal Pay Act was that, over the first two and a half decades following the Second World War, the increased reliance by the British economy upon female labour was not being paralleled by an increasing share for females in either the financial rewards of the labour market or the job opportunities offered by that market. The relative distribution of earnings between the sexes for manual workers is shown in Table 12.2.[31] According to these figures, prior to the 1970s women's increasing participation in the labour market was not yielding commensurate shares in labour rewards. But it would be naïve to conclude immediately that this was only a consequence of sex discrimination. To date, deficiencies of data have precluded detailed investigations of the female labour market in the United Kingdom, and evidence from the United States does not provide unambiguous results. Moreover, microeconomic principles permit several explanations of the male/female wage differential, and often the various factors operate together. It proves difficult to differentiate deliberate sexist-motivated discrimination from neutral, objective attempts to maximize profits by offering different wages to men and women, and supply-side influences may be at least partly responsible for the earnings differential which presents serious obstacles to efforts to achieve equality by legislative measures.

Table 12.2. Relative shares (earnings and hours) of female workers 1950–77 (manual earnings)

Year	Women's earnings (weekly) as percentage of men's	Women's earnings (hourly) as percentage of men's	Women's hours as percentage of men's
1950	55	62	88
1960	51	60	84
1970	50	61	83
1977	61	72	86

SOURCE: Figures for 1950 to 1970 from *Equal Pay*, First Report on the Implementation of the Equal Pay Act 1970, Tables C and F. The 1977 figures are calculated from data given in *New Earnings Survey*, 1977.

Broadly, there are as many as five possible separate explanations for a wide divergence between male and female earnings: (a) women are less capable than men in doing certain types of job; (b) the labour market is monopsonistic, to the detriment of female workers; (c) employers discriminate against women because they have a preference for male employees; (d) investment in females is less profitable for employers than investment in males; and (e) women under-invest in their own labour market skills.

The first argument, that women are naturally inferior to men in the exercise of certain abilities, is not particularly contentious. It is true that the range of jobs which women could undertake, given their physical and mental stamina, is probably larger than the labour market makes available to them, probably as a reflection of society's conceptions and norms. Women do tote guns to the battlefield and drive heavy goods lorries and so on in several countries. On the other hand, it may well be true that 'natural' factors either preclude women from certain jobs or that pay based on productivity will be lower for women than for men doing the same job in certain instances. After surveying the available evidence on this point, Phelps-Brown concludes that 'in many employments there are objective reasons for the work of women being of lower net value than that of men; and employers do estimate such net value and take it into account'.[32] The observation that certain occupations will lie always beyond the grasp of most females was acknowledged also in the United Kingdom by the White Paper, *Equality for Women*;[33] and it is probably true to say that even the most ardent feminist would accept this as being a fact of life, although she (or he) might disagree strongly about the extent of 'natural' preclusion. Earnings differentials which result from a comparative advantage based on sex are not at the heart of the debate over discrimination in the labour market.

A second explanation of male/female differentials concerns monopsony in the labour market. Facing an upward-sloping supply curve of labour, the monopsonist must offer higher wages to attract new labour and must pay the higher rates to his existing labour force. Thus, if women, for whatever reason, offer to work at lower rates of pay than men, profit-maximizing employers will hire more women than men, but at lower rates of pay. Such a possibility raises some thorny normative problems. For example, if employers do behave in this way, the resulting exploitation of women does not stem from a sexist viewpoint but is 'non-deliberate'[34] in the sense that it results from profit-maximizing behaviour. Consequently, any legislation which forces employers to pay women the same rates as men for the same employment penalizes employers for following the profit motive. To distinguish between efficiency and equity in this context requires a full investigation of the reasons for women offering to work at lower rates than men, and/or the reasons why the range of female occupational opportunities should be narrower than that for men.

Unfortunately, there is no clear evidence about the extent of monopsony in the market for female labour in the United Kingdom. However, there does appear to be an indication that monopsony is not a feature of the UK scene from the structure of 'concentrated' manufacturing industry where females have been distributed in approximately the same way as men.[35] As noted in Chapter 9, the major employer of women is the service sector, where small enterprises predominate. In this sector, wages of all employees are kept relatively low by several forces: market competition, declining demand for final products and prohibitive costs of organizing labour into unions and associations.

The most provocative explanation of the differential treatment of female workers is that it reflects deliberate, or 'pure', discrimination. According to this viewpoint, the demand side of the labour market is prepared to exercise a trade-off between profits and the employment of female labour. This trade-off is compatible with maximizing behaviour since the employer's utility function includes a discrimination argument. Such is the basis of the seminal model of discrimination (racial), advanced by Becker[36] and extended by Arrow,[37] which predicts that, in equilibrium, males are paid more than equally productive females, males receiving at least the value of their marginal product.

Several empirical investigations have been undertaken, mainly in the United States, and evidence has been advanced of apparent discrimination, in terms of either wage payments to women, or women being assigned to much lower job levels than men. But two points should be borne in mind in relation to empirical studies. First, many investigations have been 'macro' in nature, relying on aggregate data across broad occupational groupings.[38] The nature of such studies makes it impossible to isolate homogeneous groups – where a large number of males and females are employed in the same occupation using the same, or very similar, skills. Furthermore, aggregating across occupational groups, or even across a given industry, does not permit the investigator to isolate the importance of on-the-job experience.[39] As pointed out by Chiplin and Sloane, 'it is only at the very lowest level of disaggregation that we can hope to isolate the pure discrimination of the sex wage differential'.[40]

Another criticism of many empirical investigations is that they adopt a 'residual' approach whereby an attempt is made to isolate supply-side differences between the sexes. In this way, a part of the female/male wage differential is 'explained', the remainder being a consequence (by assumption) of discrimination. Unfortunately, while this approach does recognize and take account of alternative causes, it does not take account of any feedback from the labour market to the household. For example, it does not take account of wage discrimination discouraging women from investing in education and training and thus contributing to the perpetuation of male/female differentials. On a broader front, the residual approach tends to ignore most of the discrimination (social, educational and so on) which moulds labour characteristics prior to entry into the labour market, nor does it take account of other social influences, such as the possibility that a lower attachment to the labour market by married women may dull their desire for job improvement.[41]

The influence of factors outside the labour market is discussed presently, but first it should be noted that researchers are aware of the obstacles facing empirical investigation. The only real attempt at a disaggregated study for the United Kingdom is that of Chiplin and Sloane,[42] in which the data base relates to a single large enterprise. Results from this study lend support to the view that at least part of the wage differential between the sexes can be explained by discrimination, and the authors go so far as to suggest that their results 'are broadly in line with comparable studies undertaken in the United States, which perhaps implies that some generalizations might be made from this particular case and that the results are not dominated by the peculiarities of the individual enterprise'.[43] However, since this study attempts to isolate discriminatory practices as a residual cause of the unequal position of female workers, it is subject to the criticisms already levelled at this approach.

Finally, there are the arguments suggested by human capital theory. From the employers' point of view, women might be perceived (rightly or wrongly) to be a higher employment risk than men because of the demands of motherhood, and hence employers may be loath to underwrite appropriate training programmes. Furthermore, social conditioning might foster under-investment by women in their own training and acquisition of skills. If such a cycle of under-investment persists, the horizon of employment opportunities for women is likely to remain very much narrower than that for men.

The fact that employers of women face lower expected benefit-cost ratios from employment than those faced by employers of men has been used to predict that women will earn lower wages than men of equal productivity in those occupations where individual wages are negotiable, and also that men will tend to be employed in those occupations where women demand wages equal to those of equally productive men. Both these predictions are made as well by the pure discrimination hypothesis, and the hiring costs argument is advanced as an alternative explanation. Such is the attempt of an often-quoted exercise undertaken by Mancke,[44] in which the predictions are formulated into testable hypotheses on the assumption that, since training outlays raise initial employment costs to a level above that of initial revenue productivity, non-discriminatory employers will be indifferent between males and females 'only if these employers expect that, on the average, women are likely to remain with the firm as long as equally productive men'.[45] On the basis of this hypothesis, it can be expected that women's employment opportunities will be highest in those jobs for which training is shortest and cheapest, and lowest where training programmes are lengthy and expensive. Only where training costs are borne by the employee will employers be indifferent between males and females.

Using data pertaining to employment opportunities for women in the United States, Mancke offers five tests of the basic hypothesis. First, looking at thirty occupations in which women accounted for more than 70 per cent of the labour force in 1960 (more than 50 per cent of the total female labour force being employed in these thirty occupations), he finds these female-dominated areas of employment to be those in which either any special skills are acquired quickly or the employee acquires skills prior to employment. Secondly, the proportion of women employed in top management jobs within large American corporations is very small. Such corporations, according to Mancke, usually offer the same starting salary to new management trainees and also put potential managers through a lengthy job-training programme. Thirdly, teaching, an occupation in which the employee acquires skills prior to employment, is an occupation in which there is no significant sex-related difference in the salaries received by male and female teachers, and women hold a far greater percentage of all teaching jobs than is predictable from their share of the total college-educated labour force. Fourthly, the fact that a woman invests in postgraduate business training – for example, the Master of Business Administration (MBA) degree – suggests to a potential employer that she anticipates a long-term attachment to the labour force. Taking the average starting salaries of men and women MBA graduates of the University of Chicago in 1970 as proxies for this test, single women's starting salaries were 94 per cent of those received by single men, while those for married women were 90 per cent of those received by married men. In both cases, the male/female differential is small and the single/married differential also bears out the basic hypothesis. Finally, in technical areas of employment where undergraduate training is of a highly specific nature which offers few alternative employments, the female/male initial salaries differential for the year 1969–70 was lower than the average differential for all college graduates of that year.

A detailed survey of the above type has not been undertaken for the United Kingdom, but from various studies broad hints emerge that some sort of payback principle could be at work in the hiring practices of certain employers, although, again, the extent of social conditioning and its influences on women's own decisions about training and gaining qualification may be able to explain better some of the patterns of female employment.

Additional support for Mancke's hypothesis must be gleaned from varying sources. The Ministry of Labour report found that, among women in the sample who had ever worked, the proportion of individual types of work for which on the job training had been achieved was only 15·3 per cent. Moreover, only one type of work in fifty had involved an apprenticeship; only one in a hundred a 'learnership'; and less than one in twenty types of work involved training lasting more than six months.[46] Looking at census data from 1951 and 1961, Pauline Pinder has found that women employees were relatively concentrated in manual occupations and were seriously under-represented in the professions, with little change occurring between the two dates. In 1951, nearly 64 per cent of all women in civil employment were occupied in manual work, and in 1961 the proportion was almost 58 per cent; while, for the same respective years, the proportions employed in the professional and managerial classes were only 14 per cent and 16 per cent.[47]

It must be said, of course, that evidence quoted on this explanation can be a double-edged sword. A low proportion of women employed in the professions and in managerial capacities may signify employers' unwillingness to underwrite training programmes for women, but it may also suggest either discrimination in occupational opportunities or promotional opportunities, or the occupational choices of women given social conditioning, marital arrangements and other factors. For example, a study by Greenhalgh,[48] using data from the General Household Survey of 1971, has found that while single women in the sample have higher qualifications than married women, they still tend to follow 'female careers' and do not seem to have gained any real foothold in industries employing large proportions of the male labour force. Further, 60 per cent of the husbands in the sample with qualifications higher than A-level have professional or managerial occupations, while the proportion for similarly qualified single women is only 16·4 per cent. Such findings would seem to conflict with Mancke's hypothesis. The one profession where females do make up the majority of the work-force is teaching, which would seem to support Mancke's views regarding 'pre-entry' training. However, there might well exist substantial 'post-entry' discrimination in that the number of senior posts held by women in the teaching profession is small in relation to the number of female teachers,[49] though this fact would also be consistent with a female disinterest in promotion, possibly because of the importance attached to domestic responsibilities.

Within some of the evidence which supports the Mancke hypothesis, there lies possible support for another view which introduces a variation on the discrimination argument: the so-called 'crowding' hypothesis. According to this view of the labour market, women are concentrated in, or crowded into, specific occupations, the resulting excess supply lowering the female marginal product and helping to push women's wages below those of men.[50] Again, however, such a feature of the labour market does not result necessarily from discrimination against the employment of women in male-dominated occupations. Rather a demand-side explanation could be akin to that of Mancke's view, already discussed, while on the supply side social factors, including family responsibilities, may encourage women to seek employment in given areas of the labour market – where training requirements are low, shift-working and part-time employment are possible and so on.

Whatever the reason for a separation of the sexes within the labour market, there has emerged a view that it presents a major obstacle to policies aimed at lowering male/female differentials since 'hiring and firing' arrangements can become institutionalized, leading to a permanent market segregation of the sexes. This view of the labour market is part of a wider concept of a 'dual labour market', divided into a primary sector – high skills, high wages – and a secondary sector – low skills, low wages. Dualism is self-perpetuating, since employees enter the labour market by either one sector or the other, and once they have made their 'choice', future prospects concerning promotion, pay and so forth are ruled by conditions prevailing within the sector where they are employed. In other words, any mobility which takes place does so only within one sector and not between sectors. Clearly, such a view of the labour market parallels that of the poverty cycle discussed in an earlier chapter: job determines income, which determines lifestyle, which determines opportunities for children, which determines their future jobs. Supporters of the dualism hypothesis place female workers in the secondary sector, given their loose attachment to the labour force. According to the theory, women help to perpetuate the system by adopting the characteristics and aspirations which keep them within the secondary sector.

A very simple test for the existence of dualism is to consider the age/earnings profiles for various groups of workers, including females.[51] Given segregation in the labour market, wages will, within each 'internal' labour market, tend to be a function of age, since the promotions ladder determines prospects; and once on the ladder the worker is to some extent cushioned against market forces. However, market forces will tend to hold more sway over those workers whose attachments to the labour force are relatively loose. A reasonable expectation would be that, with age, female wages will become lower relative to male wages and will approximate more closely the state of the 'external' market for labour. The earnings profiles for both males and females according to the 1977 *New Earnings Survey* are shown in Figure 12.1 This figure demonstrates that, for 1977, the earnings profiles for females are much flatter than those for males, so suggesting that women's prospects of promotion are narrower than men's. Both the female profiles tend to flatten after the age group 25–29, while the male profiles continue to rise beyond this age, with manuals reaching a peak at 30–39 and non-manuals at 40–49.[52]

The age earnings profiles provided by the *New Earnings Survey* do not, however, offer a comprehensive test for the existence of a dual labour market. At best, they offer a descriptive summary of how earnings move with age, for each sex, within the chosen labour groupings. The actual shapes of the profiles may reflect discrimination, in terms of training offers and promotion chances, or relative education effects, or even productivity differences between the sexes. A more sophisticated test for dualism, based on data from the *General Household Survey* has been undertaken by Psacharopoulos.[53] He is unable to find evidence for dualism; on the contrary, splitting his sample into two segments –

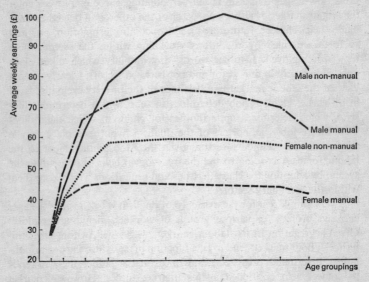

Figure 12.1. Age/earnings profiles for male and female workers (full time), April 1977.

upper occupation and earnings and lower occupation and earnings – he finds that education is a slightly better investment for workers in the lower segment than for those in the higher. The career pattern which emerges from Psacharopoulos's sample is normal: young people enter *initially* less desirable jobs and later advance into better ones – evidence of intra-generational socio-economic mobility – while he further finds evidence of considerable upward (inter-generational) mobility.

Even if the concept of a dual labour market were to be accepted as a reasonable description of reality, it does not explain how and why the segmentation occurs. But it is in the concept's favour that it does force attention on to the supply side of the female labour market, which has to date been neglected somewhat in the discrimination literature. To the extent that supply-side characteristics do further labour market segmentation, anti-discrimination legislation alone can only put women on to an equal footing with men in relation to opportunities and earnings over the longer run, since the effects of legislation (if successful) feed back to households and help to change attitudes towards women's participation in the labour market. An eminent labour economist, Sir Henry Phelps-Brown, is worth quoting on this point:

> ... it seems highly probable that the disabilities of women workers spring far more from ... two forms of discrimination, in upbringing and in opportunity, rather than ... discrimination by monopsony and according to status.[54]

To distinguish the independent variables in any labour supply function is a most difficult task and, not surprisingly, few researchers have dared to tackle the job. A brave exception in this respect is the work of Christine Greenhalgh,[55] who has emphasized the importance of marital status as a proxy for work effort and for motivation towards work, promotion and so forth. Using data derived from the *General Household Survey* of 1971, Greenhalgh has analysed average hourly earnings by marital status for women in Great Britain, trying to view male/female wage differentials, not just in terms of pure discrimination but also by taking account of sex differences in education and qualifications and the extent to which occupational choices are independent of social coercion.

Some of Greenhalgh's findings were referred to earlier. But, in the present context, other results are notable, including the observations that the 'pursuit of higher education and marriage were, to some considerable extent, alternatives',[56] and that participation rates by age 'follow patterns which are consistent with the traditional division of functions within families'.[57] The pattern of participation – a 'discontinuous labour market attachment' – is reflected also in higher unemployment rates for women aged 15–35, when compared to husbands of the same age and to older men or women. Similarly, the data on hours worked per year demonstrate discontinuity and the fact that part-time work is more normal among married women than among their husbands. As a consequence of married women's employment patterns, the mean value of average hourly earnings for married women is found to be about half that for husbands, while the value for single women is found to be about three quarters that for husbands.[58] But, in terms of human capital theory, the most interesting results follow from Greenhalgh's estimated earnings functions – regression analysis, which relates the natural logarithm of average hourly earnings to a set of variables designed to capture quality differences and other causes of differentials. What emerges from the estimates is a further endorsement of the importance of qualifications and experience as passports to better earnings, with the two variables often acting as interdependent determinants of earnings patterns. The importance of qualifications to a woman's market prospects is clearly underlined. For example, the gain in earnings per year of experience appears to be greatest for single women, with married women taking second place, but this is only true for single women with qualifications; and a bachelor's degree raises earnings by 80 per cent in all cases, with the largest differential being observed for married women: 105 per cent of mean earnings of the unqualified.

In terms of female attitudes to work, home and so on, Greenhalgh's results on average hourly earnings, based on *industry* wage differences, offer some guide. One very important finding is that there seems to be little evidence of married women having a preference against market work, but some indication of an effect from differences in the opportunities facing single and married women, the former enjoying higher actual average earnings than the latter. Unfortunately, the regression analysis does not permit determination of whether or not the cause of the opportunities differential is married women's inability to undergo further training when young children are in their care, or employers' reluctance to hire married women. However, the predicted wages for single and married women are almost equal, suggesting that 'single women, whatever their level of qualifications, are no better off than married women, in spite of their higher probability of continuous participation'.[59]

It would seem, then, that studying the hours and earnings patterns of married women *vis-à-vis* their husbands and single women gives some hints regarding attitudes towards market work and the effort that married women are prepared to put into work outside the home. Unfortunately, the hints cannot be translated into harder facts because it remains impossible to separate employer's reluctance or prejudice from married women's inability or reluctance to train, work longer hours and so forth as explanations of relatively different treatment meted out to the various groups chosen for study. Greenhalgh does seem to believe that demand-side considerations hold the trump card, since 'whereas married women are partly constrained by domestic responsibilities – which have been voluntarily contracted, they were in 1971, also substantially affected by a narrow choice of occupation and industry and by discrimination in wages to an extent suffered equally by single women'. She concludes that, on the whole, 'including the satisfaction to be derived from family life and assuming no rapid changes since 1971, ... marriage may still be the best of a rather limited set of choices facing women in Great Britain'.[60]

In relation to several of the points underlined in this section, any final comments should note that, according to Table 12.2, the overall ratio of women's wages to men's, both hourly and weekly, has risen substantially since 1970. It is tempting to conclude that demand-side determinants have been the historical culprits, and that the anti-discrimination legislation has bitten hard. However, the 1970s have also been a period of hardening feminist attitudes, with possibly a different view of the home/market trade-off emerging, fed by the experience of a generation of female workers who have come on to the labour market after gaining their education and forming many of their attitudes during the turbulent 1960s – the first five years of the 1970s saw a three-fold increase in the number of working women in the 24–9 age group. Again, there is a strong warning not to ignore supply-side considerations. Furthermore, the 1970s have been years of stringent incomes policies which have attempted to control overall wage increases but have allowed relatively larger percentage increases for lower wage-earners.

Taxing the Family

One means by which the state can influence household decisions regarding choices between market employment and housework for each spouse is through the income tax. In particular, there are three aspects of the income tax system which are likely to modify household decisions in this way: (a) the choice of the tax unit; (b) the definition of income; and (c) the method and degree of differentiation among tax units of different size.[61] The ensuing discussion maintains the assumptions that taxes levied on incomes follow the 'ability-to-pay' principle and that the revenue authority tries to uphold the criteria of equity ('equal treatment of equals') and neutrality (revenues should be raised without interfering with resource allocation as determined by private economic processes).

From a feminist viewpoint, one of the most contentious aspects of the UK income tax is its use of the marital unit wherein the incomes of spouses are aggregated and the total is treated as if it were the income of a single individual. This approach has been regularly criticized by feminists, both by the 'old' at the turn of the century and by the 'new' of the period since the 1960s, as a denial of the separate identity of a wife. On occasion, this argument has even been adopted in party political discussion papers. According to an Opposition Green Paper of 1972:

> The case against taxing a wife's separate income as part of her husband's income rests upon the demand for emancipation of the married woman. She has a claim to be treated as a person in her own right, to control her own income and to privacy in her own money matters.[62]

Despite such opinion, the case for the marital unit does not rest on a sexist premise, but on the 'ability-to-pay' principle as it relates to a cohabitory unit in which incomes are pooled and shared. Assuming that most married couples do behave as a single income and expenditure unit, the economic power of each member of such units can be seen as a function of joint, rather than separately received and used, income. Thus, following the equity principle, a married couple should be treated as a single unit for determining their ability to pay income tax. Of course, the basic argument rests on an assumption about the real world – that married couples pool and share their incomes – and it might be claimed that this proposition has not been tested properly. Such evidence as is available, however, does offer strong support to the case for a joint, marital, tax unit.

A comprehensive sample survey, undertaken in 1972 on behalf of the Law Commission by the Social Survey Division of the Office of Population Censuses and Surveys, found that the majority of marital arrangements include joint ownership of such major household assets as house, car or furniture.[63] The case of home ownership is particularly interesting, since it demonstrates that legal convenience does not necessarily imply *de facto* arrangements: 52 per cent of sample couples who were owner-occupiers had accommodation in joint names; furthermore, of the couples who had accommodation in the name of only one spouse, 87 per cent of both husbands and wives thought of the accommodation as belonging to them both. Even stronger support for a view of marriage as a sharing arrangement comes from the finding of a 'general' view that, even in the case of possessions owned by one spouse, prior to marriage, such assets become merged into the shared property of the married couple; and this opinion extended even to inheritances, a majority view holding that an inheritance by one spouse became a joint possession of the couple.[64]

Such facts of life as those suggested by the findings of this survey, together with the results of various court deliberations, have led the Law Commission to move in the direction of an explicit law of joint marital property for, at least, that most important of family assets, the matrimonial home.[65] According to the commission, existing property law,

... takes little account of the realities of family relationships. The concept of separate property does not seem apt when applied to property which is jointly used, and to a situation where there is often a mingling of assets and where restraint is necessary in the interests of the other spouse and the family.[66]

Such a view lends further support to opinions about the criteria by which the tax unit should be defined as expressed by two Royal Commissions on personal taxation.[67]

Even more difficult to resolve than the question of how to allocate marital incomes for tax purposes is how to measure them. The criteria of equity and neutrality can be satisfied only if the income definition is sufficiently broad to embrace non-monetary elements. Such components of income are those which do not carry a price tag because they have not resulted from market transactions and therefore a monetary value must somehow be imputed to them. For simplicity, such elements are referred to as 'imputed income'.

All individuals receive imputed income when they supply themselves with various services, and any tax unit enjoys imputed income when any one member renders services to that unit.[68] Failure to include this imputed income in the tax base will underestimate a unit's taxable capacity, and such miscalculation could be severe if one spouse eschews market employment. When this happens, both the equity and neutrality criteria are violated. A tax levied solely on money income will treat favourably a married couple with only one spouse earning, relative to a married couple with the same income but both spouses gainfully employed, since the imputed value of the 'nonworking' spouse's services will escape tax. In addition the exclusion of imputed elements from the tax base lowers the (post-tax) price of 'leisure' relative to that of market work.[69]

In the case of marital tax units, the main source of such income is likely to be the services of a full-time housewife. Conceptually, the full value of a wife's contribution to the tax unit is the minimum amount of income that the unit would demand in compensation for the loss of such services. But if it is decided for tax purposes to measure only those services which are marketable, then the wife's contribution to the tax unit is measured by her transfer earnings: that market rate of return at which the tax unit is indifferent between the wife remaining at home and working in the market-place. Levying tax on imputed income so measured would remove, for many marital units, the tax-induced incentive for a wife to remain at home, although to the extent that any housewife's services to the tax unit constitute an economic rent, both the neutrality and the equity criteria could still be violated.

However, at the practical level it is likely to prove impossible to impute a value to the many services rendered to a tax unit by a wife.

Transfer earnings will differ according to both geographical location and level of aggregate demand. Many wives have received no formal training in market skills; others possess obsolete skills; many have only worked on a part-time basis; housewives may be acquiring skills while engaged in domestic activities; and so on. In all these cases there are overwhelming difficulties facing any attempt to assess corresponding labour market values. Such problems preclude accurate evaluation of domestically produced services, and without some alternative compensating tax device, 'housework' enjoys an implicit subsidy.

As a compromise on some of the problems created by imputed income, revenue authorities have introduced systems of tax deductions for working wives to permit, for purposes of income tax assessment, the deduction of expenses incurred by engaging in market activities. In principle, such a deduction can re-establish tax neutrality in relation to the work/leisure choice, but, in practice, the computational difficulties almost match those which surround imputed income. Complete tax neutrality makes the impossible demand of a deductions system to fit every individual case, and the only practical possibility is consequently that of a standard deduction which offers an approximation to employment costs. Inevitably, measurement problems determine that such a deduction can be no more than an arbitrary allowance against the real costs of increased household expenditures on market goods and services which arise from the reduction in time available for domestic production. Furthermore, even if neutrality could be satisfied, any tax allowance based on an accurate computation of any costs incurred when both spouses are gainfully employed must be inequitable in relation to the treatment of single taxpayers who do not receive the benefits of a spouse's services.

The traditional method of dealing with the above problems adopted by the UK authorities, dating back to the end of the nineteenth century, has been to offer special tax treatment to working wives. In 1894, working wives in professions or vocations were granted a separate exemption or abatement of their own earned income (provided that aggregate marital income did not exceed £500 per annum). This exemption was in recognition of the extra expenses incurred by working wives, and three years later a similar special treatment was extended to wives deriving incomes from trades (provided that the wife's trade was unconnected with that of her husband). But the real foundations of the modern system were laid by a 1920 Royal Commission which recommended a special consideration for working wives where marital income was low. This recommendation included abolition of separate treatment of husband and wife,[70] but also suggested a deduction from gross income of an amount representing the extra expenditure incurred by a marital unit when the wife chooses market employment.[71] Following these recommendations, a special wife's earned income relief was introduced in 1920. Extensions to the system of reliefs awaited the Second World War and the necessity for increased participation in the labour force by both sexes. An inducement to women was offered in 1942 when the special relief was increased to the same value as that of the single personal allowance. Post-war, the system of encouraging wives to work outside the home has continued, and a wife's earned income allowance remains in operation at the present time.

The final way in which the tax system can influence domestic work/leisure decisions is by the method of differentiation among differing-sized tax units with equal net incomes.[72] Such differentiation is necessary to adjust the degree of income tax progression to the personal circumstances of all tax units. Many of the problems raised in this context were met in earlier discussions of the problem of poverty and income maintenance. Real-world tax systems exhibit a wide variety of approaches to this problem,[73] but it is possible to distinguish broadly two types of differentiation system: *unit* and *per capita*.[74]

Under a unit approach, a single individual and a married couple pay taxes at the same marginal rate if their net incomes are equal, differentiation among units of different size being achieved through exemptions. The main difficulty associated with this approach concerns the magnitude and type of exemption to be used. As was noted in the discussion on poverty, standards of minimum necessity are relative to the customs of the various income groups, and hence the discretionary components of income vary with the group's margin of wants satisfaction. In the absence of accurate and flexible standards, a unit approach must treat harshly the married couple and the family relatively to the single individual in terms of cost experience at different levels of income.

Under a *per capita* approach, the marginal tax rates for a married couple and a single person are equalized if per capita net incomes are equal. Such a system faces the difficult task of reconciling two opposing considerations: incremental income (in excess of any exemptions level) has a taxable capacity which varies directly with the size of the unit on a per capita basis, while in the upper income ranges a steadily declining percentage of income is required to maintain an 'adequate' standard of living. Inevitably, such a system will mete out relatively harsh treatment to the single individual.

In the United Kingdom, differentiation between single people and married couples with the same net income has been attempted by means of personal allowances – basically a unit approach. The problems already mentioned about this system can be seen in the historical development of the UK income tax. The first attempt to differentiate between single individuals and married couples was made in 1918 with the introduction of a wife allowance. Like the child allowance (reintroduced in 1909), the wife allowance was restricted to lower incomes on the grounds that 'dependency' as a real drain on family resources is not a problem beyond a certain level of income.[75] The Royal Commission of 1920 upheld the view that married couples have a lower taxable capacity than single persons (of equal income) and proposed a differentiation between the two in the form of an extra continuing tax exemption for married couples: not a wife allowance as such, but a higher personal allowance for a married man. A further endorsement of the principle of differentiation by personal allowances was offered by the 1954 Royal Commission, and to date the system remains operative in the United Kingdom.[76]

Given the social and economic changes of the post-war period, the continued adherence to a system which treats a wife as a dependant in order to differentiate married couples from single individuals, in terms of relative treatment under the income tax, is surprising. Apart from the untaxed imputed income enjoyed by the marital unit – and one might even accept Prest's consideration that such an item is unlikely to result in a total income per capita which is equal (after tax) to that of a single person with the same money income[77] – there are economies of scale from cohabitation. If maintenance of a given standard of living for two individuals living together costs less than twice the amount of resources required to establish this standard for two separate individuals, then the separate individual has a relatively lower taxable capacity.[78] Given the advances in household technology and the increased opportunities for bulk buying offered by the post-war market economy, such economies of cohabitation may well have increased relatively to the pre-war years.

A more serious challenge to the doctrine of differentiation by dependency allowances stems from the increased labour force participation of married women. In a world of increasing market opportunities for married women, the case for a higher personal allowance for a married man diminishes. Of course, this is not true for cases of true dependency which are the result, for example, of physical disabilities, or because there are small children to rear; but where this is not the case and a wife chooses to stay at home because she prefers to do so, a higher personal allowance merely subsidizes 'leisure'.

Indeed, it is on the question of dependency that several anomalies might be corrected as well as a feminist argument being formulated properly. The major problem, so far as society is concerned, relates to children. It would seem indisputable that children are dependants, and that mothers, at least for a short period of their children's lives, will prefer working at home to market employment. Society must decide, therefore, on what sort of home/market choices should be made available to mothers. The nature of such a decision must depend on the extent to which children confer social benefits. If children are viewed as purely private consumption goods, yielding benefits to their families and no one else, than a dependency tax allowance for children and mothers is unlikely and a system of taxing imputed income will impose a relatively heavier burden on those families with many children. But if society recognizes that its future depends upon the efficient rearing of successive generations of children, some non-market arrangements will be made to further this end.

If society does opt for a non-market arrangement, this does not require a necessary use of the income tax system. The discussion so far has raised many difficulties encountered by trying to mould the income tax to satisfy the dual criteria of equity and neutrality. A more direct and efficient way to differentiate among different-sized marital units is to offer a direct payment to the spouse who stays at home to rear children – a 'housewife's wage'.[79] Such a payment, which must be offered by the state since there is no trading agent available within the marital unit, would be made only in the case of parenthood and would not be available to the childless couple. Further, the payment could be made proportional to the number of children in the family unit subject to a maximum defined by the 'optimum' size of family.

Supposing such a scheme were adopted, the abolition of any dependant's allowance for wives could be implemented simultaneously. Thus, this combined programme would differentiate among tax units with the same market incomes in a way which does not raise the problems of a system of allowances or a *per capita* system of income tax treatment for marital units. Assuming that an 'adequate' wage for housewifery can be defined, any differences in the disposable incomes out of total earnings between marital (or family) units of different size and equal market earnings would be a reflection of the housewife's wage only.

In terms of neutrality, the proposed system removes the indirect subsidy to leisure enjoyed by the childless couple under the wife's tax allowance regime, and makes a definite, non-neutral, attempt to increase the attractions of domestic work. Where a spouse remains at home to rear small children, the household is compensated for earnings forgone. Where a childless spouse chooses to remain at home, no such compensation is forthcoming and the tax system provides no indirect subsidy to leisure.[80] Indeed, any consumption of leisure is financed by the marital unit itself. This argument may have to be qualified if no means of taxing imputed income is introduced since this would again offer an indirect subsidy to leisure consumption, though a tax allowance against the extra costs from market employment could offset this.

Finally, it must be re-emphasized that the trading agent is the state. The deal is between marital units and the rest of society. It assumes that playgroups, child-minders and the like are only partial substitutes for parental care, and that parental skills should be encouraged and subsidized. If this is a weak assumption, then the case outlined is correspondingly reduced. The discussion has also tended to assume that the spouse most likely to elect for housework will be female. This may be the likely case in a world where market opportunities for men are superior to those for women and/or maternal deprivation is believed to retard seriously the development of children. When society is convinced that efficient child rearing does not depend on a particular sex remaining at home, and the labour market opportunities for women match those for men, the arguments presented can apply equally to either parent.[81]

Conclusions

Perhaps the only clear indication to emerge from the lengthy discussion in this chapter is the need for a coordinated programme to help women fulfil simultaneously the several roles expected of them by the modern industrial society. The United Kingdom has made some important steps in this direction through a flurry of legislation during the 1970s, but, as yet, coordination of all programmes – covering the labour market, taxing the family unit and social insurance arrangements – has not been achieved. Part of the problem arises from a confusion over what 'woman's role' is actually meant to be. Clearly some women will have stronger preferences for home than for market employment, others will prefer the labour market, while others will want to combine both possibilities. Society must know the strengths of such preferences if it is to weigh them against the needs of the economy in terms of supplies of productive resources and also against social goals concerning the best means of rearing children and of maintaining harmonious lasting relationships between the sexes. Some answers are being offered by the Chicago model of marriage and family formation, but acceptance of this model has not been unqualified and it remains untested for the United Kingdom.

The safest conclusion to be reached from the welter of opinions expressed about the treatment of women in the labour market concerns the folly of being dogmatic. While there is apparent discrimination on the demand side of the market, in terms of both wages and opportunities offered, it remains unclear whether or not such discrimination is based on tastes or on expected returns from employing women, despite empirical investigations. If it *is* based on estimates of female value product coloured by prejudice which stems from women's traditional role in the household sector, then the increasingly familiar picture of the 'working woman', married or single, should lead to a change in employer attitudes over the long run. But if differentials result from women opting for the household sector and a consequent downgrading of market skills, then the future picture is less clear. To the extent that women have articulated their wants, it would appear that opportunities to choose freely between home and market is the key demand. Greenhalgh has neatly captured the broad scope of recent legislation:

... preservation of the opportunity to be either the same or different according to one's tastes requires that individuals be presented with the same range of external constraints, and this is the objective of the equal opportunity legislation in both Britain and the US.[82]

Clearly labour market arrangements can be made to further continuity of work experience for female workers. Indeed, such arrangements do exist in the United Kingdom, where, under the Employment Protection Act of 1975, 'maternity leave' permits a pregnant woman to leave work for her confinement and to return to the same job after three months, receiving nine tenths of normal pay (minus any maternity allowance received) during this period.[83] However, the payback to the employer from employing females will always depend upon the length of the period in which women intend to nurture their children fulltime. If this time period covers at least pre-school years, it is unlikely that employers will consider women and men as equivalent investment prospects, and some sort of earnings or opportunities differential may always persist. As yet it is not clear how far society is prepared to go to counteract such a possibility, given that any policy which involves preventing employers from behaving in this way penalizes profit-maximizing behaviour rather than sexism. It may well be that equitable treatment is seen to be combined with efficiency only when a new approach is adopted to social and economic policy which relies on an overview of the needs and habits of both sexes, in and out of marriage, rather than on a programme of separate pieces. If income taxation and income maintenance policies affect the relative time costs facing the sexes, and this in turn affects the roles adopted by spouses and how they behave relative to single individuals, then policy-makers should be so aware.

In a mixed economy, the interrelationship between market opportunities and social policies introduced by the state must be understood and accounted for in framing such policies.

Notes and References

Chapter 2: Normative Ground Rules

1. As developed in his classic, *The Economics of Welfare*, first published in 1920 as a revised version of his original *Wealth and Welfare* (1912).

2. L. C. Robbins, *An Essay on the Nature and Significance of Economic Science*, 2nd edn, Macmillan, London, 1935.

3. A. K. Sen, *Collective Choice and Social Welfare*, Oliver & Boyd, Edinburgh, 1970, p. 22.

4. James M. Buchanan and Craig Stubblebine, 'Externality', *Economica*, vol. 29, 1962.

5. As demonstrated in the famous Samuelson papers of the mid 1950s. See P. A. Samuelson, 'The Pure Theory of Public Expenditure', *Review of Economics and Statistics*, vol. 36, 1954; and 'A Diagrammatic Exposition of a Theory of Public Expenditure', *Review of Economics and Statistics*, 1955.

6. For a discussion of both the methodological and pragmatic problems facing cost-benefit analysis, see A. H. Williams, 'Cost-Benefit Analysis: Bastard Science? And/Or Insidious Poison in the Body Politick?', *Journal of Public Economics*, vol. 1, 1972.

7. The famous example of the 'new' Victoria Line of the London underground system is the most oft-quoted example of this danger. In an exercise undertaken to identify the full costs and benefits of the proposal, Foster and Beesley estimated that the line would not be viable if evaluated on commercial criteria – *private* costs and benefits. But on a broader calculation, accounting for social gains (reduction in congestion, time savings, etc.), benefits were found to outweigh costs. See C. D. Foster and M. E. Beesley, 'Estimating the Social Benefits of Constructing an Underground Railway in London', *Journal of the Royal Statistical Society*, vol. 126, 1963.

8. M. S. Feldstein, 'Net Social Benefit Calculation and the Public Investment Decision', *Oxford Economic Papers*, New Series, vol. 16, No. 1, pp. 114–31.

9. For a lucid and informative summary account of the avenues adopted by economists faced by the problems of a world which does not fit neatly into the paradigm of perfect competition, see A. J. Culyer, Introduction, Chapter 1 of A. J. Culyer (ed.), *Economic Policies and Social Goals*, Martin Robertson, London, 1974.

10. For the classic statement of the liberal position on all of these issues, see Milton Friedman, *Capitalism and Freedom*, University of Chicago Press, 1962. In Friedman's view, government itself is the most important source of monopoly power. See ibid., pp. 121–9.

11. Amartya Sen, 'The Impossibility of a Paretian Liberal', *Journal of Political Economy*, 1970; and 'Liberty, Unanimity and Rights', *Economica*, 1976.

12. This contrasts with Arrow's 'social welfare function' (K. J. Arrow, *Individual Values and Social Choice*, Wiley, New York, 1951), which is a collective choice rule which has a range restricted to orderings. Sen suggests a weaker requirement in 'The Impossibility of a Paretian Liberal', loc. cit., pp. 152–3. See also Sen's 'Quasi-transitivity, Rational Choice and Collective Decision', *Review of Economic Studies*, 36, No. 3, 1969, pp. 381–93.

13. Modified to 'libertarianism' in his 1976 paper.

14. See Charles K. Rowley and Alan T. Peacock, *Welfare Economics (A Liberal Restatement)*, Martin Robertson, London, 1975.

15. ibid., p. 79.

16. ibid., p. 83.

17. Charles K. Rowley, *Antitrust and Economic Efficiency*, Macmillan, London, 1973, p. 68.

18. ibid.

19. ibid.

20. See W. D. Glasgow, 'The Contradiction in Ethical Egoism', *Philosophical Studies*, vol. XIX, No. 6, 1968.

21. ibid., p. 84.

22. See K. E. Boulding, 'Notes on a Theory of Philanthropy', in F. G. Dickinson (ed.), *Philanthropy and Public Policy*, New York, 1962; and Harold H. Hochman and James D. Rodgers, 'Pareto Optimal Redistribution', *American Economic Review*, vol. 59, 1969.

23. Alternatively, β's general consumption level as measured by his income could appear in α's utility function. See Hochman and Rodgers, 'Pareto Optimal Redistribution', loc. cit.

24. E. J. Mishan, 'The Futility of Pareto Efficient Distributions', *American Economic Review*, December 1972, 62, pp. 971–6.

25. ibid., p. 972.

Chapter 3: More on Externalities

1. A. C. Pigou, *The Economics of Welfare*, 4th edn, Macmillan, London, 1932.

2. R. H. Coase, 'The Problem of Social Cost', *Journal of Law and Economics*, vol. 3, 1960.

3. See Peter A. Victor, *Economics of Pollution*, Macmillan, London, 1972, Chapter 2, for an account of this criticism as well as the diagrammatic analysis of the Coase theorem adopted in this chapter.

4. W. J. Baumol and W. E. Oates, 'The Use of Standards and Prices for Protection of the Environment', *Swedish Journal of Economics*, LXXIII, 1971, pp. 42–54. See also Chapters 10 and 11 of W. J. Baumol and W. E. Oates, *The Theory of Environmental Policy*, Prentice-Hall, Englewood Cliffs, NJ, 1975.

5. James M. Buchanan, *The Inconsistencies of the National Health Service*, IEA Occasional Paper No. 7, November 1965.

6. For example, see A. J. Culyer, *The Economics of Social Policy*, Martin Robertson, London, 1973, Chapter 6.

7. I. M. D. Little, *A Critique of Welfare Economics*, Oxford University Press, 1950.

8. See Nicholas Georgescu-Roegen, 'Choice, Expectations, and Measurability', *Quarterly Journal of Economics*, LXVIII, 1954, reprinted in N. Georgescu-Roegen, *Analytical Economics*, Harvard University Press, 1967, p. 198.

9. N. Georgescu-Roegen, 'Economic Theory and Agrarian Economics', *Oxford Economic Papers*, XII, 1960, pp. 1–40, reprinted in Georgescu-Roegen, *Analytical Economics*, pp. 360–97.

10. ibid., p. 286.

11. Mark V. Pauly, 'Efficiency in the Provision of Consumption Subsidies', *Kyklos*, vol. 23, 1970, pp. 33–57.

12. Though, as Pauly points out, he may be able to reach points to the left of P_4 if we assume that x has close substitutes. If B responds to an offer of free medical services by reducing his own purchases of preventive 'medicines' – adequate diet, personal hygiene, etc. – then, conceivably, he could consume negative amounts of the transferred commodity.

13. Cotton M. Lindsay, 'Medical Care and the Economics of Sharing', *Economica*, New Series, 1969, pp. 351–62.

14. As Lindsay himself admits. See his conclusion, ibid., p. 362.

15. A. J. Culyer, 'On the Relative Efficiency of the National Health Service', *Kyklos*, 1972, pp. 266–87.

16. For a comprehensive survey of both research already completed and problems which await empirical analysis, see Alan Williams, 'Health Service Planning', in M. T. Artis and A. R. Nobay, *Studies in Modern Economic Analysis*, Basil Blackwell, Oxford, 1977.

17. M. S. Feldstein, 'Net Social Benefit Calculation and the Public Investment Decision', *Oxford Economic Papers* New Series, vol. 16, No. 1, pp. 114–31.

18. See *Nationalized Industries: A Review of Economic and Financial Objectives*, Cmnd 3437, HMSO, London, 1967.

19. A sample of useful readings on applications of cost-benefit analysis would include: Trevor Newton, *Cost-Benefit Analysis in Administration*, Allen & Unwin, London, 1972, esp. Parts III and IV; M. G. Beesley, 'The Value of Time Spent Travelling: Some New Evidence', *Economica*, May 1965; M. Blaug, 'The Private and Social Returns on Investment in Education: Some Results for Great Britain', *Journal of Human Resources*, Summer 1967; J. D. Pole, 'Mass Radiography: A Cost-Benefit Approach', *Problems and Progress in Medical Care*, vol. 5, 1971; R. F. F. Dawson, *The Cost of Road Accidents in Great Britain*, Road Research Laboratory Report, LR79, HMSO, London, 1967; and A. D. J. Flowerdew, 'Choosing a Site for the Third London Airport: The Roskill Commission's Approach', in Richard Layard (ed.), *Cost-Benefit Analysis*, Penguin Modern Economics Readings, Penguin Books, Harmondsworth, 1972.

20. Detailed expositions of what PPB tries to do, and what success it has

met with, can be found in Charles L. Schultze, *The Politics and Economics of Public Spending*, Brookings Institution, Washington, DC, 1968; Peter Else, *Public Expenditures, Parliament and PPB*, PEP Broadsheet 522, November 1970; David Coombes, *et al.*, *The Power of the Purse*, Allen & Unwin, London, 1976; and P. K. Else and G. P. Marshall, *The Mananagement of Public Expenditure*, Policy Studies Institute, London, 1979, Ch. 7.

21. For details of the police experiment, see G. J. Wasserman, 'Planning, Programming, Budgeting in the Police Service in England and Wales', *O. and M. Bulletin*, vol. 25, No. 4, 1970.

22. Department of Education and Science, *Output Budgeting for the Department of Education and Science*, HMSO, London, 1970. See also Second Report from the Expenditure Committee, Session 1970–71, HMSO, London, July 1971, paras. 18 ff.; and the Second Memorandum by the DES to this Report, p. 91.

23. See, for example, Eighth Report from the Expenditure Committee, Session 1971–2.

24. DHSS, *Priorities for Health and Personal Social Services in England: A Consultative Document*, HMSO, London, 1976; and *Priorities in the Health and Social Services, The Way Forward*, HMSO, London, 1977.

25. Else, *Public Expenditures, Parliament and PPB*, pp. 60–67.

Chapter 4: Inequality (1): Some Conceptual Difficulties

1. Some of the problems of unequal opportunities for women are considered in the concluding chapter.

2. Or vice versa – political power being derived from economic power.

3. H. C. Simons, *Personal Income Taxation*, University of Chicago Press, 1938, p. 49.

4. *The Structure and Reform of Direct Taxation*, Report of a Committee Chaired by Professor J. E. Meade, Allen & Unwin for the Institute for Fiscal Studies, London, 1978, p. 31. Hereafter this report is referred to in the text as the 'Meade Report'.

5. For example, see A. B. Atkinson, *The Economics of Inequality*, Clarendon Press, Oxford, 1975, Chapter 3.

6. For a full summary of the characteristics of the new series, see D. Ramprakesh, 'Distribution of Income Statistics for the United Kingdom, 1972/3: Sources and Methods', *Economic Trends*, August 1975, pp. 78–96.

7. In particular, see R. M. Titmuss, *Income Distribution and Social Change*, Allen & Unwin, London, 1962. Of course, much of the criticism has been acknowledged, e.g. see Royal Commission on the Distribution of Income and Wealth, Report No. 1, *Initial Report on the Standing Reference*, HMSO, July 1975, Chapter 4.

8. A good discussion of the various indices of inequality is provided in F. A. Cowell, *Measuring Inequality*, Philip Allan, Oxford, 1977.

9. A. B. Atkinson, 'On the Measurement of Inequality', *Journal of Economic Theory*, vol. 2, 1970, pp. 244–63.

10. John Rawls, *A Theory of Justice*, Oxford University Press, 1973.

11. H. Dalton, 'The Measurement of the Inequality of Incomes', *Economic Journal*, vol. 30, 1920.

12. Atkinson's quibble might be considered of vital importance only if we are concerned about the cardinal properties of an index. For Sen, the really important characteristic of Dalton's index is its ordering property, which is quite unaffected by Atkinson's qualification. See Amartya Sen, *On Economic Inequality*, Clarendon Press, Oxford, 1973, p. 37.

13. For a more detailed numerical example, see A. B. Atkinson (ed.), *Wealth, Income and Inequality*, Penguin Modern Economics Readings, Penguin Books, Harmondsworth, 1971, Reading 3, p. 67.

14. There are also further theoretical problems to be resolved. See Sen, *On Economic Inequality*, pp. 39–76.

Chapter 5: Inequality (2): The Post-war Distribution of Incomes in the United Kingdom

1. For estimates of income distribution in pre-war Britain, see L. Soltow, 'Long-run Changes in British Income Inequality', *Economic History Review*, vol. 21, 1968.

2. Royal Commission on the Distribution of Income and Wealth (Diamond Commission).

3. Diamond Commission, Report No. 1, *Initial Report on the Standing Reference*, Cmnd 6171, HMSO, London, 1975, para. 1.

4. See Diamond Commission, Report No. 4, *Second Report on the Standing Reference*, Cmnd 6626, HMSO, London, 1976, para. 20.

5. Diamond Commission, Report No. 5, *Third Report on the Standing Reference*, Cmnd 6999, HMSO, London, 1977, Tables 1–4, Appendix F.

6. See Diamond Commission, Report No. 1, Chapter 3 and Appendix F, for detailed descriptions of the various sources.

7. See D. Ramprakesh, 'Distribution of Income Statistics for the United Kingdom, 1972/73: Sources and Methods', *Economic Trends*, August 1975, pp. 78–96.

8. Following recommendations in Report No. 1 from the Diamond Commission, the CSO has widened the income definition to try and account for this factor.

9. F. W. Paish, 'The Real Incidence of Personal Taxation', *Lloyds Bank Review*, January 1957.

10. H. F. Lydall, 'The Long-Term Trend in the Size Distribution of Income', *Journal of the Royal Statistical Society*, Series A, 122, Part 1, 1959.

11. R. J. Nicholson, 'The Distribution of Personal Income', *Lloyds Bank Review*, January 1967.

12. A. J. Walsh, 'Tax Allowances and Fiscal Policy', in P. Townsend and N. Bosanquet (eds.), *Labour and Inequality*, Fabian Society, London, 1972.

13. As underlined by Paish, 'The Real Incidence of Personal Taxation', loc. cit.

14. Diamond Commission, Report No. 1, Table 15.

15. Royal Commission on the Distribution of Income and Wealth, Back-

ground Paper No. 3: Robert Dinwiddy and Derek Reed, *The Effects of Certain Social and Demographic Changes in Income Distribution*, HMSO, London, 1977.

16. Note, however, that as a result of the educational expansion and population bulge among the 15–24 group having little impact outside the bottom income ranges, the Gini coefficient was not severely affected. See Dinwiddy and Reed, *The Effects of Certain Social and Demographic Changes in Income Distribution*, para. 278. Note also that here we see one argument for the life-cycle approach to income distribution, since many within the student age group will eventually enjoy large rewards in the labour market.

17. See ibid., para. 207. For most of their analysis, Dinwiddy and Reed derive and contrast distributions based on two different data sources: the Family Expenditure Survey and the income follow-up to the 1971 Census.

18. ibid., para. 258.

19. ibid., para. 262.

20. Lydall, 'The Long-Term Trend in the Size Distribution of Income', loc. cit.

21. Nicholson, 'The Distribution of Personal Income', loc. cit. p. 19. Nicholson calculated that, for the period 1957–63, the rates of growth of the various income components were as follows (1957 = 100): employment income, 140; self-employment income, 125; rent, dividends and interest, 142; transfers, 179.

22. Diamond Commission, Report No. 5, paras. 87–90.

23. A. B. Atkinson, *The Economics of Inequality*, Clarendon Press, Oxford, 1975, p. 168. For a survey of empirical estimates of trends in the growth of factor shares, see ibid., pp. 161–8.

24. H. F. Lydall, *The Structure of Earnings*, Oxford University Press, 1968, pp. 66–7.

25. ibid.

26. For a thorough and comprehensive study of the structure of earnings and the nature of changes in the distribution of earnings in the UK during this century, see G. Routh, *Occupation and Pay in Great Britain, 1906–1960*, Cambridge University Press, 1965. See also Lydall, *The Structure of Earnings*. Lydall makes use of Routh's findings in relation to changes in earnings dispersion and presents some data comparisons in appendices.

27. ibid., p. 184.

28. Atkinson, *The Economics of Inequality*, p. 76.

29. Diamond Commission, Report No. 5, para. 68.

30. ibid., para. 74.

31. For example, see G. F. Break, 'Effects of Taxation on Incentives', *British Tax Review*, June 1957; and D. B. Fields and W. J. Stanbury, 'Incentives, Disincentives and the Income Tax: Further Evidence', *Public Finance*, No. 3, 1970.

32. ibid. But see also the important survey by C. V. Brown and E. Levin, 'The Effects of Income Tax on Overtime: The Results of a National Survey', *Economic Journal*, December 1974.

33. Diamond Commission, Report No. 4, para. 88. See also ibid., Table 18.

34. For a detailed account of these assumptions, see *Economic Trends*, No. 278, December 1976.

35. J. L. Nicholson, 'The Distribution and Redistribution of Income in the United Kingdom', in D. Wedderburn (ed.), *Poverty, Inequality and Class Structure*, Cambridge University Press, 1974.

36. Diamond Commission, Report No. 1, para. 160.

37. In considering the data shown in Tables 5.8 and 5.9, we should bear in mind the point noted by the Diamond Commission – that 'the distributions are unlinked so not all the households in the bottom decile of original income will be in the bottom decile of final income. Some households may have moved upwards and others down to take their places.' See Diamond Commission, Report No. 5, para. 120.

38. Diamond Commission, Report No. 1, Table 25.

Chapter 6: Inequality (3): The Concentration of Wealth in the United Kingdom

1. See Diamond Commission, Report No. 1, *Initial Report on the Standing Reference*, Cmnd 6171, HMSO, London, 1975, para. 44.

2. A. B. Atkinson and A. J. Harrison, *Distribution of Personal Wealth in Britain*, Cambridge University Press, 1978, p. 6.

3. For some examples, see ibid., p. 30.

4. ibid., p. 35.

5. See Diamond Commission, Report No. 1, paras. 44–5.

6. For a detailed discussion of the estate multiplier method, see ibid., Appendix J.

7. Chapter 3 of Atkinson and Harrison, *Distribution of Personal Wealth in Britain*, suggests that while variations in multipliers are sufficiently important to be taken into account, the effects are not large.

8. Revell's estimates are based on estate duty returns; they relate to the population aged 25 and over in England and Wales, and they are derived by using mortality multipliers for the general population. The estimates of Atkinson and Harrison are also based on the application of mortality multipliers to estate data with appropriate adjustments to render them comparable with earlier studies, but they relate to the 'economically independent' population – 18 and over for 1973, 20 and over for 1953, and, by linear extrapolation, 23 and over in 1923 – *Distribution of Personal Wealth in Britain*, pp. 153–5.

9. See Diamond Commission, Report No. 5, *Third Report on the Standing Reference*, Cmnd 6999, HMSO, London, 1977, Table 33, p. 76.

10. The analysis originates in J. E. Meade, *Efficiency, Equality and the Ownership of Property*, Allen & Unwin, London, 1964; and is modified and extended in J. E. Meade, *The Just Economy*, Allen & Unwin, London, 1976.

11. Meade, *Efficiency, Equality and the Ownership of Property*, p. 28.

12. ibid., Table 1, p. 27.

13. ibid., p. 27.

14. H. F. Lydall and D. G. Tipping, 'The Distribution of Personal Wealth in Britain', *Bulletin of the Oxford Institute of Economics and Statistics*, 1961.

15. Diamond Commission, Report No. 1, para. 240.

16. See Diamond Commission, Report No. 4, *Second Report on the Standing Reference*, Cmnd 6626, HMSO, London, 1976, paras. 115–17.

17. Atkinson and Harrison, *Distribution of Personal Wealth in Britain*, p. 240.

18. Meade, *Efficiency, Equity and the Ownership of Property*, p. 46.

19. For a fascinating attempt to describe in detail this complex network of determinants, including a diagrammatic interpretation, see James Meade's paper, 'The Inheritance of Inequalities', Third Keynes Lecture in Economics, *Proceedings of the British Academy*, vol. LIX, 1973; and *The Just Economy*, Chapter 10.

20. See the survey of evidence presented in A. B. Atkinson, *Unequal Shares*, Allen Lane The Penguin Press, London, 1972, Chapter 4, pp. 65–8.

21. J. A. Kay and M. A. King, *The British Tax System*, Oxford University Press, 1978, p. 69.

22. C. D. Harbury, 'Inheritance in the Distribution of Personal Wealth', *Economic Journal*, 1962.

23. See J. Wedgwood, *The Economics of Inheritance*, Penguin Books, Harmondsworth, 1939.

24. Atkinson, *Unequal Shares*, pp. 70–72.

25. C. D. Harbury and P. C. McMahon, 'Inheritance and the Distribution of Personal Wealth in Britain', *Economic Journal*, 1973.

26. C. D. Harbury and D. M. Hitchens, 'The Inheritance of Top Wealth Leavers', *Economic Journal*, 1976.

27. It should be pointed out that the 1973 sample is subject to estate duty, and to the extent that gifts *inter vivos* were made to immediate relatives in an effort to avoid the duty, the actual estates passed on at death might suggest a distribution pattern more equal than the true situation.

28. See Diamond Commission, Report No. 5, Chapter 8, 'The Pattern of Inheritance'.

29. 'Capital Taxes 1: Taxes on the Transfer of Wealth', *The Structure and Reform of Direct Taxation*, Allen & Unwin for Institute for Fiscal Studies, London, 1978, Chapter 15, pp. 318–20.

30. For a more detailed analysis of the theoretical comparison of taxes on wealth and income, see J. F. Due, 'Net Worth Taxation', *Public Finance*, 1960, reprinted in R. W. Houghton, *Public Finance*, Penguin Modern Economics Readings, 2nd edn, Penguin Books, Harmondsworth, 1973; and C. V. Brown and P. M. Jackson, *Public Sector Economics*, Martin Robertson, London, 1968, pp. 318–25.

31. O. Lange, 'On the Economic Theory of Socialism', in O. Lange and F. Taylor, *On the Economic Theory of Socialism*, University of Minnesota Press, 1938.

32. For a good discussion of the compensation issue, see Atkinson, *Unequal Shares*, pp. 210–18.

Chapter 7: Income Maintenance (1): Income Maintenance and Social Insurance

1. The importance of making this distinction cannot be over-emphasized. See, e.g., James M. Buchanan, 'Social Insurance in a Growing Economy: A Proposal for Radical Reform', *National Tax Journal*, vol. XXI, No. 4, 1968, pp. 386–95.

2. This type of argument, which is essentially bound up with the concept of individual freedom, is forcibly presented by Milton Friedman, *Capitalism and Freedom*, University of Chicago Press, 1962, Chapter XI.

3. See Joseph A. Pechman, Henry J. Aaron and Michael K. Taussig, *Social Security: Perspectives for Reform*, Brookings Institution, Washington, DC, 1968, Chapter 8.

4. See R. A. Musgrave, 'The Role of Social Insurance in an Overall Programme of Social Welfare', in W. G. Bowen (ed.), *The American System of Social Insurance*, McGraw-Hill, New York, 1968.

5. P. A. Samuelson, 'An Extract Consumption Loan Model of Interest with or without the Social Contrivance of Money', *Journal of Political Economy*, 1958. See also A. P. Lerner, 'Consumption-Loan Interest and Money', *Journal of Political Economy*, October 1959, and Samuelson's 'Reply' in the same issue.

6. Samuelson, 'An Exact Consumption Loan Model of Interest . . .', loc. cit.

7. *Social Insurance and Allied Services* (The Beveridge Report), Cmd 6404, HMSO, London, 1942.

8. Fairly detailed accounts of the development of social security in Britain are given in B. B. Gilbert, *The Evolution of National Insurance in Great Britain*, Michael Joseph, London, 1966; G. Rhodes, *Public Sector Pensions*, Allen & Unwin, London, 1965, Chapter 1; Walter Hagenbuch, *Social Economics*, Cambridge University Press, 1958, Chapters VI–X.

9. The full Beveridge Plan, of course, included provisions outside the so-called 'insurance scheme'. Such provisions, e.g. family allowances and national assistance, are discussed in Chapters 10 and 11.

10. The major part of the cost of earnings-related supplements were met by increased graduated contributions for employees not contracted out. Employees contracted out began to pay graduated contributions at a rate equivalent to the increase. In 1977, an estimated 23 million employees were contracted out of the scheme. (Information provided by the Department of Health and Social Security.)

11. Since we are attempting to comprehend the broader principles involved, we shall not present a detailed analysis. Fairly detailed studies of the British scheme and the financial organization of the National Insurance Funds are to be found in A. T. Peacock, *The Economics of National Insurance*, W. Hodge & Co., London, 1952; and V. George, *Social Security: Beveridge and After*, Routledge & Kegan Paul, London, 1968, Chapter 3.

12. The argument is directly analogous to the case of a unit tax on output, the difference being that, in the present case, the imposition of the tax causes

a leftward shift in the employer's demand curve. The neoclassical case, as traditionally represented, can be found in H. G. Brown, *The Economics of Taxation*, Lucas Brothers, 1924; and Seymour E. Harris, *Economics of Social Security*, McGraw-Hill, New York, 1941.

13. M. S. Feldstein, 'Incidence of a Capital Income Tax in a Growing Economy with Variable Savings Rates', *Review of Economic Studies*, vol. XLI, 1974.

14. John A. Brittain, 'The Incidence of Social Security Payroll Taxes', *American Economic Review*, March 1971; and *The Payroll Tax for Social Security*, Brookings Institution, Washington, DC, 1972.

15. ibid, p. 11.

16. Wayne Vroman, 'Employer Payroll Tax Incidence: Empirical Tests with Cross-Country Data', *Public Finance*, 1974.

17. Johannes Weitenberg, 'The Incidence of Social Security Taxes', *Public Finance*, 1969.

18. Musgrave's study of the American payroll tax would seem to support such a conclusion. See R. A. Musgrave, *et al.*, 'Distribution of Tax Payments by Income Groups: A Case Study for 1948', *National Tax Journal*, vol. 4, No. 1, 1951.

19. Weitenberg, 'The Incidence of Social Security Taxes', loc. cit.

20. ibid., p. 208.

21. Philip Cagan, *The Effect of Pension Plans on Aggregate Saving: Evidence from a Sample Survey*, NBER Occasional Paper No. 95, Columbia University Press, 1965; George Katona, *The Mass Consumption Society*, McGraw-Hill, New York, 1964, Chapter 19. See also Roger F. Murray, *Economic Aspects of Pensions: A Summary Report*, NBER General Series No. 85, Columbia University Press, 1968, Chapter IV.

22. Martin J. Feldstein, 'Social Security and Private Savings: International Evidence in an Extended Life-Cycle Model', in M. S. Feldstein and R. P. Inman (eds.), *The Economics of Public Services*, Macmillan Press, London, 1977.

23. R. F. Harrod, *Towards a Dynamic Economics*, Macmillan, London, 1948.

24. Franco Modigliani, 'The Life-Cycle Hypothesis of Saving and Inter-country Differences in the Savings Ratio', in W. A. Eltis, *et al.* (eds.), *Induction, Growth and Trade. Essays in Honour of Sir Roy Harrod*, Clarendon Press, Oxford, 1970.

25. The argument must also apply in reverse; neither is the contribution likely to induce workers to work more in order to maintain their pre-tax levels of income.

26. See Mark M. Hauser and Paul Burrows, *The Economics of Unemployment Insurance*, Allen & Unwin, London, 1969, p. 97.

27. ibid., p. 103. Hauser and Burrows (pp. 103–10) attempt to estimate the disincentive effects of unemployment benefit by using rough pointers to the likely effect of increases in unemployment benefit: whether flat-rate benefit increases led to an 'unusual' increase in the level of unemployment during the

period 1948–65; whether benefit increases led to an increase in numbers receiving unemployment benefit during the period 1960–65; and for the same period, whether benefit increases had any effect on the duration pattern of employment. All three measures indicate that benefit increases did not create disincentive problems.

28. H. G. Grubel and D. Maki, 'The Effect of Unemployment Benefits on US Employment Rates', Department of Economics and Commerce Discussion Paper, Simon Frazer University, December 1974; and H. G. Grubel, D. Maki and S. Sax, 'Real and Insurance Induced Unemployment in Canada', *Canadian Journal of Economics*, May 1975.

29. ibid.

30. D. Maki and Z. A. Spindler, 'The Effect of Unemployment Compensation on the Rate of Unemployment in Great Britain', *Oxford Economic Papers*, New Series 27, 1975.

31. ibid., p. 448.

32. See, for example, Ernest Bloch, 'Automatic Fiscal Stabilizers in the 1957–1958 Business Contraction', *Review of Economics and Statistics*, XLI (August 1959), pp. 312–16; M. O. Clement, 'The Concept of Automatic Stabilizers', *Southern Economic Journal*, XXV (January 1959), pp. 303–14, and 'The Quantitative Impact of Automatic Stabilizers', *Review of Economics and Statistics*, XLII (February 1960), pp. 56–61; and Pechman, Aaron and Taussig, *Social Security*, pp. 183–5. Pechman, *et al.*, seem rather less emphatic on the issue than other researchers, mainly because of what they consider to be the poor performance of the American payroll tax relative to the personal income tax.

33. Hauser and Burrows, *The Economics of Unemployment Insurance*, Ch. IV.

34. ibid., p. 151.

35. ibid., p. 152.

36. For example, see J. C. R. Dow, *The Management of the British Economy 1945–1960*, Cambridge University Press, 1964.

Chapter 8: Income Maintenance (2): The Concept of Poverty

1. This relationship is more fully explored and described in diagrammatic form in G. C. Fiegehen, P. S. Lansley and A. D. Smith, *Poverty and Progress in Britain 1953–73*, National Institute of Economic and Social Research Occasional Papers, XXIX, Cambridge University Press, 1977, Chapter 2.

2. ibid., pp. 7–8.

3. For two vigorous denials of the possibility of an absolute poverty standard, see A. B. Atkinson, *The Economics of Inequality*, Clarendon Press, Oxford, 1975, p. 186; and A. J. Culyer, *The Economics of Social Policy*, Martin Robertson, London, 1973, p. 91.

4. Dudley Jackson, *Poverty*, Macmillan, London, 1972, p. 13.

5. ibid., p. 16.

6. ibid., Chapter 4.

7. For a more detailed account of this approach than is presented in *Poverty*,

see Dudley Jackson and Ann Fink, 'Assets, Liabilities and Poverty', *Social and Economic Administration*, vol. 5, No. 4, 1971. An interesting attempt to quantify how earnings are affected by certain 'assets' – length of full-time education, father's education, racial characteristics, health – is attempted in the excellent study of poverty submitted to the Diamond Commission by R. Layard, D. Piachaud and M. Stewart, *The Causes of Poverty*, Background Paper No. 5 to the Diamond Commission's Report No. 6, *Lower Incomes*, HMSO, London, 1978, Chapter 4.

8. Peter Townsend, 'Poverty as Relative Deprivation: Resources and Style of Living', in Dorothy Wedderburn (ed.), *Poverty, Inequality and Class Structure*, Cambridge University Press, 1974, p. 15. The term 'relative deprivation' was introduced into the literature by S. A. Stouffer, *et al.*, *The American Soldier*, Princeton University Press, 1949, but has been largely developed as an analytical device in studying social problems, as a result of the work by W. G. Runciman, *Relative Deprivation and Social Justice*, Routledge & Kegan Paul, London, 1966. Since the present book went into proof, Professor Townsend has made a further, major contribution to research into poverty in Peter Townsend, *Poverty in the United Kingdom*, Allen Lane: Penguin Books, London and Harmondsworth, 1979.

9. Townsend, 'Poverty as Relative Deprivation', loc. cit., p. 15.

10. ibid., pp. 25 and 26.

11. ibid., pp. 30–31.

12. ibid., p. 31.

13. ibid., pp. 35–6.

14. Fiegehen, Lansley and Smith, *Poverty and Progress in Britain*, Chapter 6.

15. ibid., Table 6.1.

16. ibid., Table 6.6 and p. 80.

17. ibid.

18. ibid., p. 83.

19. Charles Booth, *Life and Labour of the People of London*, Macmillan, London, 1902.

20. B. S. Rowntree, *Poverty: A Study of Town Life*, Macmillan, London, 1901.

21. B. S. Rowntree, *Poverty and Progress: A Second Social Survey of York*, Longmans, Green, London, 1941; B. S. Rowntree and G. R. Lavers, *Poverty and the Welfare State: A Third Social Survey of York Dealing Only with Economic Questions*, Longmans, Green, London, 1951.

22. *Social Insurance and Allied Services* (The Beveridge Report), Cmd 6404, HMSO, London, 1942.

23. For sources, see ibid., p. 19.

24. B. Abel-Smith and P. Townsend, *The Poor and the Poorest*, Occasional Papers on Social Administration No. 17, Bell, London, 1965; Ministry of Social Security, *Circumstances of Families*, HMSO, London, 1967; and A. B. Atkinson, *Poverty in Britain and the Reform of Social Security*, Cambridge University Press, 1969.

25. ibid., p. 16.

Chapter 9: Income Maintenance (3): Poverty and Market Solutions

1. The seminal work on this approach is K. E. Boulding, 'Notes on a Theory of Philanthropy', in F. G. Dickinson (ed.), *Philanthropy and Public Policy*, NBER, Columbia University Press, 1961.

2. See Mark V. Pauly, 'Efficiency in the Provision of Consumption Subsidies', *Kyklos*, vol. 23, 1970. Pauly also points out (ibid., p. 37) that the introduction of interdependence changes the trading equilibrium. If there is only a fixed amount of x available, every unit of x obtained by α is one unit less available to β. Thus when α gets another unit of x he receives a joint product – a 'good' (dx^α) and a 'bad' (dx^β). Assuming separability in α's utility function, the total change in α's utility as the result of obtaining an additional unit of x is:

$$\frac{\partial U^\alpha/\partial x^\alpha}{\partial U^\alpha/\partial y^\alpha} - \frac{\partial U^\alpha/\partial x^\beta}{\partial U^\alpha/\partial y^\alpha}$$

which modifies the trading equilibrium to:

$$\frac{\partial U^\epsilon/\partial x^\alpha}{\partial U^\alpha/\partial y^\alpha} - \frac{\partial U^\alpha/\partial x^\beta}{\partial y^\alpha/\partial y^\alpha} = \frac{\partial U^\beta/\partial x^\beta}{\partial U^\beta/\partial y^\beta}$$

3. For a more detailed analysis of problems in this area, see G. Tullock, 'Information without Profit', in G. Tullock (ed.), *Papers on Non-Market Decision Making*, Thomas Jefferson Centre for Political Economy, University of Virginia, 1966. See also G. P. Marshall, 'The Control of Private Charities', *Public Administration*, Autumn 1978.

4. Report of the Committee on the Law and Practice Relating to Charitable Trusts, Cmd 8710, HMSO, London, 1952.

5. Tenth Report from the Expenditure Committee, *Charity Commissioners and Their Accountability*, vols. I and II, H.C. 495–1 and 495–11, HMSO, London, 30 July 1975, para. 15.

6. ibid., vol. II, *Minutes of Evidence*, p. 18, para. 9.

7. Report of the Charity Commissioners for England and Wales for the Year 1970.

8. Report of the Committee on the Law and Practice Relating to Charitable Trusts, para. 39.

9. The same diagram can be used to illustrate a *national* minimum wage. In this case, the demand and supply curves would refer to the whole economy.

10. While the Department of Employment publishes data about the earnings of certain groups of workers, including those who are covered by minimum wage legislation, there are no comparable employment or price data published which would enable us to test the neoclassical prediction about the effects of a higher minimum being set. The main source of data on these problems appears annually in the *New Earnings Survey*.

11. John M. Peterson, 'Employment Effects of Minimum Wages, 1938–50', *Journal of Political Economy*, vol. LXV, 1957.

12. H. M. Douty, 'Some Effects of the $1.00 Minimum Wage in the United States', *Economica*, New Series, vol. 27, 1960.

13. Colin B. Campbell and Rosemary G. Campbell, 'State Minimum Wage Laws as a Cause of Unemployment', *Southern Economic Journal*, vol. 35, 1968–9.

14. Yale Brozen, 'The Effect of Statutory Minimum Wage Increases on Teen-Age Employment', *Journal of Law and Economics*, vol. XII, 1969.

15. Marvin Kosters and Finis Welch, 'The Effects of Minimum Wages on the Distribution of Changes in Aggregate Employment', *American Economic Review*, vol. LXII, 1972.

16. ibid., p. 350.

17. B. J. McCormick and H. A. Turner, 'The Legal Minimum Wage, Employers and Trade Unions: An Experiment', *Manchester School of Economic and Social Studies*, vol. 25, No. 3, September 1957, p. 285. For a full account of the historical developments of minimum wage legislation in Britain, see F. J. Bayliss, *British Wage Councils*, Blackwell, Oxford, 1962.

18. Trade Boards Act 1909, Section 1(2).

19. McCormick and Turner, 'The Legal Minimum Wage, Employers and Trade Unions', loc. cit., p. 287; and Bayliss, *British Wage Councils*, p. 56.

20. John Greenwood, 'The Case for Retaining Legal Minimum Wages', *Institute of Manpower Studies Monitor*, vol. 3, July 1975, pp. 119–30.

21. See F. Field and S. Winyard, 'Low Pay in Public Employment and the Wages Council Sector', in F. Field (ed.), *Low Pay*, Arrow Books, London, 1973.

22. For example, see Report of a Royal Commission on Trade Unions and Employers Associations (The Donovan Commission), Cmnd 3623, HMSO, London, 1968, pp. 65–6, and various Reports by the National Board for Prices and Incomes.

23. Nicholas Bosanquet, 'The Real Low Pay Problem', in Field (ed.), *Low Pay*, p. 31.

24. Field and Winyard, 'Low Pay in Public Employment . . .', loc. cit., p. 47.

25. E. G. A. Armstrong, 'Minimum Wages in a Fully Employed City', *British Journal of Industrial Relations*, vol. 4, 1966, pp. 22–38.

26. Field and Winyard, 'Low Pay in Public Employment . . .', loc. cit., p. 50.

27. Greenwood, 'The Case for Retaining Legal Minimum Wages', loc. cit., p. 122.

28. ibid., p. 123.

29. Field and Winyard, 'Low Pay in Public Employment . . .', loc. cit., p. 56.

30. J. Marquand, 'Which are the Low Paid Workers?', *British Journal of Industrial Relations*, November 1967.

31. R. H. Tawney, *The Establishment of Legal Minimum Rates in the Chain-Making Industry*, London, 1914; and *The Establishment of Legal Minimum Rates in the Box Making Industry*, London, 1915.

32. B. J. McCormick, 'The Royal Commission, Low Paid Workers and the Future of the Wages Councils', *Journal of Economic Studies*, 1968, pp. 83–91.

33. Report of the Committee of Enquiry into the Working and Effects of the

Trade Boards Acts (The Cave Committee), Cmd 1645, HMSO, London, 1922.

34. National Board for Prices and Incomes, *Laundry and Dry Cleaning Charges*, Report No. 20, Cmnd 3093, HMSO, London, 1966 p. 2; and *Road Haulage Rates*, Report No. 1, Cmnd 2695, HMSO, London, 1965, p. 9.

35. One estimate suggests that, at any level of general unemployment, the unemployment rates for the unskilled are about two and a half times the general rate for men. See N. Bosanquet and G. Standing 'Government and Unemployment 1966–70; a Study of Policy and Evidence', *British Journal of Industrial Relations*, 1972.

36. A. B. Atkinson 'Low Pay and the Cycle of Poverty', in Field (ed.) *Low Pay*, pp. 101–17.

Chapter 10: Income Maintenance (4): State Programmes and the UK Experience in the Post-war Period

1. *Social Insurance and Allied Services* (The Beveridge Report), Cmnd 6404, HMSO, London, 1942. For useful surveys of developments since Beveridge, see Victor George, *Social Security: Beveridge and After*, Routledge & Kegan Paul, London, 1968; and Alan Maynard, 'A Survey of Social Security in the UK', *Social and Economic Administration*, vol. 7, No. 1, January 1973.

2. B. Abel-Smith and P. Townsend, *The Poor and the Poorest*, Occasional Papers on Social Administration No. 17, Bell, London, 1965. The term 'National Assistance' was replaced by 'Supplementary Benefit' in 1966.

3. I. Gough and T. Stark, 'Low Incomes in the United Kingdoms', *The Manchester School*, June 1968; A. B. Atkinson, *Poverty in Britain and the Reform of Social Security*, Cambridge University Press, 1969; 'Conflict in Social Security Policy', in N. Kaldor (ed.), *Conflicts in Policy Objectives*, Blackwell, Oxford, 1971, and 'Poverty and Income Inequality in Britain', in D. Wedderburn (ed.), *Poverty, Inequality and Class Structure*, Cambridge University Press, 1974; G. C. Fiegehen, P. S. Lansley and A. D. Smith, *Poverty and Progress in Britain 1953–73*, National Institute and Economic and Social Research Occasional Paper, XXIX, Cambridge University Press, 1977; Ministry of Pensions and National Insurance, *Financial and Other Circumstances of Retirement Pensioners*, HMSO, London, 1966; Ministry of Social Security, *Circumstances of Families*, HMSO, London, 1967; R. Layard, D. Piachaud, and M. Stewart, *The Causes of Poverty*, Background Paper No. 5 to the Diamond Commission's Report No. 6, *Lower Incomes*, HMSO, London, 1978.

4. According to the NIESR researches, the difference between this estimate for 1953/4 and that of Abel-Smith and Townsend is the result of three main reasons: (a) the NIESR study applies a single poverty line – that for married couples – to the 'estimated' composite distribution of income per equivalent couple, while Abel-Smith and Townsend apply the relevant National Assistance scale separately to each household; (b) the NIESR study adopts a poverty line of National Assistance Scale plus 30 per cent in its 1953/4 cal-

culation, while Abel-Smith and Townsend use the actual returns for 1953/4 and employ the National Assistance Scale plus actual housing costs; and (c) the NIESR estimates are based on gross income while those of Abel-Smith and Townsend are based on 'expenditure widely defined to include mortgage payments, life assurance and other forms of saving, but excluding income tax and national insurance contributions'. See Fiegehen, Lansley and Smith, *Poverty and Progress in Britain 1953–73*, p. 30.

5. Of course, this method may also mislead, as acknowledged by the NIESR report, in so far as there may be 'an element of artificiality in applying so far away from the time when they were implemented standards which do not allow for changes in social habits' – ibid., p. 28.

6. It should be pointed out at this stage that the NIESR found that in *relative* terms there had been little change over the period so that the decline in the numbers in poverty so measured 'reflects essentially the growth of the economy rather than a redistribution of income' – ibid., p. 110. While we are primarily concerned with *absolute* poverty in this chapter, such findings do provide a means of tempering our observations.

7. B. Seebohm Rowntree, with G. R. Lavers, *Poverty and the Welfare State: A Third Social Survey of York Dealing Only with Economic Questions*, Longmans, Green, London, 1951.

8. See CSO, *Social Trends*, No. 3, 1972, Table 1, p. 6.

9. Fiegehen, Lansley and Smith, *Poverty and Progress in Britain, 1963–73*.

10. ibid., Table 5.5, p. 60, and p. 62.

11. ibid., p. 62, Table 5.6. This table provides a complete breakdown of both risk and accountability for the various types of household.

12. *Department of Employment Gazette*, vol. LXXXI, No. 11, November 1973, p. 1086.

13. G. P. Marshall 'Income Taxation and the UK Flat-Rate Retirement Pension', *Social and Economic Administration*, 1979.

14. Ministry of Pensions and National Insurance, *Financial and Other Circumstances of Retirement Pensioners*, HMSO, London, 1966, Table 11.4, p. 12.

15. ibid.

16. One estimate is that, even by the end of the century, the proportion of pensioners' households in receipt of an occupational pension will not exceed two thirds. See Department of Health and Social Security, *National Superannuation and Social Insurance*, Cmnd 3883, HMSO, London, 1969.

17. *Financial and Other Circumstances of Retirement Pensioners*.

18. A forceful protest is made by A. B. Atkinson in *Poverty in Britain and the Reform of Social Security*, Cambridge University Press, Chapter 1, and subsistence pensions form an integral part of his 'Back to Beveridge' plan advanced as a scheme to correct inadequacies within the Welfare State. See ibid., Chapter 7.

19. Ministry of Pensions and National Insurance, *Financial and Other Circumstances of Retirement Pensioners*, para. 84.

20. *The Poor and the Poorest*.

21. D. Cole and J. Utting, *The Economic Circumstances of Old People*, Occasional Papers on Social Administration No. 4, Codicote Press, Welwyn, 1962.

22. Atkinson, *Poverty in Britain and the Reform of Social Security*, p. 57.

23. Beveridge Report, p. 155.

24. Ministry of Social Security, *Circumstances of Families*.

25. Atkinson, *Poverty in Britain and the Reform of Social Security*, Table 5.2, p. 82.

26. ibid. Net income is defined in this context to include Family Allowance.

27. See Abel-Smith and Townsend, *The Poor and the Poorest*, Table 19.

28. Fiegehen, Lansley and Smith, *Poverty and Progress in Britain, 1953–73*, p. 114.

29. ibid., p. 60.

30. Atkinson, *Poverty in Britain and the Reform of Social Security*, p. 84 and Table 5.5.

31. Maynard, 'A Survey of Social Security in the UK', loc. cit., Table 3, p. 48.

32. Atkinson, *Poverty in Britain and the Reform of Social Security*, p. 88. Atkinson bases his calculations on the findings of a survey conducted by the Department of Employment and Productivity, 'Results of a New Survey of Earnings in September 1968', *Department of Employment and Productivity Gazette*, 1969.

33. It might be pointed out here that, prior to the introduction of Family Income Supplement, the only positive action directed by the social security system towards low earners was negative! Prior to its abolition in 1975, the 'wage stop' achieved some notoriety. This was a rule which operated to prevent a claimant of social security from receiving in benefits, while unemployed or sick, more than his previous take-home earnings. This puritanical device, designed to discourage the malingerer, meant that many low earners would not receive full supplementary benefit when out of work.

34. M. Meacher in *The Times*, 29 December 1971.

35. Recent social security changes have recognized this fact and made some amends. For example, when family allowance was raised to £1.50 for the second child of the two-parent family in 1975, this rate was extended to the first child of the one-parent family. Under the child benefits scheme, the proposed rates for April 1978 included an additional £1 payable for the first child of the one-parent family.

36. R. Layard, D. Piachaud and M. Stewart (in collaboration with N. Barr, A. Cornford and B. Hayes), *The Causes of Poverty*, Background Paper to the Diamond Commission's Report No. 6, *Lower Incomes*, HMSO, London, 1978. This excellent study of the causes of poverty was published too late for proper discussion by the author.

Chapter 11: Income Maintenance (5): State Programmes and the Alternatives to Beveridge

1. Discussion at this point follows the classification presented by Carl S. Shoup, 'Negative Taxes, Welfare Payments and Subsidies', *Revista di diritto finanziario e scienza delle finance*, December 1967.

2. For a further discussion of some of the issues involved, see G. P. Marshall, 'The UK Retirement Pension and Negative Taxation', *Bulletin of Economic and Social Research*, vol. 30, 1978.

3. For a detailed and thorough examination of the various negative income tax schemes, see Christopher Green, *Negative Taxes and the Poverty Problem*, Brookings Institution, Washington, DC, 1967.

4. Some examples include G. F. Break, 'Income Taxes and Incentive to Work, an Empirical Study', *American Economic Review*, vol. 47, 1957; C. V. Brown, 'Misconceptions about Income Tax and Incentives', *Scottish Journal of Political Economy*, vol. 15, 1968; C. V. Brown, and E. Levin, 'The Effects of Income Taxation on Overtime: the Results of a National Survey', *Economic Journal*, December 1974. For a useful survey of potential effects on low earners, see C. V. Brown, 'Survey of the Effects of Taxation on Labour Supply of Low Income Groups', *Fiscal Policy and Labour Supply*, Conference Series No. 4, Institute for Fiscal Studies, London, 1977.

5. Brown, 'Surveys of the Effects of Taxation on Labour Supply of Low Income Groups', pp. 23–7.

6. Although Brown, in ibid., does see a consensus beginning to emerge that the experiments have produced income and substitution effects of expected size.

7. A. J. Culyer, *The Economics of Social Policy*, Martin Robertson, London, 1973, p. 102.

8. Milton Friedman, *Capitalism and Freedom*, University of Chicago Press, 1962, pp. 191–5.

9. D. Lees, 'Poor Families and Fiscal Reform', *Lloyds Bank Review*, October 1967.

10. *Proposals for a Tax-Credit System*, Cmnd 5114, HMSO, London, 1972.

11. Those excluded from the scheme were to include: the self-employed, those with low earnings and those receiving supplementary benefits but not national insurance benefits.

12. A. B. Atkinson, *The Tax Credit Scheme and the Redistribution of Income*, Institute for Fiscal Studies, London, 1973.

13. *Policy for Poverty*, IEA Research Monograph No. 20, London, 1970.

14. A comprehensive scheme of this type for Britain was first outlined by Lady Juliet Rhys Williams in *Something to Look Forward To*, Macdonald, London, 1943.

15. J. E. Meade, 'Poverty in the Welfare State', *Oxford Economic Papers*, vol. 24, 1972.

16. This would represent an extension of an earlier proposal by Meade in *Planning and the Price Mechanisms*, Allen & Unwin, London, 1948.

17. *The Structure and Reform of Direct Taxation*, Report of a Committee chaired by Professor J. E. Meade, Allen & Unwin for the Institute for Fiscal Studies, London, 1978.

18. See A. B. Atkinson, *Poverty in Britain and the Reform of Social Security*, Cambridge University Press, 1969, pp. 276–94.

Chapter 12: Women in the Mixed Economy

1. Gary S. Becker, 'A Theory of the Allocation of Time', *Economic Journal*, 1965.

2. Gary S. Becker, 'A Theory of Marriage: Part I', *Journal of Political Economy*, vol. 81, 1973, pp. 813–46.

3. Another way to view (6) is to think of 'full' income as being that amount of money income which could be realized if *all* available household time were to be allocated to market work.

4. K. Lancaster, 'A New Approach to Consumer Theory', *Journal of Political Economy*, 1966.

5. The term 'marriage' is mainly used to describe all cohabitory arrangements between two adults, whatever the legal status of such arrangements or the sex ratio within them.

6. Such predictions are reversed for the case of a rise in the female wage rate.

7. Indeed, the implication relates also to inter-temporal allocation. If the husband's real wage rate is expected to increase (relatively) over time, present goods, including child services, will be substituted for future ones. See Gilbert R. Ghez and Gary S. Becker, *The Allocation of Time and Goods over the Life Cycle*, NBER, Columbia University Press, 1975, Chapter 1.

8. An impressive collection of Chicago papers and critical comments on them is presented in T. W. Schultz (ed.), *Economics of the Family: Marriage, Children and Human Capital*, Chicago University Press for the NBER, 1974. Most of the papers in this volume were first presented at two NBER conferences and originally published as supplements to the *Journal of Political Economy:* 'New Economic Approaches to Fertility', March/April 1973; and 'Marriage, Family Human Capital and Fertility', March/April 1974.

9. Robert J. Willis, 'Economic Theory of Fertility Behaviour', in Schultz (ed.), *Economics of the Family*, pp. 25–80. This elegant paper clearly explains some theoretical extensions of Becker's model.

10. See Bruce Gardner, 'Economics of the Size of North Carolina Families'; Dennis N. De Tray, 'Child Quality and the Demand for Children'; Yoram Ben-Porath, 'Economic Analysis of Fertility in Israel'; and Masanori Hashimoto, 'Economics of Postwar Fertility in Japan'; all in Schultz (ed.), *Economics of the Family*.

11. See Robert T. Michael, 'Education and the Derived Demand for Children', in ibid., pp. 120–56.

12. In ibid., pp. 160–83.

13. In ibid., pp. 120–56.

14. In ibid., pp. 189–220.

15. In ibid., pp. 225–49.

16. G. S. Becker and H. Gregg Lewis, 'Interaction between Quantity and Quality of Children', in ibid., pp. 81–90.

17. In ibid., pp. 91–116. De Tray's findings are based on the assumption, acknowledged to be dubious by the author, that the extent of a child's education is a proxy measure of the 'quality' of that child.

18. Audrey Hunt, *A Survey of Women's Employment*, vols. 1 and 2 (a survey undertaken on behalf of the Ministry of Labour by the Government Social Survey in 1965), HMSO, London, 1968.

19. ibid., vol. 1, p. 181.

20. ibid.

21. ibid.

22. ibid., p. 15.

23. Trevor Noble, *Modern Britain: Structure and Change*, Batsford, London, 1975, pp. 30–31.

24. ibid. This statement is based on the findings of studies which Noble admits to be less than wholly reliable. For an interesting example of surveying fertility expectations, see Myra Woolf, *Family Intentions*, Office of Population Censuses and Surveys, Social Survey Division, HMSO, London, 1971.

25. Noble, *Modern Britain*, p. 31.

26. Becker, 'A Theory of Marriage, Part I', also reprinted in Schultz (ed.), *Economics of the Family*; and 'A Theory of Marriage, Part II', *Journal of Political Economy*, vol. 82, 1974, pp. 11–26 of Supplement.

27. Alan Frieden, 'The US Marriage Market', in Schultz (ed.), *Economics of the Family*, pp. 352–71.

28. Lee Benham, 'Benefits of Women's Education within Marriage', in ibid., pp. 375–93.

29. For some interesting details of both the patterns of female employment and female attitudes to labour market opportunities, see Hunt, *A Survey of Women's Employment*, vols. 1 and 2; and Pauline Pinder, *Women at Work*, PEP Broadsheet No. 512, May 1969.

30. CSO, *Social Trends, 1977*, HMSO, London, 1977, Table 5.3, p. 82. The increase in participation rates for married women more than affects the decline in the rates for unmarried women over the same period (from 55 per cent in 1951 to 42 per cent in 1976).

31. Comparable data for non-manuals are not available. However, for salaried employees the pattern of change between 1950 and 1970 was very similar to that shown in Table 12.2. See *Equal Pay*, First Report on the Implementation of the Equal Pay Act 1970, Office of Manpower Economics, HMSO, London, 1972, Table F, p. 13.

32. Henry Phelps-Brown, *The Inequality of Pay*, Oxford University Press, 1977, p. 158.

33. Cmnd 5724, September 1974, para. 35.

34. To use the term suggested by Gordon Bloom in 'A Reconsideration of the Theory of Exploitation', *Quarterly Journal of Economics*, 1942.

35. Brian Chiplin and Peter J. Sloane, *Sex Discrimination in the Labour Market*, Macmillan, London, 1976, pp. 98–9.

36. G. S. Becker, *The Economics of Discrimination*, University of Chicago Press, 2nd edn, 1971.

37. K. Arrow, 'Models of Job Discrimination', and 'Some Mathematical Models of Race Discrimination in the Labour Market', in Anthony H. Pascal (ed.), *Racial Discrimination in Economic Life*, D. C. Heath, Boston, Mass., 1972.

38. See, for example, H. Sanborn, 'Pay Differences Between Men and Women', *Industrial and Labour Relations Review*, 1964; V. R. Fuchs, 'Differences in Hourly Earnings between Men and Women', *Monthly Labor Review*, 1971; and J. Mincer and S. Polachek, 'Family Investments in Human Capital: Earnings of Women', *Journal of Political Economy*, 1974.

39. See B. G. Malkiel and J. A. Malkiel, 'Male-Female Pay Differentials in Professional Employment', *American Economic Review*, 1973.

40. B. Chiplin and P. J. Sloane, 'Personal Characteristics and Sex Differentials in Professional Employment', *Economic Journal*, vol. 86, 1976, p. 730.

41. See Mincer and Polachek, 'Family Investments in Human Capital', loc. cit.

42. Chiplin and Sloane, 'Personal Characteristics and Sex Differentials . . .', loc. cit.

43. ibid., p. 744.

44. Richard B. Mancke, 'Lower Pay for Women: A Case of Economic Discrimination?', *Industrial Relations*, vol. 10, 1971, pp. 316–26.

45. ibid., p. 320.

46. Hunt, *A Survey of Women's Employment*, vol. 1, p. 158.

47. Pinder, *Women at Work*, p. 546.

48. Christine Greenhalgh, *Is Marriage an Equal Opportunity?* Discussion Paper No. 14, Centre for Labour Economics, London School of Economics, 1977.

49. Pinder, *Women at Work*, p. 557.

50. This hypothesis was first advanced to explain the labour market consequences of racial discrimination. See Barbara R. Bergmann, 'The Effect on White Incomes of Discrimination in Employment', *Journal of Political Economy*, 1971.

51. For example, see N. Bosanquet and P. B. Doeringer, 'Is There a Dual Labour Market in Great Britain?', *Economic Journal*, 1973.

52. The relationship between manual and non-manual profiles seems in line with the predictions of human capital theory. See Chiplin and Sloane, *Sex Discrimination in the Labour Market*, pp. 68–70.

53. George Psacharopoulos, 'Labour Market Duality and Income Distribution: The Case of the UK', Discussion Paper No. 5, Centre for Labour Economics, London School of Economics, February 1977.

54. Phelps-Brown, *The Inequality of Pay*, pp. 158–9.

55. Greenhalgh, *Is Marriage an Equal Opportunity?*

56. ibid., p. 15.

57. ibid., p. 18.

58. ibid., p. 25.

59. ibid., p. 42.

60. ibid., p. 43.

61. For a more detailed discussion of these issues than is presented here, see G. P. Marshall and A. J. Walsh, 'Marital Status and Variations in Income Tax Burdens', *British Tax Review*, 1970.

62. *Discrimination against Women*, Opposition Green Paper (Labour Party), 1972, p. 26.

63. J. E. Todd and L. M. Jones, *Matrimonial Property*, HMSO, London, 1972, pp. 10–11.

64. ibid., pp. 23 and 25.

65. See Law Commission, *Family Property Law*, Working Paper No. 42, October 1971; and *First Report on Family Property: A New Approach*, Working Paper No. 52, May 1973. Comments on these papers, as they relate to the supply of female labour and to taxing the marital unit, can be found in G. P. Marshall, 'Some Economic Aspects of Family Property Rights Reform', *British Tax Review*, 1974.

66. Law Commission, *First Report on Family Property*, para. 13.

67. Royal Commission on the Income Tax Report, Cmd 615, HMSO, London, 1920; and Royal Commission on the Taxation of Profits and Income, Second Report, Cmd 9105, HMSO, London, 1954.

68. It is interesting to note that the value of such services is generally recognized by married couples. According to the survey by Todd and Jones, 'the wife's effort in running the home was mentioned as a contribution to the home as frequently as earnings' – *Matrimonial Property*, p. 28.

69. So far 'leisure' and 'housework' have been used as synonyms, both referring to non-market employment. Where it is necessary in later discussion, 'leisure' will be employed in its everyday usage.

70. Operative since 1914 as a concession to the feminist movement.

71. The allowance was to equal the wife's earnings, subject to a maximum. See Royal Commission on the Income Tax Report, 1920, para. 261.

72. 'Net' income being defined as taxable income plus any personal allowances granted to the tax unit.

73. See O. Oldman and R. Temple, 'Comparative Analysis of the Taxation of Married Persons', *Stanford Law Review*, vol. 12, 1960, pp. 585–605.

74. Modifications to these approaches have been advanced in the literature. See Marshall and Walsh, 'Marital Status and Variations in Income Tax Burdens', op. cit., p. 244.

75. See Royal Commission on the Income Tax Report, 1920: C. G. Spry, Minutes of Evidence, para. 2822.

76. Despite changes in the intervening period, the system of a higher personal allowance for a married man, currently operative, closely resembles that of 1920.

77. A. R. Prest, *Public Finance in Theory and Practice*, 3rd edn, Weindenfeld & Nicolson, London, p. 286.

78. On this view, the 1971 decision by the UK authorities to permit separate assessment for a married couple once their incomes make it worthwhile for the couple to elect to be treated in this way was erroneous.

79. See Marshall, 'Some Economic Aspects of Family Property Rights Reform', op. cit., pp. 36–7; and also B. Abel-Smith, 'Equity and Dependency', in *Conference on Proposals for a Tax-Credit System*, Publication No. 5, Institute of Fiscal Studies, March 1973, pp. 34–5.

80. A system of unemployment compensation can cater for involuntary domesticity in the case of a childless spouse.

81. It might also be noted that the term 'marital' has been used for convenience. The laws relating to the tax treatment of jointly-owned property and income usually assume a legal definition of marriage. Clearly such a definition is not essential to the arguments presented in this chapter, and the tax treatment of cohabitory arrangements should not vary with legal status.

82. Greenhalgh, *Is Marriage an Equal Opportunity?*, pp. 4–5.

83. To safeguard a woman's health during the later stages of pregnancy, the financial arrangements are extended to all pregnant women, whether or not they intend to return to work. Nine tenths of normal pay, adjusted for maternity allowance payments, is payable from the eleventh week prior to confinement to any woman who chooses to cease market work from that time.

Subject Index

Name Index

More About Penguins
and Pelicans

Penguinews, which appears every month, contains details of all the new books issued by Penguins as they are published. It is supplemented by our stocklist, which includes almost 5,000 titles.

A specimen copy of *Penguinews* will be sent to you free on request. Please write to Dept EP, Penguin Books Ltd, Harmondsworth, Middlesex, for your copy.

In the U.S.A.: For a complete list of books available from Penguins in the United States write to Dept CS, Penguin Books, 625 Madison Avenue, New York, New York 10022.

In Canada: For a complete list of books available from Penguins in Canada write to Penguin Books Canada Ltd, 2801 John Street, Markham, Ontario L3R 1B4.

In Australia: For a complete list of books available from Penguins in Australia write to the Marketing Department, Penguin Books Australia Ltd, P.O. Box 257, Ringwood, Victoria 3134.

'This momentous book will rank as the contemporary successor to the classic works of Booth and Rowntree; its case histories alone should put paid to those who still assert that there is no longer poverty in Britain' – Barbara Wooton

Poverty in the United Kingdom
A survey of household resources and standards of living

Peter Townsend

'The chief conclusion of this report is that poverty is more extensive than is generally or officially believed, and has to be understood not only as an inevitable feature of severe social inequality but also as a particular consequence of actions by the rich to preserve and enhance their wealth and so deny it to others . . . The extremely unequal distribution of wealth is perhaps the single most notable feature of social conditions in the United Kingdom.'

Professor Townsend's massive and controversial survey is the most comprehensive investigation into poverty and wealth in Britain ever undertaken. It has virtually the scope and prestige of a Royal Commission, and will stand as the seminal work on the subject for years to come.

'Not only presents the results of the most extensive survey of poverty carried out in Britain, but also brings together Townsend's thinking over the last 25 years on the subject of poverty, the position of social minorities, and the role of social institutions. It is a veritable tour de force.' – *Guardian*

'The contribution to knowledge and understanding is great indeed, and covers so many topics and correlations that it will provide material for discussion for years to come.' – *New Society*

Recently published in Penguin Education

The Economics of Women and Work
Edited by Alice H. Amsden

The number of married women in paid employment has dramatically
increased. Sexual inequality in the labour force remains static. This is
just one paradox that has come to light in the recent spate of articles
and books by economists on the subject of women and work. The four
major schools of thought represented in these readings – neoclassical,
institutional, Marxist and radical – treat almost all this new information
differently, and have seldom before confronted each other with their
opposing views. In addition the editor introduces this volume with an
admirable résumé of each economic school of thought.

The World of Goods
Towards an Anthropology of Consumption
Mary Douglas and Baron Isherwood

Modern Western society is, if nothing else, a consumer society; a society
that lives, moves and has its being in a commodities environment. *The
World of Goods* is cast as a debate between anthropology and economics
on the question of *why* people want goods; and it not only presents new
facts about consumer demand, but also provides the theory to explain
what we already know about the subject.

Geographical Economics
Patrick O'Sullivan

Is the unrestricted operation of the market economy compatible with the
best interests of all society? If not, what are the economic and political
implications? With these basic questions in mind, Professor O'Sullivan
builds up an equilibrium model of the geographical economy, and then
examines the geographical aspects of economic growth. His lucid analysis
provokes questions of equity and efficiency, and their implications for
political decision-making at both regional and national level.